Market Risk and Financial Markets Modeling

Didier Sornette • Sergey Ivliev • Hilary Woodard
Editors

Market Risk and Financial Markets Modeling

Perm Winter School

Springer

Editors
Prof. Didier Sornette
D-MTEC
ETH Zürich
Zurich, Switzerland

Ph.D. Hilary Woodard
D-MTEC
ETH Zürich
Zurich, Switzerland

Asst. Prof. Sergey Ivliev
Prognoz Risk Lab
Perm State University
Perm, Russia

ISBN 978-3-642-27930-0 e-ISBN 978-3-642-27931-7
DOI 10.1007/978-3-642-27931-7
Springer Heidelberg Dordrecht London New York

Library of Congress Control Number: 2012930390

Printed on acid-free paper

Springer is part of Springer Science+Business Media (www.springer.com)

market
risk
model
time
funds
price
hedge
financial
fund
stock
information
management
liquidity
prices
approach
dynamics
alpha
capital
analysis
data
value

Contents

Introduction

Market Risk and Financial Markets Modeling

Introduction

Financial Market and Systemic Risks

Didier Sornette

ETH Zurich, Chair of Entrepreneurial Risks, Department of Management, Technology and Economics, Kreuzplatz 5, CH-8032 Zurich, Switzerland. email: dsornette@ethz.ch

Susanne von der Becke

ETH Zurich, Chair of Entrepreneurial Risks, Department of Management, Technology and Economics, Kreuzplatz 5, CH-8032 Zurich, Switzerland.
email: svonderbecke@ethz.ch

The ongoing financial crises since 2007 painfully reminded us that systems can develop what scientists often refer to as "emergent" dynamics that are fundamentally different to what can be expected by studying their parts. The assumption that the economy as a whole can be understood by solely focusing on the equilibria resulting from utility optimization of its economic agents constitutes one of the major shortcomings of economics. A mantra in academic circles, exploited by bankers and policy makers to excuse their failures, is that, with the rise of recent technological and financial innovations, societal and economic networks have never been more complex and this complexity has reached unmanageable levels within the current understanding and methodologies. Many scholars as well as professionals call for novel and ambitious initiatives to improve our understanding of the dynamics of the financial and economic systems, using a transdisciplinary approach, typically based on adding system theory from various branches of the natural sciences, network analysis, and out-of-equilibrium agent-based models to traditional economics.

While these are crucial to advance the disciplines of finance and economics in the medium to long term, they are overlooking much needed short-term operational solutions. Rather than putting our hope in tackling the super complexity with super high tech solutions, we should remember simple truths that demonstrated their value in the past but have been by and large forgotten. Academic and institutional memory loss includes the role of banks in credit creation, the benefits of certain (lost) forms of regulations, and the crucial role of central banks as fighters (rather than promoters) of bubbles.

In macro-economic models such as the class of Dynamic Stochastic General Equilibrium (DSGE) models used by central banks, the banks as separate agents directly influencing the economy are conspicuously absent, apart from their influence through interest rates. Why should then taxpayers' money bail them out if they are just transparent economic conduits? In contrast, stressing the role of banking in the wider context of economic systems was central to Austrian economists and scholars such as Hayek and Schumpeter. While not without weaknesses, the Austrian economic school emphasised correctly the role of banks and their cre-

D. Sornette et al. (Eds.), *Market Risk and Financial Markets Modeling*,
DOI 10.1007/978-3-642-27931-7_1, © Springer-Verlag Berlin Heidelberg 2012

ation of credit through the fractional reserve system. Too much credit, encouraged by artificially low interest rates set by central banks for instance, can lead to an unsustainable boom and the creation of economic and financial bubbles. This is exactly what happened in the run up to the current financial crises. The concept that banks are in large part responsible for credit creation was well understood 30 years ago and discussed and taught in major economic textbooks. This knowledge seems to have been forgotten in mainstream macroeconomics. This is a fundamental loss. Indeed, the forgotten problem is the misaligned interests between the credit creation chosen by banks in order to maximize their utility versus the amount of credit required by the real economy. Schumpeter also emphasised the crucial role of banks and credit markets through their function of active allocators of capital to entrepreneurs and hence fostering economic development. The reason for this memory loss may have been the inability and even resistance to apply these concepts in mathematical models. It seems, though, that much wisdom can be derived from revisiting these ideas, which carry valuable lessons on the role of banks within the financial and economic system.

What we are currently witnessing could be described as a system that has become unstable because some of its constituents act as mutually reinforcing destabilizers through positive feedback loops. That banks serve their own interests on the one hand and play a key role in lubricating the economy, thus serving as public good entities, on the other hand has been widely recognized in recent debates. Many discussions, with different emphasis across the Atlantic, focus of what kind of regulations should therefore be imposed to align the private interests of banks with the public interests. The recent Dodd-Frank act (2010) enacted in the US can be seen as a rather timid step towards a working solution, if not just because many of the changes implied by its implementation are not expected to be fully enacted until 2015 (five years is really like eternity for financial markets!). Consider in contrast that the fifty years following WWII have constituted arguably the most stable economic period in the history of the United States and of Europe. Most scholars attribute a key role for this stability to the Glass-Steagall Act of 1933, which successfully prevented the occurrence of systemic instabilities, by separating by law investment banking, commercial banking, retail banking and insurance. This disaggregation provided completely separated waterproof compartments to prevent any Titanic like event of crisis spreading. Only with deregulation that started taking place in the 1980s culminating in the repelling of the Glass-Steagall act by the Gramm–Leach–Bliley Act of 1999, banking mutated into a new highly interconnected form that recovered basically its pre-1929 role within the ecosystem. Much of the risks that we currently face both in Europe and in the US originate from too much leverage and uncontrolled indebtedness spreading across all networks that build on the incorrect belief that transfers of debts to bigger and bigger entities will solve the problem.

We cannot afford and do not need to wait another decade or more until new super high tech models are developed. Faster solutions are possible by revisiting policies that worked in the past and by relearning and expanding some of the old wisdom in economics, specifically related to the role of banks. These theories should be anchored on rigorous analyses of empirical evidence and enhanced by fertilization with various branches of the natural sciences, network analysis, and out-of-equilibrium agent-based models.

The main bottleneck is not technical but political due to the control exerted by an oligarchy of bankers in effective control of the economy. But this essential truth is hidden in the smoke of complexity and loss of memory of past solutions. It is also convenient to foster the belief of an illusion of the "perpetual money machine", promising unending economic growth from expanding leverage and indebtedness. It is due time that we stop being lulled by these sirens and used either as scapegoats or future prophets. Only then might a genuine science of out-of-equilibrium system economics become credible and useful.

In this context, the Proceedings of the International annual event "*Perm Winter School*" held in February, 2011 on Financial Market Risks is a demonstration of the progresses obtained in the last decade to rejuvenate the financial and economic culture among Russian university students, as well as among practitioners from the private and public sectors. The contributions are varied and cover a large spectrum of important problems with examples and applications relevant to the Russian market, from high-frequency trading, asset pricing models, hedging and liquidity issues, hedge-fund characteristics, models of interest rates, the influence of derivatives, role and limits of present regulation rules, the psychology of traders, the influence of strategic behaviors and the ubiquitous problem of insider trading, agent-based models aiming a reproducing stylized facts and emphasizing the critical behavior of markets and bifurcations, and more. These contributions illustrate that the Russian school of economics and finance has a lot of potential to grow in the future, building on its great mathematical tradition, its reservoir of excellent natural scientists and its growing business oriented economy. In that respect, the co-organization of the conference by Perm State University and the company Prognoz is exemplary even by western standards of the win-win situation provided by close ties between university and companies who share a same vision of achieving professional excellence and individual growth, training and fulfilling lifetime realizations.

References

Bogle, J. C., The fiduciary principle: no man can serve two masters. The Journal of Portfolio Management 36 (1), 15-25 (2009).

Haldane, A. G. and R.M. May, Systemic risk in banking ecosystems. Nature 469, 351-355 (2011).

Johnson, N., Proposing policy by analogy is risky, Nature 469, 302 (2011). T. Lux, Network theory is sorely required, Nature 469, 303 (2011).

Johnson, S., The quiet coup, The Atlantic Online (May 2009) (http://www.theatlantic.com/magazine/archive/2009/05/the-quiet-coup/7364/).

Sornette, D. and R. Woodard, Financial Bubbles, Real Estate bubbles, Derivative Bubbles, and the Financial and Economic Crisis, in Proceedings of APFA7 (Applications of Physics in Financial Analysis), M. Takayasu, T. Watanabe and H. Takayasu, eds., (Springer 2010) (http://arxiv.org/abs/0905.0220).

Werner, R. A., New Paradigm in Macroeconomics (Basingstoke: Palgrave Macmillan 2005).

On the Development of Master in Finance & IT Program in a Perm State National Research University

Dmitry Andrianov

Chair of information systems & mathematical methods of economy,
Department of Economics, Perm State University, and Prognoz, Perm, Russia.
email: adl@prognoz.ru

Natalya Frolova

Chair of information systems & mathematical methods of economy,
Department of Economics, Perm State University, Perm, Russia.
email: nvf_psu@mail.ru

Sergey Ivliev

Chair of information systems & mathematical methods of economy, Department of Economics, Perm State University, and Prognoz Risk Lab, Perm, Russia.
email: ivliev@prognoz.ru

Currently, according to new Russian educational standards in higher education system there is a transition from qualification model to professional competence model. Areas of Higher School modernization associated with the adoption of Russia Bologna Declaration includes: the transition to a two-tiered "the bachelor – master" system of education, the introduction of ECTS credits for the convertibility of diplomas and international educational mobility, the creation of a system of certification and quality control in education (introducing a rating system for both teachers and students alike), development of scientific environment.

In the innovation economy specialist must be able not only to apply the knowledge and skills acquired during education, but also have the necessary competences such as creativity, ability to understand and identify problems and find solutions, teamwork, the ability to structure large amounts of information, etc. Competence that students must master after graduation is settled in the standards for both bachelors and masters. They are divided into competencies related to the subject area (profile, special) and universal (general).

Perm State University participated in the All-Russian competition in 2010 and received the status of a national research university (NRI). The educational process at NRI includes:

- strengthening the role of an independent and practical work of students;
- expansion of the teaching and use of foreign language;
- creation of a world-class laboratories, which conduct the major research work;
- active participation of students in research and development;

D. Sornette et al. (Eds.), *Market Risk and Financial Markets Modeling*,
DOI 10.1007/978-3-642-27931-7_2, © Springer-Verlag Berlin Heidelberg 2012

- transformation of the educational process, providing students with practical competencies, reducing the load of classroom teachers, individualized educational trajectories;
- opening of new educational programs on an international level.

Department of Information Systems and Mathematical Methods in Economics (ISMME) is deeply involved in the modernization of the educational process in connection with the introduction of a new generation of standards for higher professional education and the assignment of PSU status of a national research university. The department has formed a unique R&D cluster with Joint-Stock Company "PROGNOZ". The main activity is held in the development of Decision Support Systems for various industries and tasks, including, the analysis of financial markets as a complex systems. Such integration of academic and applied research and information technologies is even more important in nowadays economy of knowledge.

In the 2011/2012 academic year there were openings of two master's programs, *"Information-analytical systems in forecasting and management processes of socio-economic development of countries and territories"* and *"Master in Finance & Information Technologies (MiFIT)"*. Both programs are implemented within the framework of scientific-educational complex (SEC) "*Predicting and managing the processes of socio-economic development of countries and territories on the basis of modern information technologies*", which is a structural unit of NRI. Implementation of master's programs provides an opportunity for further development of quality scientific and educational processes of the department. But at the same time it requires active human resources policy, stimulating research and educational performance, attraction of leading scientists and experts, professionals, economists, experts in the field of information technology to ensure competitiveness on the international level of academic and labor markets. One of the major challenges faced by the department and JSC "PROGNOZ" is the merger of the educational and R&D processes, assuming the attraction of students to research teams from the first grade.

The curriculum structure of the program is the key competitive point. Studying at the ISMME programs must master a variety of disciplines in three major areas: Math, Finance and Computer Science (IT). We analyzed several masters and undergraduate courses of the following universities and business school: Carnegie Mellon University, Princeton University, Baruch College, London School of Economics and Political Science, Cass Business School, Warwick Business School, Imperial College Business School, etc. So our programs were constructed to address the broader range of fields including:

- Stochastic processes;
- Operation research and optimization;
- Financial engineering;
- Data mining;
- Simulation and copula theory;
- Risk management;

- Data management;
- Information system design and programming;
- E-Commerce.

As part of the MIFIT program the international annual event "*Perm Winter School*" was introduced. The first school was held in February, 2011, organized jointly by PSU and "PROGNOZ" with the support of the Government of Perm Region, National Research Unviersity Higher School of Economics and Professional risk managers' international association (PRMIA).

3-day school program focusing on market risks included lectures, master classes, round tables with participation of renowned researchers and representatives of major financial institutions, as well as evening student sessions.

At a roundtable organized at the second day of the school hot issues of financial market development and risk management were discussed by the Federal Financial Markets Service of Russia, National Bank of Belarus, Sberbank of Russia, investment companies and software vendors.

The school was attended by more than 140 participants from 38 universities and organizations from 6 countries (Belarus, India, Italy, Switzerland, etc.). Additionally 70 people joined the Perm Winter School online.

The successful experience of 2011 had proven this event to be efficient and consistent model of education. Direct communication with outstanding academics, leading practitioners and top managers, allows students to see the problems that still need to be addressed involving young scientists in the world of financial research.

Questions of Top Management to Risk Management

Sergey Chernov

Vitus Asset Management, Perm, Russia. email: chernov@vitus.ru

Nothing is more desirable and frightening for a human as uncertainty. It is the source of all our hopes and fears, victories and defeats. We unite, create companies to reach new heights, great opportunities, but at the same time also multiply and grow our risks. And there is probably no business in the world that is not looking for the answer to the question: "What risks he is prepared to take to achieve the desired result?"

Risks are surrounding the business from all sides, but does business need risk management?

I was lucky enough to come to the Russian business in 1992 and participate in the development of Russian financial market since its inception, through all crises of the last two decades, and see in my company and partner companies the evolution of risk management.

Of course, I cannot answer the question of whether the necessary risk management on behalf of the entire professional community, conducting operations in the financial market and my answer reflects more personal point of view with regard to risk management.

I believe that the risk management system should be in every company, but:

- Each company must come to that decision independently. Forced imposition of risk management in companies with the regulatory bodies will not lead to positive results, as the saying goes: "A horse can be forced to enter into the water, but you cannot make it drinking the water",
- Each company is individual and therefore for each of the risks prioritizing will be individual, this does not allow determination of unified risk prioritization even within a single industry,
- Requirements for the risk management system in the company must comply with its size and scope of business.

In spite of my conviction about the benefits of risk management for the company I feel conflicting opinions about risk management.

If you need absolute confidence in the effectiveness and practical application of various methods of risk management and risk reduction, including minimizing risk, diversification, hedging and other techniques I have doubts on the adequacy of models to measure risks. And the reasons for these doubts are several:

1. There are still vivid memories of the 2008 financial crisis, which led to the collapse of many financial institutions worldwide, who's risk management systems

D. Sornette et al. (Eds.), *Market Risk and Financial Markets Modeling*,
DOI 10.1007/978-3-642-27931-7_3, © Springer-Verlag Berlin Heidelberg 2012

were much better than most financial institutions in Russia can have. It unwittingly doubts the correctness of applied risk assessment models.

2. No matter how good the model is in any case it will contain certain assumptions, limitations within a certain confidence intervals and, therefore, by default will not contain a complete measurement of all cases.
3. The Russian stock market is evolving and improving at a good pace, but it still has enough assets that have no liquidity, not enough historical data, so the risks cannot be adequately assessed by standard valuation models.

One can try to look flaws of existing models of risk measurement for long, some of which will be objectively and realistically reflect system-wide unresolved issues, and some possibly will reflect issues of a particular company. But this is not my task. All these doubts are caused more by the fact that I see a number of unsolved problems:

1. **Methodological support.** For all the sophistication of risk management methodology on a global scale, at the largest financial institutions in Russia, we have to admit that the penetration of risk management by other market participants is significantly lower.
2. **The presence of a moderate skepticism.** The collapse of one large financial institution can be classified as an error of risk-management system of the institution. The collapse of several financial institutions at the same time suggests that the applied models of risk management did not work at the system level, and therefore are subject to detailed analysis of the methodology itself.
3. **Risk management education.** Financial market in Russia is developing so fast that universities are not currently able to ensure full training of the necessary market specialists. This is even more acute for the education in risk management.
4. **The mutual influence of several risks.** While performing operations on all asset classes in financial markets, in many cases we have to deal with the problem of liquidity of assets, which makes a qualitative assessment of market risks of the assets. In this case, there is a challenge to adapt the models to take into account low liquidity of the Russian market.

I hope that what I describe her will be not be considered as the announcement of doubts, but as a landmark of opportunities for further development of risk management, opportunities for new research and new discoveries.

No matter how big is the business, it will not be able locally or remotely by joining professional associations solve their problems without the help of the scientific community. In this regard, Perm Winter School was an amazing event for me, which I'm sure, will give new impetus to the development of risk management, a new platform for interaction between experts, a new place to find common ground between science and business, to engender interest in risk management in young professionals.

Market Risk and Financial Markets Modeling

Estimation of Market Resiliency from High-Frequency Micex Shares Trading Data

Nikolay Andreev

National Research University Higher School of Economics, Moscow, Russia.
email: nick.my.mail@gmail.com

Abstract This article presents an engineering approach to estimating market resiliency based on analysis of the dynamics of a liquidity index. The method provides formal criteria for defining a "liquidity shock" on the market and can be used to obtain resiliency-related statistics for further research and estimation of this liquidity aspect. The developed algorithm uses the results of a spline approximation for observational data and allows a theoretical interpretation of the results. The method was applied to real data resulting in estimation of market resiliency for the given period.

Keywords: liquidity, portfolio liquidation, resiliency, transaction costs, bid-ask spread.

JEL classification: C65; G12.

Introduction

Market liquidity is a point of interest for many practical applications. This paper demonstrates an approach to estimating one of the characteristic of liquidity – market resiliency. This concept was introduced by Kyle (1985) along with two other concepts, tightness and depth, and defined as the rate at which prices recover from the uninformative shock. One of the main applications of this work's result is estimating the minimal time interval between consequent trades during portfolio liquidation, as described, for example, in Almgren & Criss (1999). The main optimal condition of the approach is minimizing transaction costs by dividing the portfolio volume into N parts and liquidating one part per trade. The problem is that each trade will lead to a price impact and large transaction costs, thus making it ineffective to participate in the market immediately after that. Estimating market resiliency will prove important in measuring the time of replenishment for the market and, therefore, the minimal interval between trades.

Measuring resiliency is a relatively new field of research in financial engineering. One of the first approaches in literature was the so-called γ coefficient, the time of a market's returning to "normal" state. "Returning to normal" in this framework means that the bid-ask spread takes on a pre-shock value. Such a concept doesn't take into consideration the fact that for an illiquid market, returning to the

D. Sornette et al. (Eds.), *Market Risk and Financial Markets Modeling*,
DOI 10.1007/978-3-642-27931-7_4,

same values of spread and price may not happen, but move to the new "normal" stationary state.

Another approach was developed in Large (2007), based on using parametric impulse response functions for different kinds of events in the market. In that framework, returning to "normal" state means near-zero values of impulse functions. However, the author indicates that both the bid and the ask have less than 20% of replenishment after the large order.

The approach introduced here uses historical information about MICEX share trades. We use historical data to define shock states as a significant deviation from common behavior both in the nearest past and the nearest future. The statistics obtained are used to define the longest period of continuous shock condition, which is later used as an estimator of market resiliency.

The paper proceeds as follows: Section 2 describes the formal criterion for defining shock states of the market and analyses the results, Section 3 concludes.

Method for Detecting Shock States of a Liquidity Indicator

In this section we provide an engineering approach to estimating market resiliency using high-frequency shares trading data. The method is based on analysis of a liquidity index (phase variable). In this work we focus on the Xetra Liquidity Measure, closely related to average price impact costs, as the variable. This index aggregates the market impact information on the bid and ask side of the limit order book. It describes the performance loss due to liquidity costs that occur during simultaneous opening and closing a position of volume V. Construction of the index is quite simple and can be obtained from the following algorithm: for each moment t let $B_t(V)$ be the aggregate cost of opening a position of volume V, $C_t(V)$ – the aggregate cost of closing a position of the same volume. Then, by Xetra Liquidity Measure at the moment t we mean

$$\text{Xetra Liquidity Measure}_t(V) = \frac{B_t(V) - C_t(V)}{V}.$$

The associated volume V must be rather large to avoid negligible fluctuations in the dynamics. In the following research we take V *equal to* half of the average traded volume during trading period. For more information about Xetra Liquidity Measure index see Gomber & Schweickert (2002).

In this framework we define "liquidity shock" as the deviation of the phase variable, hereafter $Y(t)$, from its typical behavior. By shock length we mean the time necessary to return to the normal state. Fig.1 shows $Y(t)$ dynamics for "Lukoil" shares for 30 minutes in the middle of the trading period (10th January, 2006).

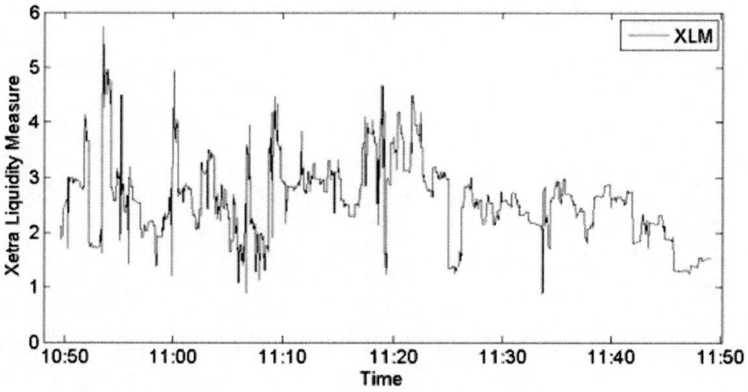

Fig. 1: Phase variable dynamics

This case already shows that intuition doesn't always allow one to detect shock states of the market (see, for example, peak at around 11:05 or 11:12). Thus a formal criterion is necessary to separate the normal and extraordinary behavior of the process. The remain of the chapter is divided into three parts

1. Estimating the trend;
2. Constructing a characteristic function for the given trajectory, and interpretation of the results;
3. Providing a criterion to detect irregular states in dynamics.

1. Estimation of common dynamics is necessary for further analysis because it allows one to neglect the influence of the global effects such as monotony or oscillation of the series. The results of the work hold under the following algorithm of defining trend $L(t)$:

Suppose we have observations of the underlying trajectory $(y_0, y_1, ..., y_n) = (Y(t_0), Y(t_1), ..., Y(t_n))$ at the discrete moments of time $t_0 < t_1 < ... < t_n \leq T$. In this case $L(t)$ on [0, T] can be found as the solution of the following minimization problem:

$$\sum_{i=0}^{n} \alpha_i (L(t_i) - Y(t_i))^2 + \varepsilon \int_0^T (L''(s))^2 ds \to \inf_{L \in W},$$

where W is the so-called Sobolev-Hilbert space of functions with an absolutely continuous first derivative and second derivative from $L_2[0,T]$. The a priori parameter ε is positive and represents the tradeoff between fidelity and smoothness (a larger values mean smoother curves). Weights α_i are found as $\alpha_i = \frac{c}{1 + |X(t_i) - \overline{X}|}$, where c is a positive constant to secure the normalization condition $\alpha_0 + \alpha_1 + ... + \alpha_n = 1$. It is shown in Wahba (1990) that the solution of the problem is a piecewise-polynomial function. Figure 2 shows the solution $L(t)$ (dashed line) for sufficiently large ε.

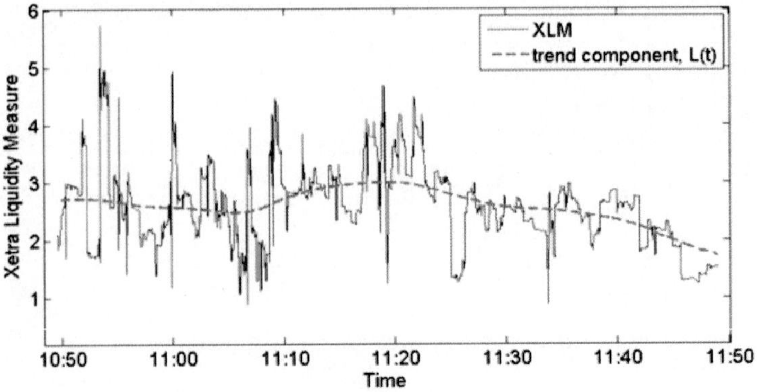

Fig. 2: Trend and trajectory of the phase variable

It is worth mentioning that the algorithm converges to the least-squares method as $\varepsilon \longrightarrow +\infty$.

2. ***Constructing a characteristic function*** of the given series requires that some assumptions hold. We formally assume that $(y_0, y_1, \ldots, y_n) = (Y(t_0), Y(t_1), \ldots, Y(t_n))$ are the noised observations of a trajectory of some general stochastic process $F(t)$. The proposed model is

$$F(t) = L(t) + bX(t), \quad t \in [0, T],$$

$$Y(t_i) = F(t_i) + \eta_i, \quad i = 0, 1, \ldots, n,$$

where $L(t)$ is a stationary component found in the previous stage;

b is an unknown positive constant;

$X(t)$ is the integrated Wiener process, i.e. Gaussian process with zero mean and known covariance function:

$$EX(t) = 0, \; R(t,s) = EX(t)X(s) = \int_0^T (t-u)_+ (s-u)_+ \, du,$$

where $x_+ = \max(x, 0)$;

$\eta_0, \eta_1, \ldots, \eta_n$ are i.i.d. random variables with normal distribution $N(0, \sigma^2)$. Under the assumptions the following statement holds:

Theorem (Kimeldorf & Wahba, 1970): let $\hat{F}(t)$ be the minimum variance, unbiased linear estimate of $F(t)$ given $(y_0, y_1, \ldots, y_n) = (Y(t_0), Y(t_1), \ldots, Y(t_n))$. Let $f_\varepsilon(t)$ be the solution of the minimization problem

$$\sum_{i=0}^{n} \alpha_i \left(f(t_i) - Y(t_i)\right)^2 + \varepsilon \int_0^T \left(f''(s)\right)^2 ds \to \inf_{f \in W}, \quad \varepsilon = \frac{\sigma^2}{b^2},$$

where W is the Sobolev-Hilbert space of functions with absolutely continuous first derivative and second derivative from $L_2[0,T]$. *Then* $\hat{F}(t) = f_\varepsilon(t)$.

From here on it is convenient to think of $f_\varepsilon(t)$ as a function of two arguments *t* and ε: $f_\varepsilon(t) \equiv f(t,\varepsilon)$. Using the statement it follows that, with the assumption of fixed $\varepsilon = \varepsilon_0$, the residual will be

$$E\left(\hat{F}(t) - F(t) \mid \varepsilon = \varepsilon_0\right)^2 =$$
$$\left(f(t,\varepsilon_0) - L(t)\right)^2 + 2b\left(f(t,\varepsilon_0) - L(t)\right)EX(t) + b^2 EX^2(t) =$$
$$= const + g^2(t,\varepsilon_0),$$

where $g(t,\varepsilon) = f(t,\varepsilon) - L(t)$ is the deviation from the "mean" function.

However, real data does not allow one to directly use the results of the Theorem, due to the unknown parameters *b*, dispersion σ^2, and, therefore, the regularization parameter ε. This problem can be avoided by allowing only a priori information about ε but **not** its **exact value**. Assuming that we know some information about **the possible values** of parameter, it is convenient to use logical interpretation of probability and consider ε as a random variable with a priori distribution. In the case of no exogenous information available, the only property of the regularization parameter is positivity. Thus the most appropriate distribution is exponential with mean λ based on the fact that among distributions on positive semi axis and with fixed mean the exponential possesses the maximal entropy. Empirical studies show that the method is robust to the choice of λ which allows a rough estimation of the parameter according to the sufficiency of the results. In this demonstration $\lambda = 1$ was used.

The stochastic nature of ε leads to finding the **expected residual** $E_\varepsilon E\left(\hat{F}(t) - F(t)\right)^2$ of the estimation:

$$E_\varepsilon E\left(\hat{F}(t) - F(t)\right)^2 = const + \int_0^{+\infty} \lambda e^{-\lambda\varepsilon} g^2(t,\varepsilon) d\varepsilon = const + \psi(t),$$

$$\psi(t) = \lambda \int_0^{+\infty} e^{-\lambda\varepsilon} g^2(t,\varepsilon) d\varepsilon.$$

The obtained function $\psi(t)$ is non-negative and has sharp deviations when the expected residual is at its maximum. Therefore, at such moments, the estimation of the phase dynamics by observations is most difficult, i.e. the variable's behavior aberrates from usual and predictable, interpreted in this framework as a shock state. Only the relative amplitude of $\psi(t)$ is important, so it is computationally easier to work with normalized values of the function. Figure 3 demonstrates the behavior of the original trajectory and the corresponding characteristic function.

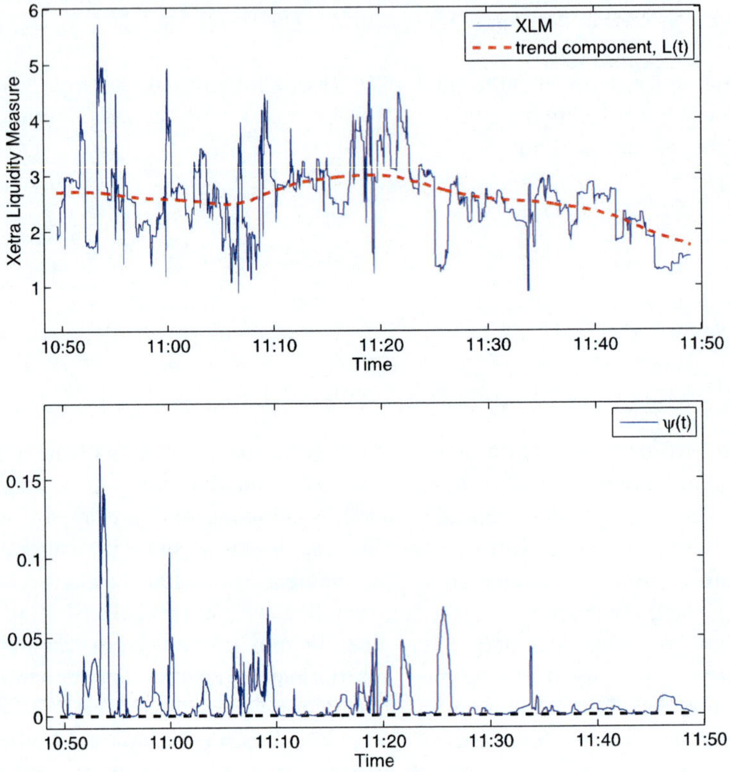

Fig. 3: Phase variable dynamics and characteristic function

The obtained results show that the stationary dynamics of the series correspond to near-zero values of $\psi(t)$. All "obvious" shock states match the function's deviations with high amplitude.

The method can be improved through classifying deviations by either ascending or descending behavior of the trajectory (hereafter upper and lower shocks correspondingly). In particular, a point of interest is detecting upward aberrations (lack of liquidity at the market), which is a direct consequence of the economic interpretation of the phase variable (Xetra Liquidity Measure). The final result of the resiliency's estimation will be based on this class of shocks.

The direction of shock for each moment t can be approximately established by using the sign of the deviation function $g(t,\varepsilon)$. For the case of the stochastic nature of ε we follow the same logic as before and derive the sign function

$$\chi(t) = sign \ \lambda \int_0^{+\infty} e^{-\lambda\varepsilon} g(t,\varepsilon)d\varepsilon \quad .$$

Then $\chi(t) = 1$ for upper shocks and $\chi(t) = -1$ otherwise. From now on the characteristic function of the trajectory can be written as

$$\psi(t) = \chi(t) \cdot \lambda \int_0^{+\infty} e^{-\lambda\varepsilon} g^2(t,\varepsilon)d\varepsilon.$$

It has the same properties as the previous one except for non-negativity. Aberrations of $\psi(t)$ in the positive half plane mean a decrease in liquidity. Figure 4 demonstrates the behavior of the original trajectory and the renewed characteristic function.

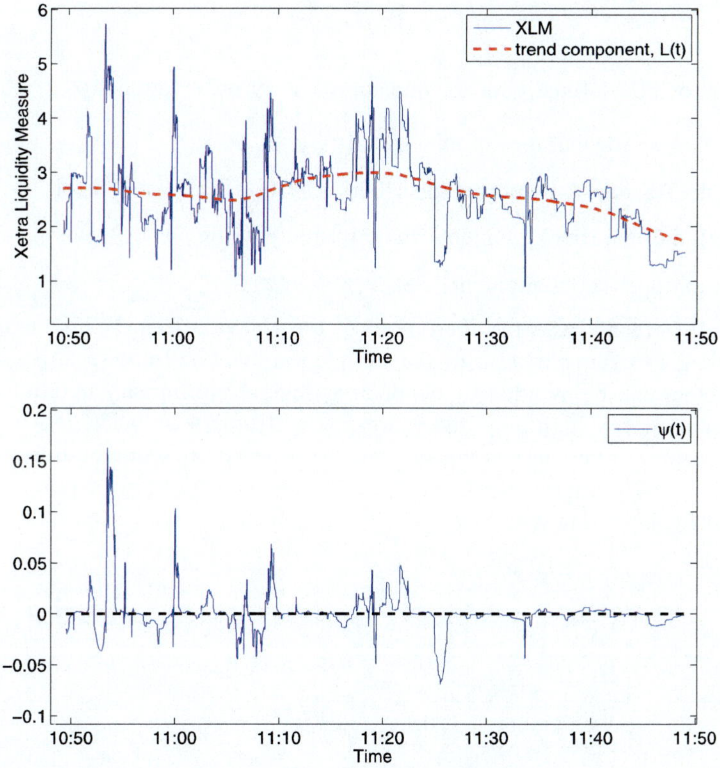

Fig. 4: Phase variable dynamics and characteristic function

$\psi(t)$ already allows visible detection of both types of shocks, and in particular a lack in liquidity. The next part of the section will provide an algorithm for an automatic strategy.

3. The formal criterion of shock will be based on constructing feasible bounds for the characteristic function. Overrunning these bounds will indicate shock behavior of the market. Instead of the continuous function $\psi(t)$ we consider a vector of its values $(\psi(t_0), \psi(t_1), ..., \psi(t_n))$ for discrete moments of time $t_0 < t_1 < ... < t_n \leq T$ (in this work the time-step is one second). The approach will be illustrated for the upper-shock bound but can be easily extrapolated for the other class.

For this purpose we consider only $(\psi_0, \psi_1, ..., \psi_k) = (\psi(t_0'), \psi(t_1'), ..., \psi(t_k'))$, where moments $t_0', t_1', ..., t_k'$ are such that $\psi(t_i') \geq 0$. The upper-shock bound $m(t)$ can be constructed with various methods. The upper confidence level concept is proposed as rather simple and simultaneously efficient. We formally assume that

$$\psi(t_i) = l(t_i) + v_i, \;\; v_i - i.i.d., \;\; N(0, \sigma_\psi^2),$$

which provides the following formula for $m(t)$:

$$m(t_i) = l(t_i) + q_\alpha \sigma_\psi,$$

where $l(t)$ can be defined with a spline approach for observations $(\psi_0, \psi_1, ..., \psi_k)$;

σ_ψ^2 is the sample variance of the series $(\psi_0, \psi_1, ..., \psi_k)$;

q_α is the fractile of the normal distribution $N(0, \sigma_\psi^2)$ for $\alpha\%$ level.

The criterion of the shock moment can be formally written as

$\{\tau$ is an upper-shock moment$\} \Leftrightarrow \psi(\tau) > m(\tau)$.

Comment: In many cases the aberrations of $\psi(t)$ have extremely high amplitude, thus leading to overestimation of the sample variance and not sensitive bounds. This problem can be avoided by conducting several preliminary iterations of the algorithm to remove high-amplitude moments t_i' from the associated set.

Fig.5 demonstrates the graphics of the characteristic function and the obtained bounds for a 99% confidence level. Fig.6 shows the trajectory of phase variable with marked shock states.

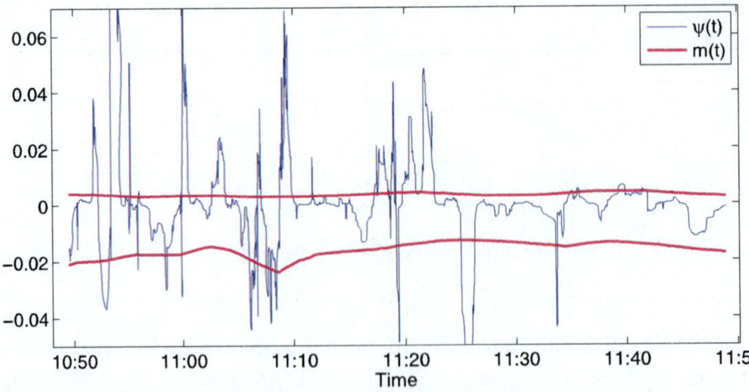

Fig. 5: Characteristic function and feasible bounds

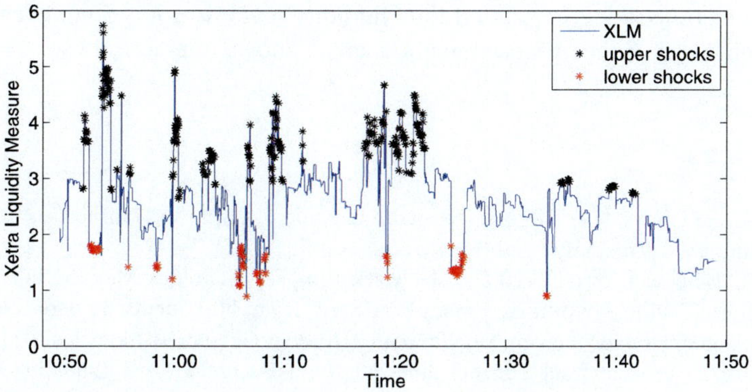

Fig. 6: Original trajectory with marked shocks

Market resiliency can now be estimated according to the statistics of continuous shock-periods. As for upper shocks, Table 1 shows that with 99.2% confidence, a 50 second period proves long enough for the market to recover after a shock. This estimate can be successfully used as a minimal time interval between consequent trades during piecewise liquidation strategy.

Table 1: Length of upper-shock states and percentage during 10th January, 2006, for "Lukoil" shares

Shock length	Percentage
< 50 seconds	99.2%
< 45 seconds	97.6%
< 30 seconds	88.1%
< 6 seconds	54.0%
< 5 seconds	49.2%

Conclusion

To quantify resiliency, a method for detecting shock states of the market was proposed. It allows automatic identification of aberrations in terms of a phase trajectory as a characteristic of liquidity. The algorithm is based on a smooth approximation approach and does not impound conditions on input data (long-term stable periods, sufficient period of time etc.). The robustness of the method and the easy interpretation of the results, correlating with the intuitive definition of shock, make it appropriate for obtaining statistics from historical data to estimate market resiliency. The method was tested on MICEX liquid shares trading data. For a period of one trading day it was shown that with a high (99.2%) level of confidence, 50 seconds are enough for the market to restore after an uninformative liquidity shock. Similar results can be derived for other periods and shares. But returning to a previous value of transaction costs, and thus liquidity level, is not a usual event at the market, which gives the proposed method an advantage in practical use.

References

Almgren, R., & Chriss, N.A. (1999). Optimal Execution of Portfolio Transactions. Retrieved from http://www.math.nyu.edu/faculty/chriss/optliq_f.pdf

Gomber, P., & Schweickert, U. (2002). The Market Impact - Liquidity Measure in Electronic Securities Trading, Working Paper. Retrieved from http://deutsche-berse.com/dbag/dispatch/en/binary/gdb_content_pool/imported_files/public_files/10_downloads/31_trading_member/10_Products_and_Functionalities/40_Xetra_Funds/30_Xetra_Liquidity_Measure/liq_wph.pdf

Kimeldorf, G.S., & Wahba, G. (1970). Spline Functions and Stochastic Processes. The Indian Journal of Statistics. Series A, Vol.32, No 2,173-180.

Kyle, A. (1985). Continuous Auctions and Insider Trading. Econometrica, 53, 1315-1336.

Large, J. (2007). Measuring the resiliency of an electronic limit order book. Journal of Financial Markets, 10, 1-25.

Wahba, G.(1990). Spline Models for Observational Data. Philadelphia, PA: SIAM.

Market Liquidity Measurement and Econometric Modeling

Viacheslav Arbuzov

Department of Economics, Perm State University, Perm, Russia.
email: arbuzov@prognoz.ru

Maria Frolova

Prognoz Risk Lab, Perm, Russia. email: frolovam@prognoz.ru

Abstract This paper presents an econometric approach to liquidity modeling. We consider transaction cost indices of market liquidity based on a full order book and then try to estimate relationships with observable market variables. The research is based on the detailed market data, which include order history and trades execution data, for Moscow Interbank Currency Exchange (MICEX) listed stocks in September, 2010.

Keywords: Liquidity measurement, market microstructure, price impact.

JEL classification: G15, G17.

Introduction

Liquidity is traditionally considered as the possibility for market participants to buy or sell any given amount of security almost instantly without significant price impact (Berkowitz, 2000). The level of liquidity of a certain security entirely depends on how the particular market is structured, i.e. market microstructure. The main objective of our research is to analyze transaction costs and their relation to observable market variables (volumes, prices, etc.).

Liquidity is a multifaceted concept. Trading liquid stocks is characterized by small transaction costs, easy trading and timely settlement, with large trades having negligible impact on market price. At the moment there is no commonly accepted indicator that solely reflects the degree of market liquidity (Cosandey, 2001; Francois-Heude, Van Wynendaele, 2001). Some of the indicators are based on the observable market data: volume, number of trades, bid-ask spread, etc., while the others are estimated from the order book data covering inner aspects of liquidity (Sarr, Lybek, 2002). The question we raise in our paper is whether an integrated metric of liquidity can be proposed and how it is related to the observable market variables.

D. Sornette et al. (Eds.), *Market Risk and Financial Markets Modeling*,
DOI 10.1007/978-3-642-27931-7_5, © Springer-Verlag Berlin Heidelberg 2012

Market Liquidity Measurement

Market liquidity is defined by the structure and the dynamics of the order book. The three major metrics as proposed by Kyle (1985) are tightness, depth and resiliency. The first two can be illustrated in a static order book snapshot (see Fig.1), while the resiliency is a dynamical measure of the order book's recovery after temporary liquidity shocks.

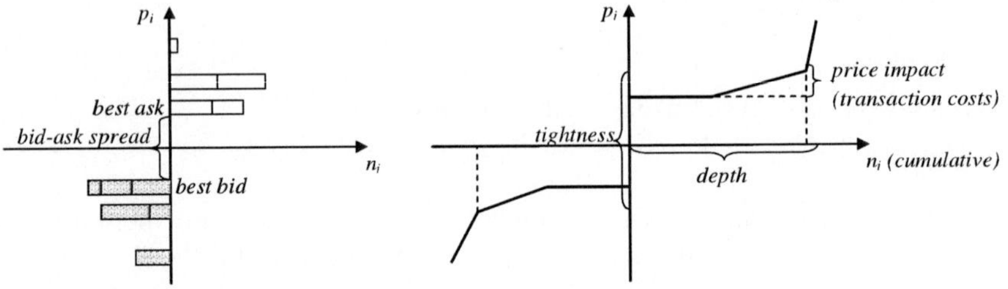

Fig. 1: Order book and liquidity characteristics representation

To integrate depth and tightness, a single metric can be calculated to represent the price impact of buying and/or selling a given amount. This is typically referred as transaction cost (Hachmeister, Schiereck, 2006). Given a roundtrip transaction the measure is widely use to estimate liquidity, e.g. the Xetra Liquidity Measure (XLM) (Krogmann, 2011). We propose a transaction cost index (TCI) for one shot buying and selling of the full order book as a measure of liquidity:

$$TCI = \sum_{i=1}^{k} |p_i - p| \cdot n_i \qquad (1)$$

where

i – order position in the order book, i=1..k,
k – total number of limit orders in the book,
p_i – price of order i,
n_i – volume of order i, n_i<0 for buy side orders,
p – current market price.

TCI represents the cash value of the price impact due to non-tightness of the full order book. In order to compare transaction costs across stocks, we introduce a relative transaction cost index (RTCI) as TCI normalized by the total value of supply and demand:

$$RTCI = \frac{\sum_{i=1}^{k} |p_i - p| \cdot n_i}{\sum_{i=1}^{k} p_i n_i} \qquad (2)$$

We have assumed a negative correlation between RTCI and trading volume, i.e. the deeper and more compact the market is (the more liquid the asset is) the less is RTCI. This assumption was confirmed by real data (see Fig. 2 with formed clusters): more liquid stocks locate in the lower right part of the plot, illiquid stocks – in the upper left part.

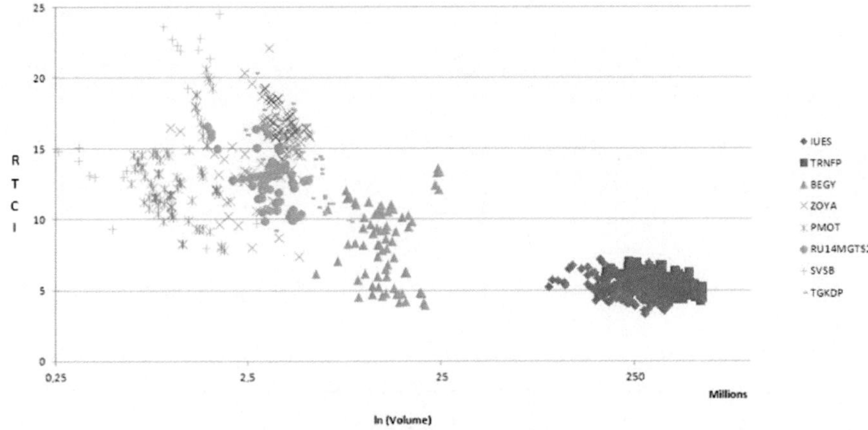

Fig. 2: Interrelation between trading volume and RTCI

RTCI can be calculated for the sell side (3) and buy side (4) orders separately. Their difference is considered to evaluate the view of market participants about subsequent market movements.

$$RTCI_{sell} = \frac{\sum_{i=1}^{k_{sell}} (p_i - p) n_i}{\sum_{i=1}^{k_{sell}} p_i n_i} \tag{3}$$

$$RTCI_{buy} = \frac{\sum_{i=1}^{k_{buy}} (p - p_i) n_i}{\sum_{i=1}^{k_{buy}} p_i n_i} \tag{4}$$

In order to obtain information about an imbalance of market costs we combined the expressions (3) and (4) to construct Preference Costs Index (PCI). PCI gives an idea about the level of sparseness asymmetry of the limit order book.

$$PCI = RTCI_{sell} - RTCI_{buy} \tag{5}$$

The scatter plot of PCI versus next minute log-return of mid price for a sample of 561 Russian equities is shown on Fig. 4.

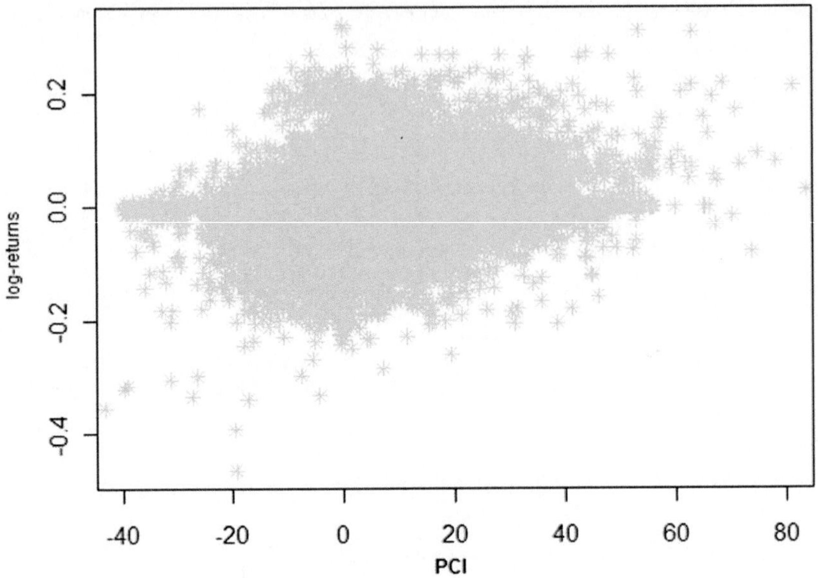

Fig. 3: PCI vs. next minute log-returns scatter plot (sample of 561 Russian equities)

To investigate a possible dependency in the tails we have filtered out log-returns less than 10% (scatter plot is shown on Fig.4).

PCI values for positive returns over the threshold significantly differ from negative returns over the threshold (Box-and-Whisker diagram is shown on Fig. 4. Two-sample t-test for PCI mean values for positive vs. negative returns is significant on 1% level.

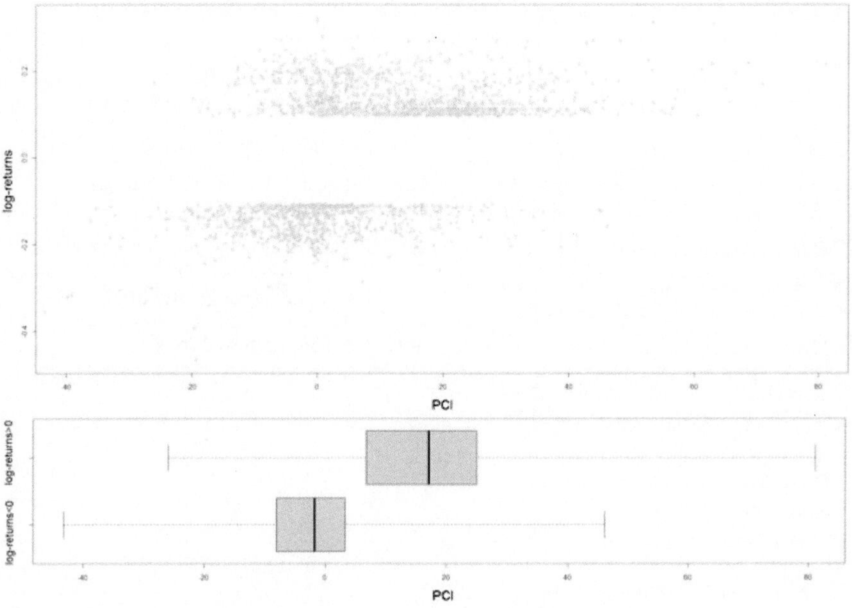

Fig. 4: PCI vs. next minute log-returns over 10% threshold scatter plot and PCI box-and-whisker diagram.

Market Characteristics and RTCI Modeling

In this section we report results of estimation of relationship between the Relative Transaction Cost Index (RTCI), which requires full order book data, and several quantitative market aggregates publicly available (such as volume of trades, number of executions, etc.). We use a linear regression on panel data to estimate these relationships.

For the analysis, we selected 19 equities of Russian companies and divided them into 2 groups: liquid and illiquid stocks. The group of liquid equities contains securities which had an average value of RTCI less than 10% during September 2010, the group of illiquid equities contains securities with the average value of RTCI above 10% (see Table 1). Further, we constructed econometric models on panel data.

Table 1: The sample of securities analyzed

Liquid	**Illiquid**
JSC "Aeroflot" (common stock)	JSC "Zoloto Yakutii" (common stock)
JSC "AVTOVAZ" (preferred stock)	JSC "Sverdlovenergosbyt" (common stock)
JSC FGC UES (Federal Grid Company of Unified Energy System) (common stock)	JSC "Udmurtskaya energosbytovaya kompaniya" (common stock)
JSC Gazprom (common stock)	JSC "Permskie motory" (common stock)
OJSC Mining and Metallurgical Company "NORILSK NICKEL" (common stock)	JSC "Kvadra" (WGC-4) (preferred stock)
JSC "RusHydro" (common stock)	JSC "MGTS" (preferred stock)
OJSC INTER RAO UES (common stock)	
OJSC Oil Company "LUKOIL" (common stock)	
OJSC The Magnitogorsk Iron and Steel Works (common stock)	
JSC "WGC-3" (common stock)	
JSC Gazprom Neft (common stock)	
JSC Transneft (common stock)	
OJSC VTB Bank OJSC (common stock)	

The following market indicators were considered as predictors:

1. *Daily average bid-ask spread.* Bid-ask spreads are the most commonly used measure of transaction (execution) costs (both implicit and explicit). Bid-ask spreads reflect the dealers' uncertainty about the equilibrium price. The bid-ask spread is a premium for market makers to compensate for the potential losses in providing a continuous market. If there are numerous participants willing to trade, transaction costs are smaller. High transaction costs reduce the demand, which could also lead to a shallow market. The percentage spread allows us to compare across markets and securities. We considered percentage bid-ask spread as a measure of depth:

$$S_i = \frac{P_{A_i} - P_{B_i}}{(P_{A_i} + P_{B_i})/2} \tag{6}$$

$$S_d = \frac{1}{N} \sum_{i=1}^{N} S_i \tag{7}$$

P_A – the lowest Ask-price at the end of ith hour of a trade day;
P_B – the highest Bid-price at the end of ith hour of a trade day;
S_i – percentage bid-ask spread at the end of ith hour of a trade day;
N – the number of hours during a trade day;
S_d – daily average percentage bid-ask spread.

2. *Daily average turnover rate*

$$TurnoverRateHour_j = \frac{\sum_{i=1}^{Q_j} p_{ij} q_{ij}}{S * p_j} \tag{8}$$

$$TurnoverRate = \frac{\sum_{j} TurnoverRateHour_j}{N} \tag{9}$$

Q_j – the number of trades during j hour;
p_{ij}, q_{ij} – prices and quantities of the i trade during j hour of a trade day;
S – the outstanding stock of the asset;
p_j – the average price of the asset during j hour of a trade day;
N – the number of hours during a trade day;
$TurnoverRateHour_j$ – turnover rate during j hour of a trade day;
$TurnoverRate$ – daily average turnover rate.

Trading volume is traditionally applied to evaluate the degree of activity of market participants. It also could be revised to be relative to the outstanding volume of the security. The daily average turnover rate is a volume-based measure that indicates the existence of both numerous and large orders in volume with minimal price impact. The turnover rate reveals the traded part of the outstanding volume.

3. *Daily average Hui-Heubel Liquidity Ratio*

$$L_{hh}\_hour_i = \frac{(p\min_i - p\max_i)/p\min_i}{TurnoverRateHour_i} \tag{10}$$

$$L_{hh} = \frac{\sum_{i=1}^{N} L_{hh}\_hour_i}{N} \tag{11}$$

$Pmax_i$ – the highest price at the end of *i* hour of a trade day;
$Pmin_i$ – the lowest price at the end of *i* hour of a trade day;
N – the number of hours during trade day of a trade day;
$TurnoverRateHour_i$ – turnover rate of *i* hour of a trade day;
$L_{hh}\_hour_i$ – Hui-Heubel Liquidity Ratio of *i* hour of a trade day;
L_{hh} – daily average Hui-Heubel Liquidity Ratio

The Hui-Heubel liquidity ratio captures the resiliency dimension of liquidity. The numerator of the ratio measures the percentage change in the price over a chosen period (here an hour). In case the prices are not available, bid-ask prices could be used as a proxy. The denominator of the the Hui-Heubel liquidity ratio is the turnover rate. This indicator reveals the volumes of trades against their price impacts: the lower the Hui-Heubel liquidity ratio, the higher the liquidity of the asset.

4. *Daily average yield (return) of asset price*

$$Yield\_hour_i = \frac{P_i - P_{i-1}}{P_{i-1}} \tag{12}$$

$$Yield = \frac{\sum_{i=1}^{N} Yield\_hour}{N} \tag{13}$$

P_i – the market price at the end of *i* hour of trade day;
N – the number of hours during trade day;
$YieldHour_i$ – yield of the asset during *i* hour of trade day;
$Yield$ – daily average yield of an asset.

5. *Daily number of trades*
6. *Daily volume*
7. *Daily average volume of a trade*
8. *Daily average price of an asset*

$$\mathrm{Pr}ice\_hour_i = \frac{(P_{A_i} + P_{B_i})}{2} \tag{14}$$

$$\mathrm{Pr}ice = \frac{\sum_{i=1}^{N} \mathrm{Pr}ice\_hour_i}{N} \tag{15}$$

P_{Ai}	– the lowest Ask-price at the end of ith hour of a trade day;
P_{Bi}	– the highest Bid-price at the end of ith hour of a trade day;
N	– the number of hours during a trade day;
$Price\_hour_i$	– the price of the asset at the end of ith hour of a trade day;
$Price$	– daily average price of an asset.

We combined the time series into 2 panel samples: for liquid and illiquid equities, and built linear regressions for these 2 groups of variables. Firstly, we constructed a correlation matrix between a dependent variable and predictors. Then, independent variables with low correlation coefficient with RTCI were excluded from the matrix. We also excluded from the matrix one of each pair of independent variables which had a high correlation coefficient between themselves. Finally, we also excluded from the final linear regressions the factors with a high p-value of the corresponding t-statistics.

The best model for group of liquid stocks that we constructed is shown at Table 2:

Table 2: Statistical parameters of the RTCI model for the group of liquid stocks

Coefficient	Value	Standard Error	t-Statistics	Probability
A0 (constant)	4.93	0.3509	14.0498	0.0000
X1 (AVERAGE VOLUME OF A TRADE[t])	-13.58	2.3518	-5.7730	0.0000
X2 (PERCENTAGE SPREAD[t])	243.68	70.2792	3.4674	0.0006
X3 (TURNOVER RATE[t])	50.31	3.0830	16.3179	0.0000
Adjusted coefficient of determination (adj R^2)	0.66			
F-Statistics (F)	189.04			

The average volume of a trade has the most influence on RTCI. The value of RTCI shrinks by 13.58 % on average as the average volume of a trade increases by 1 million units. The higher the volume of a trade the lower transaction costs. At the same time, if the percentage spread increases by 1%, RTCI rises by 2.43%. RTCI rises with the rise of transaction costs. RTCI also increases with an increasing rate of trading volume.

During the trade day, any trader can observe only the best 20 buy orders and the best 20 sell orders. Hence we also calculated the assumed repressors for the visible part of order book. We analyzed the linear relation between RTCI calculated on the base of all of the limit order book and RTCI calculated on the base of the best 20 orders for buy and sell. Thus we added to the list of regressors RTCI calculated on the base of the best 20 orders for buy and sell (Table 3).

The daily average percentage spread was excluded from the equation because of the high correlation with RTCI calculated on the base of the best 20 orders for buy and sell. The values of the F-statistics and the coefficient of determination increased, indicating an improvement in the quality of the model.

Table 3: Statistical parameters of the model for the group of liquid stocks (with RTCI calculated on the base of the best 20 orders for buy and sell as predictor)

Coefficient	Value	Standard Error	t-Statistics	Probability
A0 (constant)	3.56	0.31	11.46	0.0000
X1 (AVERAGE VOLUME OF A TRADE[t])	-4.35	2.24	-1.94	0.0531
X2 (TURNOVER RATE[t])	34.05	3.37	10.11	0.0000
X3 (RTCI FOR THE BEST 20 ORDERS[t])	3.31	0.36	9.18	0.0000
Adjusted coefficient of determination (adj R^2)	0.73			
F-Statistics (F)	258.54			

For the illiquid stocks we failed to create a model on panel data. None of the constructed models demonstrated acceptable properties. Yet we should note that construction of a sufficient model is possible for a single illiquid asset, but the set of significant factors varies between securities. As an example, the model of RTCI calculated for trading common stock of JSC "Sverdlovenergosbyt" can be seen below (Table 4).

For the case of illiquid stocks we also attempted to include RTCI calculated on the base of the visible part of the limit order book, but in all cases this factor turned out to be insignificant. See the example of JSC "Sverdlovenergosbyt" below (Table 5).

Table 4: Statistical parameters of the model for the Sverdlovenergosbyt stock

Coefficient	Value	Standard Error	t-Statistics	Probability
A0 (constant)	3.55	2.41	1.47	0.1585
X1 (PERCENTAGE SPREAD[t])	46.68	12.26	3.81	0.0013
X2 (TURNOVER RATE[t])	3 044.37	803.24	3.79	0.0013
X3 (VALUE OF THE BEST 20 ORDERS SVSB[t])	42.71	11.54	3.70	0.0016
Adjusted coefficient of determination (adj R^2)	0.61			
F-Statistics (F)	11.90			

Table 5: Statistical parameters of the model for the Sverdlovenergosbyt stock (with RTCI calculated on the base of the best 20 orders for buy and sell as predictor)

Coefficient	Value	Standard Error	t-Statistics	Probability
A0 (constant)	3.46	2.55	1.36	0.1921
X1 (PERCENTAGE SPREAD SVSB[t])	45.44	15.23	2.98	0.0083
X2 (TURNOVER RATE SVSB[t])	3 017.09	846.86	3.56	0.0024
X3 (VALUE OF THE BEST 20 ORDERS SVSB[t])	42.08	12.64	3.33	0.0040
X4 (RTCI FOR THE BEST 20 ORDERS SVSB[t])	0.02	0.17	0.15	0.8855
Adjusted coefficient of determination (adj R^2)	0.59			
F-Statistics (F)	8.44			

Conclusion

We proposed to consider the Relative Transaction Cost Indicator as a possible indicator of market liquidity that reflects such liquidity dimensions as depth and tightness and evaluates the sparseness of the limit order book. We constructed econometric models to describe the interconnections between RTCI and observable market variables. Indicators as daily average bid-ask spread, daily average volume of a trade and daily average turnover rate turned out to be the most significant factors that affect liquidity for liquid stocks. We failed to build an econometric model for illiquid stocks on panel data, yet a model for a particular illiquid security could be constructed.

For further econometric analysis of market liquidity we plan to use an enlarged sample of equities represented on the equity market of MICEX, giving a more detailed selection with different levels of equities liquidity. That will allow us to estimate the influence of different predictors on the liquidity and compare their impact on different levels of liquidity.

We also will try to construct econometric models not only for RTCI as an independent factor, but also for other indicators that represent different aspects of liquidity. Constructing an integral indicator that reflects market liquidity is an issue for further research.

References

Berkowitz, J. (2000) Incorporating Liquidity Risk Into Value-at-Risk Models. Working paper, University of California, Irvine.

Cosandey, D. (2001) Adjusting Value at Risk for Market Liquidity Risk, pp.115-118.

Francois-Heude, A., P. Van Wynendaele (2001) Integrating Liquidity Risk in a Parametric Intraday VaR Framework. Working paper.

Hachmeister A., Schiereck D. (2006) Dancing in the Dark: Post-trade Anonymity, Liquidity and Informed Trading

Krogmann M. (2011) Quantifying liquidity risk.

Le Saout E. (2002) Incorporating liquidity risk in VaR models.

Sarr A., Lybek T. (2002) Measuring liquidity in financial markets. IMF Working Paper. WP/02/232.

Modeling of Russian Equity Market Microstructure (MICEX:HYDR Case)

Tatyana Efremova

Department of Economics, Perm State University, and Prognoz Risk Lab, Perm, Russia.
email: efremova@prognoz.ru

Sergey Ivliev

Department of Economics, Perm State University, and Prognoz Risk Lab, Perm, Russia

Abstract This working paper contains quantitative and qualitative analysis and preliminary modeling of the Russian equity market using the example of RusHydro stock (MICEX:HYDR). Four major classes of agents were identified, including large long-term traders, high-frequency traders, small high-frequency traders and small manual traders. Econometric models and conditional distributions were estimated in attempt to reproduce their behavior.

Keywords: market microstructure, Russian equity market, econometric modeling.

JEL classification: G15, G17.

Introduction

Quantitative study of market microstructure is an extremely hot topic due to the increasing role of market liquidity in the family of market risks. Liquidity is determined by the particular market participants' willingness to trade. Thus, understanding the structure and behavior of market participants becomes a key source for estimation and management of liquidity risk.

Common approaches used to model market microstructure come from the field of game theory and agent-based modeling. The models which are used to describe the behavior of agents typically imply assumptions about the types of market participants and their specific features: whether they are informed (Easley, 2011), overconfident (Lin, 2003), impatient (Rosu, 2008), myopic adapting (Harras, Sornette, 2011) and so on. The problem of model calibration to the real market data remains a challenge. Agent-based models have many more parameters compared to other approaches and require sophisticated calibration procedures and deep knowledge of the real market structures (Darley, Outkin, 2007).

Our study is based on detailed market data which include orders history and deals execution data for RusHydro stock (MICEX: HYDR). RusHydro is the largest Russian hydro-generating company and the second largest in the world in terms of installed capacity. The HYDR equity is referred to as blue chip and included in the

D. Sornette et al. (Eds.), *Market Risk and Financial Markets Modeling*,
DOI 10.1007/978-3-642-27931-7_6,

MICEX index. During the observed period, on average 18100 orders arrived daily, 441 million stocks daily were bought and sold yielding a 15.6 billion rubles (approximately $502.6 million) monthly turnover. A total of 16892 market participants appeared to trade.

Model Description

Data Preparation

We have applied an econometric approach to time series that describe decision-making functions: orders submission frequency, orders average prices, orders size. The time series were aggregated from the agents' resolved order book history to the minutes frequency. Hereinafter we use term "agent" to describe a modeled market participant. The following characteristics were calculated for each agent:

- Buy/sell limit order submission frequency, orders per minute;
- Traded volume, shares per minute;
- Weighted average of order prices submitted, rubles;
- Last trade price of the minute, rubles.

Agent Clustering

In order to reverse engineer the agents' typology, we wanted to cluster the market participants to form homogeneous groups based on their behavior attributes such as intensity of order placement, average order size, deviation of order price from market price, etc.

At first, we tried to obtain clusters by algorithmic clustering (k-means, o-means, nearest neighborhood algorithms), but the output groups were not robust, highly dependant on the variables selected and algorithm's parameters. As a solution, the following primary categorization was proposed (Fig.1).

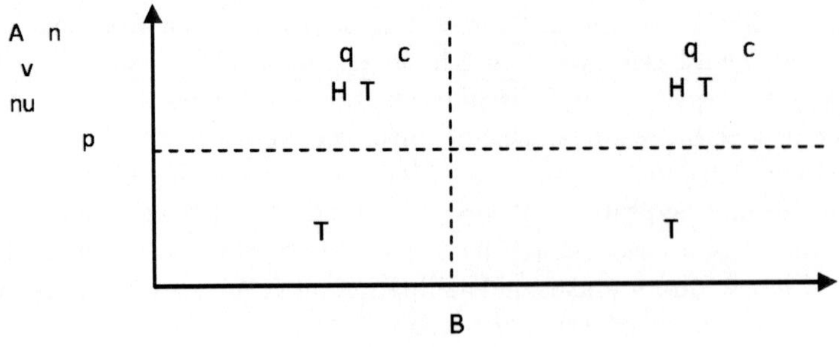

Fig. 1: Agents' 2-factor categorization

Based on empirical data the following thresholds were defined:

- order placement intensity threshold, A=16 (orders per day);
- agent's order volume to total volume threshold, B=1% (of total order volume).

The results of the categorization are provided in Table 1. Despite the relatively small number of LLT, HFT and SHFT agents relative to SMT, they generate almost half of the orders.

Table 1: Results of traders' categorization

Agents type	Number of agents (% of total)	Average orders intensity per agent per day	Average share of orders generated per agent per day	Total share of orders generated per cluster
HFT	16 (0,09%)	336,5	2,03%	32,45%
SHFT	69 (0,41%)	59,8	0,11%	7,30%
LLT	4 (0,02%)	9,5	1,52%	6,08%
SMT	16803 (99,48%)	0,5	0,003%	54,16%

For each cluster we build decision-making functions that define the agents' behavior, including:

- Decision of order type (buy/sell), size and price,
- Decision of order cancelation.

The agents have information on market price and trade volumes at previous time steps. Having such information, the agents decide whether they place or cancel orders to buy / sell at the current time step, and if they place an order, how much and at what price. We model only limit order flow. A limit order to sell with the price lower than best ask, or a limit order to buy with the price higher than best bid are considered to be market orders as they are executed immediately. Due to lack of data we ignore the history of the agent's previous orders.

The econometric equations were estimated by aggregating data from agents in each cluster. Below we provide some key dependencies for the major agent types.

High-Frequency Traders (HFT)

HFT agents are characterized by the following features:

- High intensity of order placement;
- Size of orders is relatively constant;
- Price of orders is usually significantly different from market price (see Fig. 2);
- Intraday seasonality common to the market as a whole (higher activity during the morning hours and the evening ones when market participants open and close their positions, respectively) is vastly exaggerated in this group (see Fig. 3).

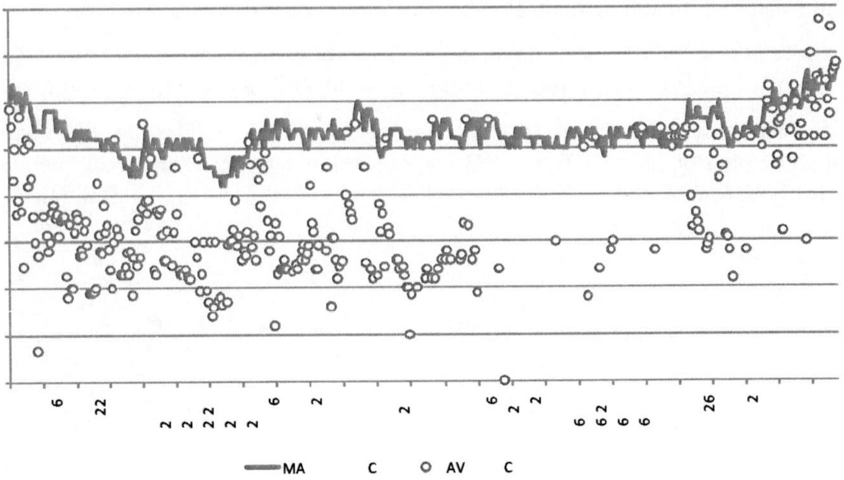

Fig. 2: Buy order price for HFTs compared to market price, 01 September, 2010

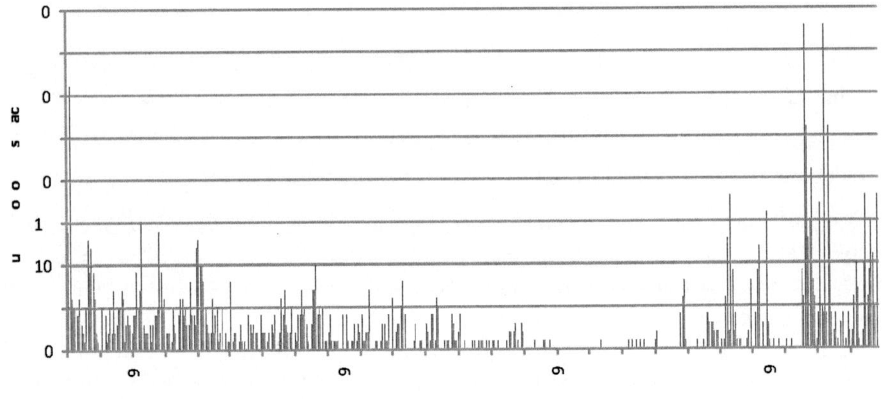

Fig. 3: Buy order intensity for HFTs, 01 September, 2010

To describe the activity of HFT order intensity equations were estimated for all agents aggregated in the HFT cluster during the following sessions:

- buy orders placed during the morning trade session (before 11:00);
- buy orders placed during the day trade session (11:00 – 16:30)
- buy orders placed during the evening trade session (16:30 – 18:45);
- sell orders placed during the morning trade session (before 11:00);
- sell orders placed during the day trade session (11:00 – 16:30);
- sell orders placed during the evening trade session (16:30 – 18:45).

A specific feature of the cluster is the fact that, at least in the dataset used for the model, no significant dependence was found between the number of orders and the market variables such as volume, price, volatility and so on for the different horizons. Thus we used autoregressions to reproduce the agents' activity (order intensity (CNT_t)). Autoregression parameters were estimated separately for each session listed above.

The autoregressive equations and adjusted R-squared are presented below (see Table 2); all the equations, as well as coefficients, are significant according to the F-test and t-test, with a 95% confidence level.

Table 2: Order submitting equations for HFTs

Session	Process equation	Adjusted R-squared
Buy orders placed in the morning time of trade session	$CNT_t = 1.33 + 0.5547 \cdot CNT_{t-1} + $ $+ 0.674 \cdot CNT_{t-90} + \xi_t - 0.797 \cdot \xi_{t-90}$	35,51%
Buy orders placed in the day time of trade session	$CNT_t = 1.068 + 0.641 \cdot CNT_{t-1} + 0.1899 \cdot CNT_{t-5} + $ $+ \xi_t - 0.208 \cdot \xi_{t-1} - 0.152 \cdot \xi_{t-5}$	31,21%
Buy orders placed in the evening time of trade session	$CNT_t = 2.74 + 0.555 \cdot CNT_{t-1} + \xi_t$	30,81%
Sell orders placed in morning time of trade session	$CNT_t = 1.93 + 0.7 \cdot CNT_{t-1} + 0.59 \cdot CNT_{t-90} + $ $+ \xi_t - 0.798 \cdot \xi_{t-90}$	57,58%
Sell orders placed in the day time of trade session	$CNT_t = 1.63 + 0.641 \cdot CNT_{t-1} + 0.155 \cdot CNT_{t-5} + $ $+ \xi_t - 0.077 \cdot \xi_{t-1} - 0.084 \cdot \xi_{t-5}$	42,91%
Sell orders placed in the evening time of trade session	$CNT_t = 2.44 + 0.589 \cdot CNT_{t-1} + \xi_t$	34,67%

where t – minute, CNT_t – number of orders placed at minute t, ξ_t – residual at minute t.

Small High-Frequency Traders (SHFT)

Order placement for SHFT is also described by an autoregressive moving average (ARMA) process (see Table 3).

Table 3: Order submitting equations for SHFTs

Session	Process equation	Adjusted R-squared
Buy orders	$CNT_t = 0.924 + 0.689 \cdot CNT_{t-1} + 0.123 \cdot CNT_{t-10} + \xi_t - 0.37 \cdot \xi_{t-1} - 0.109 \cdot \xi_{t-10}$	18,8%
Sell orders	$CNT_t = 1.061 + 0.6167 \cdot CNT_{t-1} + 0.197 \cdot CNT_{t-10} + \xi_t + 0.374 \cdot \xi_{t-1} - 0.292 \cdot \xi_{t-10}$	9,85%

where t – minute, CNT_t – number of orders placed at minute t, ξ_t – residual at minute t.

HFT and SHFT Order Quantity, Price and Volume Simulation

The estimated equations are used to simulate the conditional orders' arrival at minute t. An exponential distribution is applied to fit the data with expected intensity $\lambda = CNT_{t-1}$. The simulation is organized as an interative process: for each minute, the expected number of orders CNT_t is estimated based on econometrics and then the random number of the orders is simulated based on an exponential distribution. This procedure allows the generation of the orders' arrival time, capturing the intraday seasonality. The example of two consequent rounds of buy order count simulation for HFT at 30/09/2010 is shown on Fig.4-5.

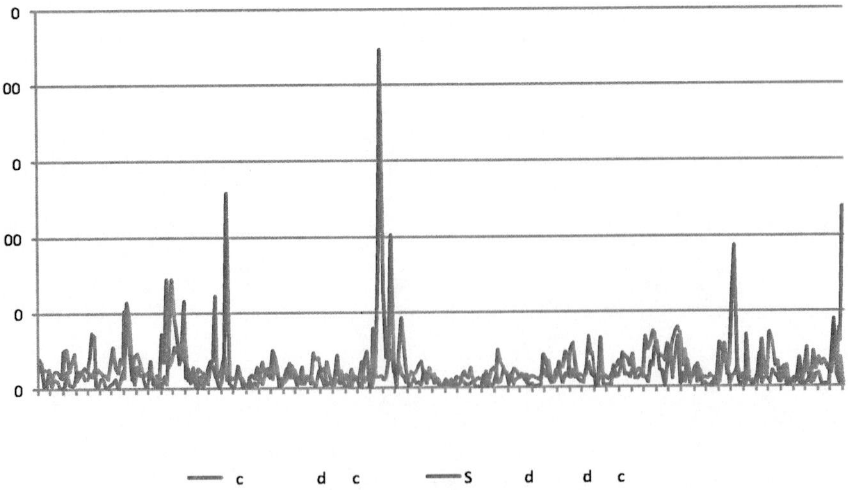

Fig. 4: Actual and simulated orders count for HFT day session (draw #1), 30.09.2010

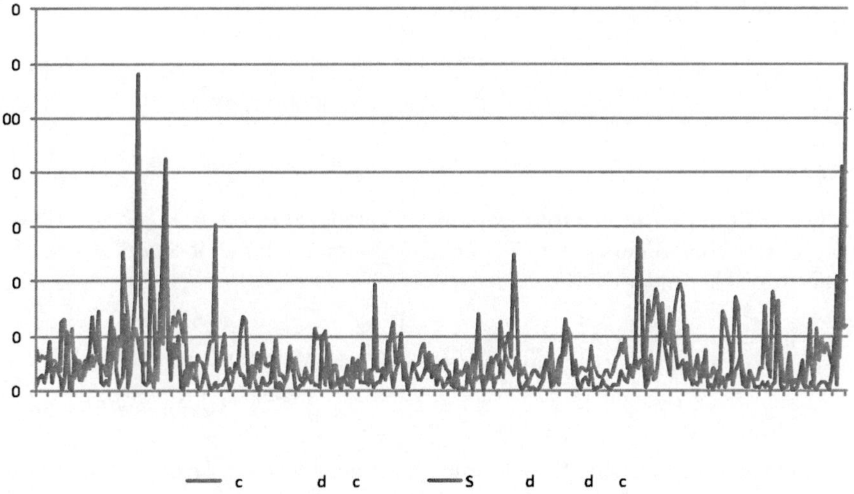

Fig. 5: Actual and simulated orders count for HFT day session (draw #2), 30.09.2010

Statistical distributions were fitted to generate prices and volumes for HFT and SHFT. For order volumes a lognormal distribution demonstrates a good fit. For heavy tailed order prices, power law and Cauchy distributions were applied. To generate dependencies between order prices and volumes, the Gaussian copula was used.

Large Long-Term Traders (LLT)

LLT are market participants with a small number of relatively large orders. LLT could be referred as the agents that provide liquidity. The share of orders executed by LLT is lower than for frequent (both HFT and SHFT) traders: 27.89% were executed against 42.16% that were executed for frequent traders. At the same time, while HFT and SHFT place orders far from the market price, LLT place orders close to the market.

The regression analysis did not recognize any dependence between the price factors (the price changes at different horizons, price trend or volatility) and the order placement frequency ($R2 < 5\%$). However, there is dependence between order placement frequency and market volumes. Thus, LLT could be considered as "volume traders".

As the orders are placed rarely, we estimated binary logit regression to model the dummy variable of order placement, Lt = {1 – order is placed at minute t, 0 – order is not placed}.

The estimated equation for buy side orders:

$$L_t = \frac{1}{1+\exp(-5.58+2.71 \cdot BUY\_SH_{t-1} + 0.000000131 \cdot MVOL_{t-1})},$$

McFadden R^2 *= 16.71%*

where L_t – dummy variable for buy order placement at step *t*, BUY_SH_{t-1} – ratio of buy orders to total orders at step *t-1*, $MVOL_{t-1}$ – total volume of orders at step *t-1*.

For sell side orders:

$$L_t = \frac{1}{1+\exp(-5.91+2.808 \cdot SELL\_SH_{t-1} + 0.000000123 \cdot MVOL_{t-1})}$$

McFadden R^2 *= 18.3%*

where L_t – dummy variable for sell order placement at step *t*, $SELL\_SH_{t-1}$ – ratio of sell orders to total orders at step *t-1*, $MVOL_{t-1}$ – total volume of orders placed at step *t-1*.

Equations for volumes and prices are provided below:

$$VOL_t = -3749277.69 + 7510510.3 \cdot BUY\_SH_{t-1} + 0.165 \cdot MVOL_{t-1}$$

where VOL_t – volume of sell orders at step *t*, BUY_SH_{t-1} – ratio of buy orders to total order volume at step *t-1*, $MVOL_{t-1}$ – total volume of orders at step *t-1*. Adjusted R-squared is 26.6%.

LLT buy order price is linearly related to market price.

$$BUYP_t = 0.998 \cdot MPRICE_{t-1},$$

Adjusted R^2 *= 74.3%*

where $BUYP_t$ – price of buy orders at step *t*, $MPRICE_t$ – market price.

For sell side:

$$VOL_t = -1672266.3 + 4997988 \cdot SELL\_SH_{t-1} + 0.2511 \cdot MVOL_{t-1}$$

Adjusted R^2 *= 36.3%*

where VOL_t – volume of sell orders at step *t*, $SELL\_SH_{t-1}$ – ratio of sell orders to total order volume at step *t-1*, $MVOL_{t-1}$ – total volume of orders at step *t-1*.

LLT sell order price is linearly related to market price as well:

$$SELLP_t = 0.089 + 0.943 \cdot MPRICE_{t-1},$$

Adjusted R^2*= 70.3%*

where $SELLP_t$ – price of sell orders at step *t*, $MPRICE_t$ – market price.

Small Manual Traders (SMT)

Small traders populate the largest heterogeneous cluster. Various sub-clusters exist in this group, following different strategies. For example, agents from the relatively stable group of **Morning Traders** place more than 80% of their daily volume before 11:00, with the typical deviation from market price. Another example is **Spread Traders** who usually place one buy and one sell order with the same volume and spread to market price. Nevertheless, we do not focus on those sub-clusters and model SMT as the aggregate cluster. Numerous statistical tests have shown that there are no significant dependencies between SMT actions and market price or volumes. We simulate SMT actions with the order price returns fitted by power law and order volumes fitted by lognormal distribution. To generate correlations for order parameters we use Gaussian copula.

Order Cancelation

The order cancel rule looks quite common for all clusters. The order is canceled if the logarithmic spread between the market price at the previous step and order price exceeds the spread between the market price step previous to the step the order was placed and order price (for buy orders) and vice versa (for sell orders). The fitted equation is the following:

$$SPREAD\_AMD = 0.00084 + 0.9887 \cdot SPREAD\_PLC\,,$$

$$R^2 = 95.7\%$$

where *SPREAD_AMD* – cancelation spread (after market price covers it, the order is cancelled at the next step), *SPREAD_PLC* – spread between market price and order price at the moment the order is placed.

Continuous Double Action Simulation

MICEX is an order-driven double auction market. Market participants submit buy and sell orders to an exchange where they are matched. The orders' priority is defined by the prices. The orders with best bid for the buy side and best ask for the sell side get higher priority. If the priority of two orders is the same, they are executed on a "first come first served" principle.

The MICEX trading rules have the following timing. The pre-trade session begins at 10:15 and ends at 10:30. The trade session lasts from 10:30 to 18:45. At 18:45 all orders that were not executed are canceled by the exchange.

The simulations were run in a special software application "Simulation engine" developed by Mikhail B. Nikulin (Prognoz). The engine allows matching of the orders according to the MICEX trading rules. "Simulation engine" was tested on the real market order data and showed to correctly reproduce the trades.

The engine was used to simulate order flow and intraday price series.

Conclusion

We have studied the microstructure of the MICX:HYDR stock, which is referred to as one of the 'blue chip' Russian stock and hence is quite liquid. The agents were clustered into four major groups according to their order submission frequency and size. The high-frequency traders show long-memory behavior and can be significantly described by an ARMA process, while large long-term traders are sensitive to the market situation and can be analyzed with multifactor regressions. The econometric approach allows one to capture the order flow's data generating process, conditional on factors across clusters.

The simulation results demonstrate that the classification of agents is still too coarse and it is suggested to use a more detailed clustering of agents to allocate even more homogeneous strategies to groups on the market.

References

Darley, V., Outkin, A.V. (2007) A NASDAQ market simulation: insights on a major market from the science of complex adaptive systems. World Scientific Publishing Co. Pte. Ltd.

Easley D, de Prado M, O'Hara M (2011) The Microstructure of the 'Flash Crash': Flow Toxicity, Liquidity Crashes and the Probability of Informed Trading. The Journal of Portfolio Management, Vol. 37, No. 2, pp. 118-128.

Glosten, L., Milgrom, P. (1985) Bid, Ask and Transaction Prices in a Specialist Market with Heterogeneously Informed Traders, Journal of Financial Economics, 14, 71–100.

Harras, G., Sornette, D. (2011) How to grow a bubble: A model of myopic adapting agents, Journal of Economic Behavior & Organization.

Lin, T. (2003) Under- and Over- Reaction from Relative and Aggregate Overconfidence. Working Paper, Fuqua School of Business, Duke University.

Rosu, I. (2008) Liquidity and Information in Order Driven Markets, Working Paper, University of Chicago.

Asset Pricing in a Fractional Market Under Transaction Costs

Vladimir Gisin

Department of Mathematics, Finance University under the Government of the Russian Federation, Moscow, Russia. email: vgisin@yandex.ru

Andrey Markov

Trust Management Department, State Corporation "The Bank for Development and Foreign Economic Affairs (Vnesheconombank)", Moscow, Russia. email: aaamarkov@gmail.com

Abstract A model of a market driven by a fractional Brownian motion is considered. We apply stochastic dominance arguments to derive a lower bound and an upper bound on the price of European options in the presence of proportional transaction costs. A numerical example with the data drawn from the Russian options market is presented.

Keywords: option, arbitrage, fractional Brownian motion, transaction costs.

JEL classification: G12, G13.

Introduction

Any consistent theory concerning the price dynamics of risky assets includes a pair of related models: a mathematical model and an economic analysis of time series. The classical Black-Scholes model is accompanied by the effective market hypothesis (*EMH*). The *EMH* assumes that market prices result from a big number of independent random factors and that the market has a short memory. These assumptions lead to the approximation of risky asset price dynamics by Brownian motion. The development of financial mathematics during the last century gives evidence that "unpaired" models appear impractical. Brownian motion was applied by L. Bachelier in order to study equity price dynamics at a stock exchange in 1900. For the period of more than sixty years Bachelier's theory remained unclaimed, but after the *EMH* was formulated Brownian motion became the basic instrument of quantitative analysis in finance.

Development of computer technologies made it possible to process a large quantity of numerical data. Analysis of financial time series revealed a number of their characteristics ("stylized facts", or "stylized features") which did not correspond with *EMH* postulates: heavy tails, long-term memory, volatility clustering, etc. (see (Mantegna and Stanley, 2000), (Sornette, 2003), (Haritonov and Ezhov

D. Sornette et al. (Eds.), *Market Risk and Financial Markets Modeling*,
DOI 10.1007/978-3-642-27931-7_7,

2007)). Basic *EMH* statements were critically reanalyzed. At the same time alternative models entered into consideration. In particular, models using the fractional market hypothesis (*FMH*) were developed. According to the *FMH,* one of the principal pricing factors is a big number of traders with various investment horizons. This factor provides financial markets with liquidity (liquidity can hardly be explained within the *EMH* framework). Moreover, over their investment horizons all traders act in a similar way. This provides a peculiar kind of invariance (self-similarity) of important market characteristics towards time scale. The Hurst parameter H is a statistical measure of scale invariance. Values of H are enclosed in the interval from zero to one. For standard Brownian motion H is equal to 0,5. If $0{,}5 < H < 1$ the time series is persistent; if $0 < H < 0{,}5$ the time series is anti-persistent.

The concept of self-similarity of stochastic processes goes back to A.N. Kolmogorov (Kolmogorov, 1940). Over the last decade, financial market models in which Brownian motion is replaced by fractional Brownian motion have been studied intensively (see (Mishura, 2008), (Biagini, Hu, Oksendal and Zhang, 2008), (Rostek, 2009)). Using fractional Brownian motion it is possible to consider long-term dependences in price dynamics and therefore to make the models more realistic.

Using fractional Brownian motion for modelling stock market prices faces a crucial obstacle. Unlike the Black-Scholes market, a market where return is driven by a fractional Brownian motion admits arbitrage possibilities. So non-arbitrage pricing is impossible. In order to overcome this obstacle the stochastic integral can be modified. However, until now no reasonable economic interpretation for such modifications has been found. The absence of arbitrage possibilities may be achieved by taking into account the peculiarities of trading in a real market. For example, a fractional market with proportional transaction costs is free of arbitrage. In such a market it is possible to estimate reasonable price bounds. In this paper an approach is suggested which allows estimation of such bounds using stochastic dominance arguments. A numerical example of the evaluation of an option for RTS index futures is given.

The paper is organized as follows. In section 1 basic definitions and facts are given. Section 2 outlines an integral representation and a discrete approximation of fractional Brownian motion. In section 3 arbitrage problems of a fractional market are discussed. In section 4 we present an approach to evaluation of a fair price of an option in a fractional market with transaction costs.

Fractional Brownian Motion

A concept of fractional Brownian motion was introduced by A.N. Kolmogorov (Kolmogorov, 1940). A stochastic process (X_t) is called self-similar (with Hurst parameter H) if $(X_{\alpha t}) = (\alpha^H X_t)$ for all $a > 0$. For Brownian motion (W_t) we have $(W_t) = (\sqrt{t} W_1)$, so Brownian motion is self-similar with $H = ½$.

Fractional Brownian motion with Hurst parameter H is a Gaussian process $B^{(H)} = (B_t^{(H)})_{t\in R}$ satisfying the following conditions:

1. $B_0^{(H)} = 0$;

2. $EB_t^{(H)} = 0$ for all $t \in R$;

3. $EB_t^{(H)} B_s^{(H)} = \frac{1}{2}(|t|^{2H} + |s|^{2H} - |t-s|^{2H})$ for all $t, s \in R$.

It can be easily seen that

$$E(B_t^{(H)})^2 = |t|^{2H} \tag{1}$$

Further

$$E(B_{s+t}^{(H)} - B_s^{(H)})^2 = |t|^{2H}. \tag{2}$$

Hence, $B_{s+t}^{(H)} - B_s^{(H)}$ and $B_t^{(H)}$ are identically distributed, i.e. $B_t^{(H)}$ is a process with homogeneous increments.

The substantial acceptance of the *FMH* is mathematically formalized by the assumption that the stochastic component of stock return is self-similar. Let S_t be the price of a stock at time t. Then the return over the time interval Δt may be presented as follows

$$\frac{S_{t+\Delta t} - S_t}{S_t} = \mu\Delta t + \sigma(B_{t+\Delta t}^{(H)} - B_t^{(H)}), \tag{3}$$

where μ is the rate of return, σ is the volatility, and $B_t^{(H)}$ is fractional Brownian motion. Equation (3) can be replaced by the stochastic differential equation

$$dS_t = S_t(\mu dt + \sigma dB_t^{(H)}). \tag{4}$$

Using (3) the autocovariance function of the reduced return

$$\rho_t = \frac{1}{\sigma}\frac{S_{t+\Delta t} - S_t}{S_t} - \mu\Delta t$$

with time lag τ can be calculated:

$$\gamma(\tau) = E(\rho_{t+\tau}\rho_t) = \frac{1}{2}((\tau+\Delta t)^{2H} - 2\tau^{2H} + (\tau-\Delta t)^{2H}).$$

For Δt small we get

$$\gamma(\tau) \approx (\tau^{2H})''(\Delta t)^2 = 2H(2H-1)\tau^{2H-2}(\Delta t)^2.$$

Stock prices are typically persistent with $H > ½$. In (Markov, 2009) H is calculated for the RTS and MICEX stock indices as well as for the DJIA, NASDAQ and

S&P500. For the RTS, H = 0.617 is estimated using daily *close* prices for the period 1995–2009. Estimation of the Hurst parameter of the other indices mentioned above also demonstrates their persistence. For the MICEX, = 0.556; for the DJIA, H = 0.568; for the NASDAQ, = 0.604; for the S&P500, = 0.570. The analysis of American stock indices was based on historical data for sufficiently long periods of time. The data range for the DJIA index includes daily *close* prices since 1928, for the NASDAQ — since 1971 and for the S&P500 — since 1952. Data for the MICEX index include prices since 1999.

Discrete Approximation of Fractional Brownian Motion

In (Norros, Valkeila and Virtamo, 1999) (see (Biagini, Hu, Oksendal and Zhang, 2008)) it is proved that

$$B_t^H = \int_0^t z(t,s)dB_s \, , \tag{5}$$

where

$$z(t,s) = c_H (H - \tfrac{1}{2}) s^{\frac{1}{2}-H} \int_s^t u^{H-\frac{1}{2}} (u-s)^{H-\frac{3}{2}} du$$

and

$$c_H = \sqrt{\frac{2H\Gamma(\frac{3}{2}-H)}{\Gamma(\frac{1}{2}+H)\Gamma(2-2H)}}.$$

Representation (5) makes it possible to obtain a discrete approximation of fractional Brownian motion in a way similar to that for the case of Brownian motion B_t. Within an N-steps approximation, increment dB_t is replaced by $\frac{1}{\sqrt{N}}\xi$, where ξ is a random variable with mean 0 and variance 1.

The unit time interval is divided into N equal intervals by the points $\frac{i}{N}$, $i = 1, \ldots, N$. We suppose that assets are traded only at these points. Let ξ_i, $i = 1, \ldots, N$, be independent random variables taking values 1 and –1 with probability 0,5. Let S_n be the price of a risky asset at time $\frac{n}{N}$.

Put

$$k(n,i) = \frac{1}{\sqrt{N}} z^{(N)}\left(\frac{n}{N}, \frac{i}{N}\right) = \sqrt{N} \int_{\frac{i-1}{N}}^{\frac{i}{N}} z\left(\frac{n}{N}, v\right) dv =$$

$$= \sqrt{N} c_H (H - \tfrac{1}{2}) \int_{\frac{i-1}{N}}^{\frac{i}{N}} \left(v^{\frac{1}{2}-H} \int_v^{\frac{n}{N}} u^{H-\frac{1}{2}} (u-v)^{H-\frac{3}{2}} du \right) dv$$

and

$$\rho_n = \sum_{i=1}^{n-1} (k(n,i) - k(n-1,i)\xi_i + k(n,n)\xi_n .$$

Then

$$S_n = (1 + \tfrac{\mu}{N} + \rho_n) S_{n-1} .$$

At time n the stock price can move up by a factor u_n (if $\xi_n = 1$) and down by a factor d_n (if $\xi_n = -1$). Unlike the classical Binomial model, up and down factors depend on the values of the random variables ξ_i at previous steps. So there are 2^n different possible paths for the stock price to evolve up to time n.

Arbitrage

The fundamental theorem of asset pricing can be interpreted as an opportunity to make the rational forecast in an arbitrage-free market (see (Babajtsev and Gisin, 2005)). If a market is not arbitrage-free it is supposed that an arbitrage income may be obtained using self-financing investment strategies under standard requirements (the strategy should be integrable and the admissible amount of borrowed funds should be limited in advance).

In a fractional market an arbitrage is possible with respect to any class of admissible investment strategies satisfying natural requirements. Taking into account long-term dependences it is possible to construct an arbitrage strategy. We need some definitions for more accurate treatment.

Let us fix a time horizon T. We will consider all processes over the time interval $[0, T]$.

Let $S = (S_t)_{0 \le t \le T}$ be the price process of a stock. The investment strategy (portfolio) is a pair of adapted stochastic processes $(\beta_t, \gamma_t)_{0 \le t \le T}$. The process β_t denotes the amount of money invested in the riskless asset and $_t$ denotes the number of stock shares in the portfolio at time t. The value of the portfolio (β_t, γ_t) at time t equals to

$$V_t = \beta_t + \gamma_t S_t .$$

Let us consider consequent time moments t_1 and t_2 at which the portfolio is rearranged. We assume that purchases and sales of assets are held without transaction costs. Let r be the risk-free interest rate. Just before rearranging at the moment t_2 the value of portfolio is $e^{r(t_2-t_1)}\beta_{t_1} + \gamma_{t_1} S_{t_2}$ and just after rearranging the value of portfolio is $\beta_{t_2} + \gamma_{t_2} S_{t_2}$. By definition, an investment strategy is self-financing if

$$e^{r(t_2-t_1)}\beta_{t_1} + \gamma_{t_1} S_{t_2} = \beta_{t_2} + \gamma_{t_2} S_{t_2} .$$

It can be easily seen that the latter condition can be presented as follows

$$e^{-t_2}V_{t_2} - e^{-t_1}V_{t_1} = \gamma_{t_1}(e^{-t_2}S_{t_2} - e^{-t_1}S_{t_1}) .$$

Further, we will consider only self-financing and exclude doubling strategies.

A strategy is an arbitrage if, starting with zero capital at favorable juncture, by the time T an investor can receive a portfolio of a positive value and in any case will not get into debt. More formally, $V_0 = 0$, $V_T \geq 0$ (a. s.) and $P(V_T > 0)>0$.

Arbitrage opportunities can be excluded if the class of admissible investment strategies is restricted. If, for example, over the interval $[0, T]$ purchases and sales of a risky asset are forbidden then arbitrage over this time interval will not occur. Normally in a fractional market with standard restrictions on admissible investment strategies there exist arbitrage opportunities (see (Bender, Sottinen and Valkeila, 2007)). In such a market hedging is impossible and therefore it is impossible to determine fair prices for derivatives.

Note that the latter arguments refer to an idealized market model. Taking into account properties of a real stock market makes it possible to exclude arbitrage. For example, trading without transaction costs a trader can hedge risks free of charge (and get an arbitrage income due to that). The Black-Scholes market is arbitrage-free because the stochastic component of a risk asset price is in a sense "absolutely stochastic". The only possible rational forecast says that tomorrow's price will be the same as today. In a fractional market such a forecast cannot be rational anymore. Moreover, in a fractional market any rational forecast is impossible, but taking into account price dynamics patterns it is possible to get an arbitrage income. The situation changes when the model includes transaction costs. Since the free rearrangement of a position is now impossible, a trader cannot construct arbitrage strategies. The absence of arbitrage opportunities in a fractional market with transaction costs has been proved in (Guasoni, 2006) (see also (Guasoni and Rasonyi, 2008)). Omitting the technical details, the main results from (Guasoni, 2006) can be treated as follows.

Let ε be the transaction costs (brokerage fee). If the market price is S_t there are traders who are ready to buy at $\overline{S}_t = (1+\varepsilon)S_t$, and there are traders who are ready to sell at $\underline{S}_t = (1-\varepsilon)S_t$. Thus, *bid* and *ask* prices define a price corridor. The main theorem states that market does not admit arbitrage opportunities if there exists a rational forecast within the price corridor. In (Guasoni, 2006) it is proved that this is exactly the case for a fractional market.

Option Price Bounds in a Fractional Market under Transaction Costs

Normally a perfect hedging of derivatives in a fractional market is impossible. Nevertheless, an estimation of derivative prices can be made. Using upper and lower hedges it is possible to evaluate a corridor where a fair price must be situated. An effective algorithm for deriving such bounds in a multi-period market is suggested in (Constantinides and Perrakis, 2002). In a multi-period market investment decisions can be taken at time moments $n = 0, 1, 2, \ldots, N$. In (Constantinides and Perrakis, 2002) it is supposed that the returns are independent. In a market driven by a fractional Brownian motion it is not so. Nevertheless, some important results from (Constantinides and Perrakis, 2002) are valid in a fractional market.

Let us consider a multi-period market with three assets: a riskless asset (account), a risky asset (stock) and a cash-settled European call-option on this stock with strike K which expires at time N. Let r be the risk-free interest rate and let ε be the brokerage fee. The investor pays $b = (1 + \varepsilon)gS_n$ from the bank account to buy g shares of stock at time t. The investor adds $(1 - \varepsilon)S_n$ to the bank account if he sells one share of stock. We assume that the expected return of the stock does not vary from period to period and exceeds the risk-free rate, that is

$$E\left[\frac{S_n}{S_{n-1}}\right] = \mu > r$$

for $n = 1, 2, \ldots, N$. The investor chooses a strategy maximizing the expected utility at the initial date (the utility function is supposed to be increasing and concave).

Put

$$\overline{C}_n = \frac{1+\varepsilon}{1-\varepsilon} \frac{E[(S_N - K)^+ \mid S_n]}{(1+\mu)^{N-n}}. \tag{6}$$

It can be shown that $\overline{C}_n$ is an upper bound of the fair price of the option at time n.

In the same way it is possible to find out that a lower bound $\underline{C}_n$ satisfies the following conditions:

$$\underline{C}_N = (S_N - K)^+;$$

$$\underline{C}_n = \frac{E[\underline{C}_{n+1} \mid S_n, S_{n+1} \le Z_n]}{1+r},$$

where Z is defined implicitly by

$$E[S_{n+1} \mid S_n, S_{n+1} \le Z_n] = \frac{1-\varepsilon}{1+\varepsilon}(1+r)S_n.$$

Outside the interval $[\underline{C}_n, \overline{C}_n]$ an arbitrage is possible.

Let us consider the dynamics of a future call option on the RTS index with strike 120 000 basis points (b.p.) and expiry date October 14, 2009, traded in the FORTS section. Option price bounds (col. 4 and 5 in Table 1) were calculated daily from September 14 until October 9, 2009. In order to make a comparison, *bid* (col.

6) and *ask* quotes (col. 7), the option price calculated by the stock exchange using Black-Scholes formula (col. 8), and the last deal price (col. 9) are also listed. We put r = 9.0079%, where 9.0079% is the annual rate of the federal loan bond OFZ-25057 at of the beginning of September 2009. One period drift and volatility of the index were 0.00213 and 0.0568 respectively. Transaction costs were taken equal to 0.01 %.

Table 1

Date	Number of days before exercise	Price of underlyin g asset (b.p.)	Upper bound of option price (b.p.)	Lower bound of option price (b.p.)	Bid	Ask	Theoretic al price	Last
1	2	3	4	5	6	7	8	9
14.09.09	30	116 340	8 435.05	1 316.69	5 530	5 810	5 705	5 425
15.09.09	29	120 780	10 661.47	4 306.88	7 105	7 230	7 270	7 185
16.09.09	28	123 590	12 447.71	6 288.69	1 055	9 000	8 550	8 400
17.09.09	27	124 960	13 143.21	7 296.29	8 070	8 700	8 585	8 400
18.09.09	26	121 730	10 698.40	4 698.39	7 310	7 705	7 535	7 635
21.09.09	23	119 805	8 734.03	3 094.13	6 500	6 600	6 535	6 500
22.09.09	22	124 045	11 207.60	6 125.49	8 330	8 895	8 525	8 000
23.09.09	21	125 010	11 600.38	6 801.86	8 370	9 075	8 990	9 200
24.09.09	20	123 720	10 443.71	5 682.46	7 435	8 170	7 925	7 700
25.09.09	19	121 190	8 501.72	3 661.69	5 815	6 375	6 035	7 090
28.09.09	16	123 640	9 257.57	5 231.83	7 125	7 545	5 500	7 310
29.09.09	15	124 145	9 303.09	5 530.50	7 100	7 625	5 500	7 400
30.09.09	14	125 720	10 065.62	6 673.29	7 860	8 385	8 145	8 250
01.10.09	13	125 370	9 517.86	6 289.06	7 185	7 700	7 700	7 600
02.10.09	12	120 750	6 168.66	2 611.52	4 205	5 555	4 595	4 610
05.10.09	9	120 485	5 019.20	2 067.98	3 625	3 700	3 615	3 580
06.10.09	8	124 070	6 973.69	4 681.80	5 570	6 025	5 875	5 900
07.10.09	7	129 000	10 471.36	8 865.79	5 000	9 980	9 550	9 800
08.10.09	6	131 880	12 738.86	11 423.88	12 150	13 350	12 335	12 300
09.10.09	5	138 460	18 965.10	17 781.01	1 555	20 000	18 515	18 135

Most *bid* and *ask* quotes as well as last deal prices are within the interval $[\underline{C}, \overline{C}]$. Several "outliers" (for example on September 16 and on October 9 when anomalously low *bid* quotes were set) are caused mainly by lack of liquidity.

The decline of the call-option price towards the lower bound can be considered as a signal on a purchase. For example, suppose that an investor buys one share of the option on September 17 at 8 070 b.p., according to the respective quote (see Table 1) and holds it up to the expiry date. On October 14, 2009 the *close* price of RTS index was 1 441.24 points, or 144 124 b.p., and exceeded the strike. Executing the call-option at this date results in the following rate of return

$$r = \frac{144124 \cdot 0.9999 - 120000 \cdot 1.0001 - 8070 \cdot 1.0001 \cdot (1 + 0.090079 \cdot \frac{27}{365})}{120000 \cdot 1.0001 + 8070 \cdot 1.0001 \cdot (1 + 0.090079 \cdot \frac{27}{365})} \cdot \frac{365}{27} \cdot 100\% = 168.52\%$$

If an investor buys one share of the option at 13 143 b.p. (close to the upper bound as of September 17), his/her profit essentially decreases, although it is high enough due to the strong growth of the RTS index over the considered period:

$$r = \frac{144124 \cdot 0.9999 - 120000 \cdot 1.0001 - 13143 \cdot 1.0001 \cdot (1 + 0.090079 \cdot \frac{27}{365})}{120000 \cdot 1.0001 + 13143 \cdot 1.0001 \cdot (1 + 0.090079 \cdot \frac{27}{365})} \cdot \frac{365}{27} \cdot 100\% = 110.24\%$$

Conclusion

The presence of proportional transaction costs makes it possible to evaluate a fair price of an option in a fractional market. The fair price is situated between upper and lower bounds of an arbitrage-free price interval. These bounds can be estimated by applying stochastic dominance arguments to the model of a multi-period market driven by a fractional Brownian motion. A numerical example with the data drawn from the Russian options market shows that most *bid* and *ask* quotes as well as last deal prices are within this arbitrage-free interval.

References

Babajtsev, V.A., & Gisin, V.B. (2005). The arbitrage concept in the mathematical theory of the effective market. Finance Academy Bulletin, 2, 64–68.

Bender, C., Sottinen, T., & Valkeila, E. (2007). Arbitrage with fractional Brownian motion? Theory of Stochastic Processes 13(29), 1-2, 23–34.

Biagini, F., Hu, Y., Oksendal, B., & Zhang, T. (2008). Stochastic Calculus for Fractional Brownian Motion and Applications. London, England: Springer-Verlag London Limited.

Constantinides, G.M. (1979). Multiperiod consumption and investment behavior with convex transactions costs. Management Science, 25(11), 1127 – 1137.

Constantinides, G.M., & Perrakis, S. (2002). Stochastic dominance bounds on derivatives prices in a multiperiod economy with proportional transaction costs. Journal of Economic Dynamics & Control, 26, 1323–1352.

Guasoni, P. (2006). No arbitrage under transaction costs, with fractional Brownian motion and beyond. Mathematical Finance, 16(3), 569-582.

Guasoni, P., & Rasonyi, M. (2008). The Fundamental Theorem of Asset Pricing under Transaction Costs, preprint.

Haritonov, V.V., & Ezhov, A.A. (2007). Econophysics. Moscow, Russia: MIPhI.

Kolmogorov, A.N. (1940). Wienershe Spiralen und einige andere interessante Kurven im Hilbertishen Raum. DAS of the USSR (Nat. Sciences), 26, 115–118.

Mandelbrot, B.B., & van Ness, J.W. (1968). Fractional Brownian motions, fractional noises and applications. SIAM Rev., 10, 422-437.

Mantegna, R.M., & Stanley H.E. (2000). An Introduction to Econophysics. – Correlations and Complexity in Finance. Cambridge, England: Cambridge University Press.

Markov, A.A. (2009). Some fractional properties of stock indices. Today and Tomorrow of Russian Economy, 30, 101-110.

Mishura, Y. (2008). Stochastic Calculus for Fractional Brownian Motion and Related Processes. Springer Lecture Notes in Mathematics, 1929, 393.

Norros, I., Valkeila, E., & Virtamo J. (1999). An elementary approach to a Girsanov formula and other analytical results on fractional Brownian motion. Bernoulli, 5, 571–587.

Rostek, S. (2009). Option Pricing in Fractional Brownian Markets. Berlin, Germany: Springer-Verlag Berlin Heidelberg.

Shiryaev, A.N. (1998). On arbitrage and replication for fractional models. MaPhySto, Department of Mathematical Sciences, Univ. of Aarhus. Research Reports, 20.

Sornette, D. (2003). How to predict crashes of the financial markets. oscow, Russia: Internet trading.

Sottinen, T. (2001). Fractional Brownian motion, random walks, and binary market models. Finance Stoch., 5, 343–355.

Influence of Behavioral Finance on the Share Market

Vadim Gribnikov

South Federal University, Rostov-na-donu, Russia

Dmitry Shevchenko

South Federal University, Rostov-na-donu, Russia. email: dimasch@mail.ru

Abstract This article concerns the behavioral finance influence on the share market. The basic reasons for investors' irrational behavior are the following: informational and emotional problems. Some behavioral aspects such as the framing effect, herding effect, illusion of control and thought contagion are indicated for analyses. Behavioral dependence in the Russian share market will be explained in this article. In conclusion, besides fundamental and technical analyses, investors should take into account psychological factors.

Keywords: Financial Markets, Share market, Behavioral Finance

JEL classification: D81, G11, G12.

Introduction

In recent years, the share market has become one of the most powerful mechanisms for allocation of short-term free capital for profit earning. There are different strategies for investing, based on fundamental or technical analysis. Different indicators, which characterize «efficiency of issuers businesses», are taken as a base for fundamental analysis. Analyzing these indicators, we can determine the change in the share prices for the long-term period. Technical analysis is based on the statement that the market contains all the necessary information. Therefore, by means of various mathematical models, one can identify trend of stock regardless of fundamental information.

The history of the development of the share market and empirical analyses of it detect a large number of situations when the approaches mentioned above turn out to be inconsistent. Changes in the share prices often do not coincide with investors' expectations and predictions. This can be explained by imperfect analysis methods, as well as by the 'luck' of relevant information at the investors' and financial analysts' disposal. Moreover, the market may form under the influence of psychological factors and behavioral characteristics due to separate market participant groups, who act irrationally under certain circumstances. This shows the necessity of

D. Sornette et al. (Eds.), *Market Risk and Financial Markets Modeling*,
DOI 10.1007/978-3-642-27931-7_8, © Springer-Verlag Berlin Heidelberg 2012

taking into account investors' psychology, when explaining and making decisions in terms of technical analysis in short- and medium- term planning.

Therefore, the actual financial research task is the analysis of psychological factor influence on individual decision-making, and therefore on the share market dynamics. Let us consider separately the most significant psychological effects, which, according to the empirical data, should be taken into account when trading on the Russian equity market.

Theoretical Foundations of the Behavioral Finance

The scope of theoretical concepts and empirical research, which reveal various psychological aspects of investment decision-making, constitutes modern behavioral financial science. Behavioral finance is a field of finance that proposes psychology-based theories to explain stock market anomalies (Bighiu Qawi, 2010). Within behavioral finance, it is assumed that the information structure and the characteristics of market participants systematically influence individuals' investment decisions as well as market outcomes.

In the second part of the 20th century a lot of research was conducted in order to reveal the reason for wrong decision-making. As a result, many basic psychological effects that have great influence on decision-making were detected [detailed review in Shefrin, 2010]. The bulk of behavioral finance work still consists of empirical studies demonstrating that markets or firms behave in ways that are anomalous with respect to traditional models, but are consistent with one of the many individual behavioral tendencies identified by psychological research. The best of this research uses psychological research to predict and demonstrate an anomaly that has not yet been previously demonstrated (Bloomfield, 2010).

There can be various reasons for investors' irrational behavior, but most of them are often based on two basic problems:

1. A problem with receiving and analyzing information
2. An emotional problem

For the first one, the main issue is overrating and selective perception of the information, i.e. the subjective nature of preliminary data selection for estimating and accounting in decision-making. Being guided by previous experience, an investor focuses on information that confirms his presumption and ignores the disproving facts (Kahneman & Tversky, 1979). By using different methods of technical analysis, he searches for things supporting his theory, and slants analysis results to find regularity where none exists. Consequently, in general, investors tend to substitute objective reality by subjective wishes.

Moreover, non-professional investors tend to simplify the existing correlation and regularity. The limited opportunities of individual investors in the course of treatment and objective evaluation of information leads to the creation of simplified models and rules of decision-making. Such models and rules do not take into account several details that play a significant part in particular situations. This phenomenon of influence is especially evident under the condition of constantly increasing economic complication and interdependency. As many non-professional markets participants are unable to reveal and correctly estimate some economic tendencies, they usually make decisions based on simplified models. In this connection, the role of an individual's emotional factors in the behavior and estimation of the received information increases. In certain situations, emotions can be more important than reasonable arguments.

Additionally, people can perceive information in different ways depending on its form and presentation method. This could be called a «framing effect». It represents the influence of message format on how information is received and shows alternative ways of investors' behavior estimation of information (Tversky & Kahneman, 1981).

Emotional factors lie in people's nature, they are connected with inner attributes. They include determination, readiness to accept great risks, excess self-confidence, objective fact ignorance, fear of losing all savings.

The main effects analyzed by the theory of behavioral finance comprise the herding effect, control illusion and thought contagion.

The herding effect was detected and described in the 19th century, but its influence on market processes when a large number of participants interact, is still relevant and important. An investor makes a decision by monitoring actions of other investors and simulating them. Under the condition of limited opportunities to receive and analyze information, investors often just follow the main crowd. Moreover, if the situation is ambiguous then this is the only way of decision-making (Scharfstein & Stein, 1990). Such an approach to decision-making is typical for beginner investors who do not take the risks of acting independently. It can be justified in some cases, but different methods of analysis should be used to catch moments of changes in trend. Only the first, who deceives the crowd, will earn money. Crowd influence on experienced investors is also large. For example, it is difficult to make the right decision to enter or leave the market, when technical and fundamental analyses show falling, whereas the crowd pushes the prices up.

The illusion of control is investors' confidence that the results fully depend on their skills (Langer, 1975). The appearance of this effect is connected with people's tendency to accept absolutely random events as controlled processes. As a result, they overrate the probability of their success, even when it depends on chance. When investors think that situation is under control, they easily make baseless and risky decisions, not worrying about new information, and show a tendency to risk when the trends goes down. The illusion of control increases when an investor is «involved into the game», with the opportunity to act independently, and gets access to large amounts of information. On the other hand, the illusion of control is manifested in the increase of investors' speculation in the share market.

However, novice investors often cannot make good efficient analysis of the future operation due to haphazard factors and incompleteness of the information used.

A good example of individual investors' susceptibility to the illusion of control is the consequence of independent trade shifting to the Internet. The typical method of investors' training starts from fundamental and technical analyses. After that, they create a beginner Internet account with a trading company that allows trading on the share market with virtual money. Investors can trade without any risk of losing real money; due to this they can afford very risky operations. In most cases, this training ends in a positive result and the investors start thinking of getting the actual profits. They invest their money and start to trade. From that moment everything is different: the decision-making is not so easy, and a profit may not appear, despite the same methods of fundamental and technical analysis.

According to some empirical research, investors' shifting to the Internet leads to increasing trade activity and decreasing profitability. It is believed to be connected with increasing investor illusion of control, as they start to be more involved and aware of the share market (Barber & Odean, 1999).

A third great influence on investors' behavior is called "thought contagion" (Frankfurter & McGoun, 2000). This effect appears when investors accept the opinion of more experienced investors or a brokerage firm, without any verification.

Psychological Effects on the Russian Share Market

This psychological influence is also manifested in some tendencies of Russian share market development. For example, the Russian share market "is afraid of" the Russian President's speeches. Before each of his "addresses to citizens", market rates decrease. Thus, over the course of several years, the President's speeches bring uncertainty to the Russian market behavior. This can affect the behavior of foreign investors' who withdraw their capital from Russian financial instruments, which causes a dramatic fall in the Russian indices.

The most famous peculiarity of the Russian share market is the correlation of its dynamics with American and Easten European indices. For this reason, investors are inactive while waiting for the opening of American tender. When America «wakes up», the activity increases significantly, and depending on the American trend can bring revolution into our market. Even if our market is showing positive dynamics all day long, the falling of American indices causes our indicies to go down until the end of the market session.

The Russian share market reacts sharply to a change in oil price. A rise in oil price can make the Russian indices increase dramatically. This information even influences the value of shares that are not connected with oil sector. Unlike foreign markets, the Russian share market does not have the division of tendencies in different sectors of economy. All "blue chips" go down or up together. On the contrary, in foreign markets oil prices affect only the oil sector.

Conclusion

In conclusion, we should take into account psychological factors in addition to fundamental and technical analyses for effective trading on both Russian and foreign share markets. Disregard of behavioral effects only leads to disappointment with trading. However, the biggest influence is manifested within a short-term period.

References

Barber B., Odean T. (1999) Online Investors: Do the Slow Die First? University of California at Davis working paper.

Bighiu Qawi R. (2010) Behavioral Finance: Is Investor Psyche Driving Market Performance? Georgia State University – Robinson College of Business, Atlanta, GA. Available at SSRN: http://ssrn.com/abstract=1598289

Bloomfield R.J. (2010) Traditional vs. Behavioral Finance. Johnson School Research Paper Series, 22.

Chen J. (2005) Information Theory and Market Behavior. ICFAI Journal of Behavioral Finance, 2(4), 25-45.

Frankfurter, G., McGoun, E. (2000) Thought contagion and Financial Economics: The Dividend Puzzle as a case Study. The Journal of Behavioral Finance, 3(4), 198-201.

Kahneman D., Tversky . (1979) Prospect theory: An analysis of decision making under risk. Econometrica, 47, 263-291.

Langer E. (1975) The Illusion of Control. Journal of Personality and Social Psychology, 32, 311-328.

Scharfstein D., Stein J.C. (1990) Herd Behavior and Investment. American Economic Review, 80(3), 465-479.

Shefrin H. (2010) Behavioralizing Finance. Foundations and Trends in Finance, 4, 1-184.

Tversky A., Kahneman D. (1981) The Framing of Decisions and the Psychology of Choice. Science, 211, 453-458.

Hedging with Futures: Multivariante Dynamic Conditional Correlation GARCH

Aleksey Kolokolov

Tor Vergata University of Rome, Italy. email: alexeiuo@gmail.com

Abstract In this paper, we apply three multivariate GARCH models for estimation of dynamic hedge ratios. We provide an empirical comparison of the effectiveness of those models in the Russian and foreign financial markets. Dynamics and interdependence between futures' and spot prices of assets are captured by vector error correction models; volatilities and correlations are modeled by dynamic conditional correlation multivariate GARCH.

Keywords: multivariate GARCH, dynamic conditional correlation, dynamic hedge ratios, Russian financial market.

Introduction

For a long time, among the approaches used for estimation of the optimal hedge ratios, a static approach developed by Johnson (1960) and Ederington (1979) dominated. Within this approach, the optimal hedge ratio is defined as the slope of the regression of changes in spot prices to changes in futures prices, and can be estimated by ordinary least squares (OLS). However, this method was subjected to intense criticism: these estimates are based on the unconditional variance and covariance, and conditional information is omitted (Myers, Thompson, 1989); the estimates obtained by the OLS are inefficient due to ignoring the autocorrelation of stock prices as well as other specific features of financial data, such as heteroscedasticity (Park, Bera, 1987).

Currently, the development of the time series theory and financial econometrics allow us to obtain estimates of conditional (with respect to all information available up to at a given point in time) hedge ratios. Such dynamic hedge ratios are calculated as a ratio of the conditional covariance between futures prices and spot prices of assets to the conditional variance of futures prices. Thus, they minimize the total variance of the position of an investor in hedging and hedged assets.

The choice of a model for the conditional covariance matrix plays an important role in estimating the optimal dynamic hedge ratios. Modeling covariance matrices began with the model VEC – direct vector generalization of a one-dimensional GARCH model (Bollerslev et al., 1988). Later, it was modified into a more compact model – BEKK (Engle, Kroner, 1995). These models, however, appeared to be inconvenient because of the complexity of restrictions that guarantee the positive

D. Sornette et al. (Eds.), *Market Risk and Financial Markets Modeling*,
DOI 10.1007/978-3-642-27931-7_9, © Springer-Verlag Berlin Heidelberg 2012

definiteness of the covariance matrix, a large number of parameters to be estimated, and ambiguities in their interpretation. Therefore, they were replaced by new models representing the dynamics of correlations and volatility separately. The first model of this kind used constant correlation (Bollerslev, 1990); then, models with dynamical correlations (Tse, Tsui, 2002 and Engle, 2002) were developed. Later, the widely used model of Engle was repeatedly modified and refined, allowing researchers and practitioners to model a variety of features of dynamics of correlations, in particular, asymmetry effects (Cappiello et al, 2006).

A substantial share of current research analyzes various models with varying conditional correlations. Bystrom (2003), Hsiang-tai Lee, Yoder (2007), Skintzi, Xanthopolous-Sisinis (2007), Yang, Allen (2004) and others repeatedly state high efficiency of such models. At the same time, there are cases where the effectiveness of the models is reduced significantly due to errors arising because of the complexity of estimation of their parameters, accumulated estimation errors, and increasing transaction costs (Tse, Tsui, 2002).

This paper compares the estimates of the optimal hedge ratios obtained using three multivariate GARCH models with different specifications of the time varying conditional correlations. The empirical study of the effectiveness of the proposed approaches is based on the data of the Russian and international financial markets.

The paper proceeds as follows: section 2 presents the methodology of modeling time-varying optimal hedge ratios. In section 3, the results of the empirical study and the effectiveness of hedging are discussed. The last section concludes.

Methodology

Definition of Optimal Hedge Ratio

According to Hull (2006), the hedge ratio is defined as "the ratio of the size of the portfolio taken in futures contracts to the size of the exposure". The main purpose of this paper is to explore the ability of multivariate GARCH models to estimate (and forecast) conditional covariances in different financial markets, rather than to develop a "realistic hedging strategy". Thus, for the purpose of the paper, the optimal dynamic hedge ratio will be defined in the simplest way possible. Such an approach makes it easier to understand how well one or another econometric model captures the conditional covariance between a hedged asset and corresponding futures. A simplified reasoning (which is, however, not a strict mathematical proof) could be, for example, that the greater the reduction in the variance of the returns on a position, the better an econometric model describes the actual data generating process. Consequently, this better model should provide more accurate estimates of optimal hedge ratios defined in a different (possibly more complex) way, provided that they are still based on the estimates of the covariances.

Assume that a hedger is long an asset and let s_t and f_t be the natural logarithms of spot and futures prices of the asset respectively. The logarithmic return at time t on an unhedged position is:

$$R_t^u = s_t - s_{t-1} \tag{1}$$

If the position is hedged with t futures contracts, it can be approximated by

$$R_t^h = (s_t - s_{t-1}) - h_t(f_t - f_{t-1}) \tag{2}$$

Here $(s_t - s_{t-1})$ and $(f_t - f_{t-1})$ are the returns of spot and futures markets respectively and h_t is the value of the dynamic hedge ratio at time t. The conditional (with respect to whole information up to time t) variance of the hedger's return can be then represented as follows:

$$V(R_t^h) = V(s_t) + h_t^2 V(f_t) - 2h_t Cov(s_t, f_t), \tag{3}$$

where $V(s_t)$ and $V(f_t)$ are the conditional variances of logarithms of the spot and futures prices respectively, and $Cov(s_t, f_t)$ is a conditional covariance between them.

To achieve the perfect hedge the optimal hedge ratio at time t is defined as a hedge ratio which gives the minimum of conditional variance of the returns on the hedger's position (see Ederington, 1979 and Hull, 2006):

$$h_t^* = \frac{Cov(s_t, f_t)}{V(f_t)} \tag{4}$$

In practice, in order to compute the optimal hedge ratio at time t, the conditional covariances are replaced by their estimates based on the sample data. Thus, the accuracy of the prediction of optimal hedge ratios depends on the accuracy of the econometric models used to forecast the conditional covariances.

Hedging effectiveness can be measured as the relative reduction of the unconditional variance of an investor's returns (Ederington, 1979):

$$u(\hat{h}_t^*) = u(model) = \frac{V(R^u)}{V(R^h)}. \tag{5}$$

The value of this measure depends on the accuracy of prediction of the optimal hedge ratio and, consequently, on the choice of an econometric model to forecast the conditional covariances. Thus, it can be used as a criterion to compare the predictive abilities of different models.

Note, however, that minimizing the variance of returns may poorly describe the strategy of a real investor, which can depend on expected income as well. Given this fact, more realistic definitions of the optimal hedge ratio can be proposed. For example, Brooks et al. (2002) define a hedge ratio such that the investor's utility function reaches its maximum.

Modeling Dynamic Covariance Matrix

Let us define a random two-dimensional vector y_t, whose components are returns on futures contracts and the corresponding financial index. It is assumed that the vector stochastic process $(y_t)_{t \in Z}$ has the following form:

$$y_t = E[y_t \mid F_{t-1}] + \varepsilon_t \,,\ \varepsilon_t = \Sigma_t^{1/2} z_t \,, \tag{6}$$

F_{t-1} represents all information available up to time t-1,

Σ_t is a positive definite matrix,

$\Sigma_t^{1/2}$ is the Cholesky decomposition of Σ_t ,

z_t are identically distributed independent vectors,

$E[z_t] = 0$,

$V[z_t] = I$ is a diagonal matrix with ones on the main diagonal.

Then the conditional variance-covariance matrix is given by

$$V[y_t \mid F_{t-1}] = \Sigma_t^{1/2} V[z_t] (\Sigma_t^{1/2})' = \Sigma_t \,. \tag{7}$$

The conditional expectation and the covariance matrix are functions of unknown parameters and observed values. Further, one needs to specify parametric forms for $E[y_t \mid F_{t-1}]$ and Σ_t. In this work, a vector error correction model is used to model $E[y_t \mid F_{t-1}]$. The conditional covariance matrix is modeled using three multivariate GARCH models of different specifications: a model with constant correlations and models of symmetric and asymmetric dynamic conditional correlations.

The covariance matrix can be decomposed as the product of three matrices:

$$\Sigma_t = D_t R_t D_t \,, \tag{8}$$

where $R_t = (\rho_{ijt})$ is a conditional correlation matrix of dimension two by two, D_t is a diagonal matrix with elements $_{iit}$ (square root of the conditional variance of the component i, i=1,2) on the main diagonal. Positive definiteness of the matrix Σ_t is ensured by positive definiteness of the matrix R_t and positivity of $_{iit}$.

In this study, all elements $_{iit}$ are assumed to follow univariate GARCH processes. However, different processes (e.g. exponential GARCH) can be used to model different univariate volatilities.

The simplest model for the conditional correlation matrix R_t is the Constant Conditional Correlation (CCC) model of Tim Bollerslev (1990), in which it is assumed that the matrix R_t is constant over time:

$$R_t = R = (\rho_{ij}) \,. \tag{9}$$

This model has an obvious interpretation and can be easily estimated in two steps: first the parameter estimates of the one-dimensional GARCH are estimated, then the sample covariance between the standardized residuals is calculated. Nevertheless, the a-priori assumption of invariability of conditional correlations is often unjustified and can lead to unacceptable inaccuracies.

A natural generalization of the CCC model, allowing the conditional correlations to change over time, is the Dynamic Conditional Correlation (DCC) model of Engle (2002). In order to provide a special form of the correlation matrix (symmetric, units on the main diagonal and smaller than unity in absolute value off-diagonal elements), R_t is represented as follows:

$$R_t = (\mathrm{diag}(Q_t))^{-1/2} Q_t (\mathrm{diag}(Q_t))^{-1/2}, \tag{10}$$

where Q_t is a positive definite symmetric matrix, evolving in accordance with the process

$$Q_t = (1-\theta_1-\theta_2)\overline{Q} + \theta_1 u_{t-1} u_{t-1} + \theta_2 Q_{t-1}. \tag{11}$$

Here

$u_t = [u_{1t}, u_{2t}]'$, $u_{it} = \dfrac{\varepsilon_{it}}{\sqrt{\sigma_{iit}^2}}$ are the standardized residuals from (1), i=1,2,

$\overline{Q}$ is the unconditional covariance matrix of u_t.

To ensure the positive definiteness of R_t and, therefore, Σ_t, the parameters θ_1 and θ_2 should be positive and their sum should not exceed one (Engle, Sheppard 2001).

The dynamics of conditional correlations in the DCC models can be explained by their dependence on previous values of the shocks (errors) standardized by the volatility. The collinear residuals increase the conditional correlations, and multidirectional residuals decrease them. However, risk-averse investors seem to be more responsive to negative information about the market. Hence, in order to describe the dynamics of conditional correlations in a more accurate way, it is reasonable to assume that changes in conditional correlations may be different for positive and negative residual values. To account for this asymmetrical effect, the DCC model can be modified to the Asymmetric Dynamic Conditional Correlation (ADCC) model.

The difference between the DCC and ADCC models is the parametric form of the matrices Q_t. For the ADCC model, matrices Q_t vary according to the following equation:

$$Q_t = (1-\theta_1-\theta_2)\overline{Q} - \theta_3 N + \theta_1 u_{t-1} u_{t-1} + \theta_2 Q_{t-1} + \theta_3 \eta_{t-1} \eta_{t-1}, \tag{12}$$

where

$\eta_t = I[u_t < 0] \otimes u_t$,

$\overline{N} = E[\eta_t \eta_t']$,

$I[u_t < 0]$ is an indicator function,

$\otimes$ stands for element by element multiplication.

The positive definiteness of R_t is ensured by the following restriction (Cappiello et al, 2006):

$$\theta_1 + \theta_2 + \delta\theta_3 < 1, \quad (13)$$

where δ is the highest eigenvalue of $\overline{Q}^{-1/2} \cdot \overline{N} \cdot \overline{Q}^{-1/2}$.

The above multivariate GARCH models belong to the class of models with time varying conditional correlations. Note that the CCC model can be regarded as DCC with $\theta_1 = \theta_2 = 0$, which in turn is the ADCC model with $\theta_3 = 0$.

The estimation theory for all above models is well studied in the literature. The vector error correction model (the model for the conditional mean) can be estimated by a two-stage least squares method (see e.g. Lutkepohl, 2005). Consistent and asymptotically normal estimates for the parameters of GARCH models are obtained by the two step (quasi) maximum likelihood method (see Newey and McFadden 1994, Engle and Sheppard, 2001, and Engle, 2001, for the DCC models; Cappiello et al, 2006, for the ADCC model).

Empirical Results and Hedging Effectiveness

For an empirical study I used historical daily values from January 1, 2008 to July 22, 2010 of the following five indices: Russian RTS index, DAX, S&P 500 (hereafter S&P), and NASDAQ COMPOSITE (hereafter NASDAQ), as well as the corresponding futures contracts.

The total number of observations is 635 for the RTS index and 668 for DAX, S&P 500 and NASDAQ. The difference in the length of the series is due to different numbers of holidays in those markets. For each series the last 60 pairs of observations, about three trading months, are used for the out-of-sample analysis. The descriptive statistics of the data are reported in Table 1.

Table 1: Descriptive Statistics

The table presents descriptive statistics for the series of the returns of indices (index) and the returns of corresponding futures contracts (future). In the rows, mean values (mean), medians (med), standard deviations (std), skewness, kurtosis, the maximum value (max), and the minimum value (min) are reported.

	RTS		**DAX**		**NASDAQ**		**S&P**	
	future	**index**	**future**	**index**	**future**	**index**	**future**	**index**
mean	0.00	0.00	0.00	0.00	0.00	0.00	0.00	0.00
med	0.00	0.00	0.00	0.00	0.00	0.00	0.00	0.00
std	0.04	0.03	0.02	0.02	0.02	0.02	0.02	0.02
skewness	-0.40	-0.23	0.31	0.29	0.11	-0.09	0.12	-0.14
kurtosis	10.87	9.91	9.08	8.19	10.17	7.02	10.30	8.17
max	0.23	0.20	0.12	0.11	0.13	0.11	0.13	0.11
min	-0.31	-0.21	-0.08	-0.07	-0.11	-0.10	-0.10	-0.09

It is worth noting that the skewnesses of returns of all indices are different from zero. For the DAX, NASDAQ and S&P they are 0.31, 0.11 and 0.12 respectively, and the skewness of return of the RTS index is -0.40. Thus, the returns of the RTS index are more likely to appear in the left tail of the distribution, and those of the DAX, NASDAQ and S&P indices in the right tail.

All five series of pairs of logarithms of index values and futures contracts happened to be cointegrated. For each pair, the two-dimensional error correction models are estimated as well as the three different GARCH models. The estimation results are not relevant for further discussion and are thus omitted here.

The competing models of correlations were tested against one another using the likelihood ratio tests. Unfortunately, the power of likelihood ratio tests can be reduced significantly due to potential misspecification of the one-dimensional GARCH models or incorrect parametric forms chosen for the conditional correlations. Therefore, in order to test the null hypothesis of constant conditional correlations against the dynamic conditional correlations, the test proposed by Engle, Sheppard (2001) is used. This test is based on consistent estimates of the CCC model only: under the null hypothesis, the standardized residuals $u_t = \overline{R}^{-1/2} D_t^{-1} \varepsilon_t$ are a sequence of independent, identically distributed, random variables. The parameters in the autoregressive vector product of the standardized residual should therefore be zero. Table 2 reports the test results.

Table 2: Tests for constant conditional correlations

The table shows the tests results for the null hypothesis of constant conditional correlations. The number of lags used in the auxiliary regression is denoted by "nlags", the test statistics are labeled "sta". The last column represents the p-values.

	nlags	sta	p-value
	2	1.92	0.59
RTS	5	2.65	0.85
	10	4.70	0.94
	2	41.84	0.00
DAX	5	63.45	0.00
	10	64.84	0.00
	2	0.21	0.98
NASDAQ	5	3.53	0.74
	10	6.10	0.87
	2	4.01	0.26
S&P	5	5.98	0.42
	10	19.22	0.06

Hedging effectiveness is measured as the reduction of unconditional variance of an investor's returns defined as in equation (5). However, since the true values of the parameters are not known, their sample estimates are used instead. Unfortunately, one cannot exclude the possibility that some models, well approximating the process of conditional covariances matrices in-sample, might turn out to be unsuitable for predictions. Therefore, for each GARCH model I calculated two estimates of the efficiency index: an in-sample estimate and an out-of-sample estimate, based on projections beyond the sample used to estimate the parameters. Estimates of this indicator, as well as the ratios of the return variances using CCC, DCC and ADCC hedges to the return variance using only the CCC hedge, are reported in Table 3.

The usage of estimates of the hedge ratios based on the DCC and ADCC models leads to a slight increase in the hedge quality in-sample and to a decrease in quality out-of-sample for the DAX, NASDAQ and S&P indices. For the RTS index, hedging effectiveness of the DCC-hedge slightly increases out-of-sample as well.

There is no significant improvement in the quality of hedging when more detailed econometric models are used. Such an effect usually arises in the framework of complicated models requiring estimation of too many parameters, and it can be explained by accumulation of the estimation errors. The ability of tests to identify the most adequate to the data model is weakened for similar reasons.

The variance reduction is much higher for the U.S. and German markets both in- and out-of-sample. This observation indicates a closer relationship between the indices and corresponding futures contracts in these developed markets due to higher liquidity, fast speed of reaction of the futures market on the behavior of the spot market, and a smaller number of speculative transactions.

Table 3: Hedging effectiveness and relative variance reduction

The table reports the estimates of the index of hedging effectiveness defined in equation (5) (u(CCC)), DCC (u(DCC)), (u(ADCC)) and ratios of estimates of variances of all hedged positions to the estimates of variance of the -hedge (CCC/CCC, CCC/DCC, CCC/ADCC).

			in-sample analysis			
	u(CCC)	**CCC/CCC**	**u(DCC)**	**DCC/CCC**	**u(ADCC)**	**ADCC/CCC**
RTS	1.646	1.000	1.639	0.996	1.637	0.995
DAX	44.668	1.000	44.997	1.007	44.973	1.007
NASDAQ	13.360	1.000	13.438	1.006	13.435	1.006
S&P	30.084	1.000	30.097	1.000	29.980	0.997
			out-of-sample analysis			
	u(CCC)	**CCC/CCC**	**u(DCC)**	**DCC/CCC**	**u(ADCC)**	**ADCC/CCC**
RTS	2.211	1.000	2.238	1.012	1.881	0.851
DAX	75.139	1.000	9.300	0.124	14.840	0.197
NASDAQ	28.487	1.000	16.473	0.578	9.249	0.325
S&P	48.586	1.000	27.776	0.572	43.881	0.903

Conclusion

The above study shows that the multivariate GARCH models with dynamic conditional correlations, such as DCC and ADCC, are not able to significantly improve the estimation of the optimal dynamic hedge ratios in comparison to the simple models with constant conditional correlations. Given the evidence of tests on the constancy of conditional correlations, it can be argued that the CCC model is a better approximation of the conditional correlations than DCC and ADCC models, which suffer due to misspecification and the accumulation of estimation errors.

Nevertheless, hedging based on the CCC models can significantly reduce the variance of positions in the indices, at least in the developed financial markets, such as the German and American markets.

For the Russian market and the specialized NASDAQ index, the designed hedges are relatively less effective. CCC, DCC and ADCC models that control for the dynamics of conditional correlations by a few parameters are not flexible enough for an exhaustive description of the process. However, the use of more bulky models is of high risk due to the aforementioned problem of accumulation of estimation inaccuracies.

References

Newey W. K., McFadden D. (1994). Large sample estimation and hypothesis testing. Handbook of Econometrics, Vol. 4, Elsevier North-Holland.

Bystrom H. N. E., (2003). The hedging performance of electricity futures on the Nordic power exchange. Applied Economics, 35, 1–11.

Bollerslev T., Engle R., and Wooldridge J.M., (1988). A Capital Asset Pricing Model with Time Varying Covariances. Journal of Political Economy, 96, 116-131.

Bollerslev T., (1990). Modelling the Coherence in Short-Run Nominal Exchange Rates: A Multivariate Generalized ARCH model. Review of Economics and Statistics, 52, 5-59.

Brooks C., Henry O. T., Persand G., (2002). The Effect of Asymmetries on Optimal Hedge Ratios. Journal of Business, 75, 333-352.

Cappiello, L., Engle R. F., Sheppard K., (2006). Asymmetric Dynamics in the Correlations of Global Equity and Bond Returns. Journal of Financial Econometrics, 4, 537-572.

Ederington L. H., (1979). The Hedging Performances of the New Futures Markets. Journal of Finance, 34, 157-170.

Engle R. F. Kroner K. F., (1995). Multivariate simultaneous generalized ARCH. Econometric Theory, 11, 122-150.

Engle R. and Sheppard K., (2001). Theoretical and Empirical Properties of Dynamic Conditional Correlation Multivariate GARCH. NBER Working Paper 8554.

Engle R. F., (2002). Dynamic Conditional Correlation. A Simple Class of Multivariate GARCH Models. Journal of Business and Economic Statistics, 20, 339-350.

Hsiang-tai Lee, Jonathan Yoder, (2007). Optimal hedging with a regime-switching time-varying correlation GARCH model. The Journal of Futures Markets, 27, No. 5, 495–516.

Hull J. (2006). Options, Futures, and Other Derivatives, 6th ed. Prentice-Hall, Englewood Cliffs, NJ.

Johnson, L. L., (1960). The theory of hedging and speculation in commodity futures. Review of Economic Studies, 27, 139–151.

Lien D., Tse Y. K., Tsui A. K. C., (2002). Evaluating the Hedging performance of the Constant-Correlation GARCH model. Applied Financial Economics, 12, 791-798.

Lutkepohl H. (2005). New Introduction to Multiple Time Series Analysis. Springer-Verlag Berlin Heidelberg.

Myers, R. J. and Thompson, S.R. (1989). Generalized Optimal Hedge Ratio Estimation. American Journal of Agricultural Economics, 71, 858-867.

Park H., Bera, A., (1987). Interest rate volatility, basis, and heteroscedasticity in hedging mortgages. American Real Estate and Urban Economics Association 15, 79–97.

Skintzi V. D., Xanthopolous-Sisinis S., (2007). Evaluation of correlation forecasting models for risk management. Journal of forecasting, 26, 497-526.

Tse Y., Tsui A. (2002). A multivariate generalized autoregressive conditional heteroscedasticity model with time-varying correlations. Journal of Business and Economic Statistics, 20, 351–362.

Yang W., Allen D., (2004). Multivariate GARCH hedge ratios and hedging effectiveness in Australian futures markets. Accounting and Finance, 45, 301–321.

A Note on the Dynamics of Hedge-Fund-Alpha Determinants

Olga Kolokolova

Manchester Business School, UK. email: olga.kolokolova@mbs.ac.uk

Abstract Various studies have analyzed the determinants of hedge fund performance. The majority of them, however, come to contradictory conclusions with respect to the direction of influence of different factors on fund performance. The key reason for the inconsistencies is the highly dynamic nature of hedge funds. This paper specifically focuses on the dynamics of the relations between hedge fund performance and various microeconomic factors. It quantifies shifts in the average fund alpha that result from changes in hedge fund style, age, size, and fee structure and investigates the time variation of these shifts. The empirical results highlight the dynamic nature of the hedge fund industry. Hedge funds seem to generate a positive and significant alpha on average; however, the alpha level varies considerably over time. It is hard to predict the exact absolute alpha level based on the hedge fund micro-factors, but it seems to be possible to rank hedge funds using the micro-information. The results suggest that large funds with high relative inflow, charging higher than median management fees, are likely to deliver a higher alpha than their peers most of the time.

Introduction

As the hedge fund industry is expanding, it is attracting more and more attention from investors and academics. The increasing quantity of research papers and reported empirical findings, although providing additional insights into the different aspects of hedge fund performance, does not yet seem to have converged to a well established and overall accepted set of results. The majority of studies that have analyzed the determinants of hedge fund performance have come to contradictory conclusions, even with respect to the direction of influence of the considered factors.

The current literature typically models hedge fund return time series using a set of common macro-factors. For example, Favre and Ranaldo (2005) use the higher-moment adjusted CAPM, where the authors introduce as additional factors the squared and cubic deviation of the return on the S&P 500 index from its average. The seven-factor model of Fung and Hsieh (2004) uses the S&P 500 as a proxy for the equity market, adds bonds, size, and credit spread factors, as well as three option-based trend-following factors based on bonds, currency, and commodities. Agarwal and Naik (2000) propose an eight-factor model based on eight tradable indices, including emerging markets and gold. Alas, these approaches ignore the

D. Sornette et al. (Eds.), *Market Risk and Financial Markets Modeling*,
DOI 10.1007/978-3-642-27931-7_10, © Springer-Verlag Berlin Heidelberg 2012

panel (cross-sectional) dimension of the data which contains micro-level information pertaining to individual funds. Such information includes variables that can help to explain the cross-section of hedge fund performance, such as the style of the fund (Brown and Goetzmann, 2003) or the level of its fees (Brown et al., 2004).

The impact of the micro-factors has been investigated in cross-sectional settings by several authors. However, since the dynamic (time-varying) nature of the considered relationships was largely ignored, these studies came to contradictory conclusions. For instance, Liang (1999) finds a positive relationship between hedge fund performance and size, as well as between performance and fees. Agarwal et al. (2004) document a negative relationship between fund performance and size, and Kouwenberg and Ziemba (2007) report a negative relationship between performance and fees. The results of the major studies on the relationship between hedge fund performance and different micro-factors are summarized in Table 1.

Table 1: Hedge Fund Performance and its Determinants: Evidence from the Literature

This table lists the central questions related to hedge fund performance and groups the research according to their findings. The reference databases and the analyzed time period are specified in brackets.

Relationship between Performance and:	Positive relationship	Negative Relationship	No Relationship
Fund size	Amenc, Curtis and Martellini (2003) [CISDM, 1996-2002] De Souza and Gokcan (2003) [TASS] Getmansky (2005), [TASS, 1994-April 2003] Liang (1999) [HFR, 1994-June 1997]	Brorsen and Harri (2004) [LaPorte Asset Allocation, up to 1998] Goetzmann, Ingersoll and Ross (2003) [US. Offshore Funds Directory, 1990-1996] Agarwal, Daniel and Naik (2004), [HFR, TASS, MAR, 1994-2000] Naik, Ramadorai and Strömqvist (2007) [HFR, TASS, CISDM, 1994 – 2002] Fung, Hsieh, Naik and Ramadorai (2008) [HFR, TASS, CISDM, 1994-2002]	Gregoriou and Rouah (2003) [ZCM and LaPorte, 1994-1999] Koh, Koh and Teo (2003) [AsiaHedge, EurekaHedge, 1999-March 2003]
Fees	Ackermann, McEnally and Ravenscraft (1999) [TASS,1988-1995] Liang (1999) [HFR, 1994-June 1997] De Souza and Gokcan (2003) [TASS] Amenc, Curtis and Martellini (2003) [CISDM, 1996 – 2002]	Kazemi, Schneeweis and Martin (2002) [TASS, HFR, 1994 -2000] Koh, Koh and Teo (2003) [AsiaHedge, EurekaHedge, 1999-March 2003]	Agarwal, Daniel and Naik (2009), [CISDM, HFR, MSCI, TASS, 1994-2002]
Age		Howell (2001) [TASS, 1994-2000] Liang (1999) [HFR, 1994-June 1997] Amenc, Curtis and Martellini (2003) [CISDM, 1996 – 2002] Agarwal, Daniel and Naik (2004) [HFR, TASS, MAR, 1994-2000]	Koh, Koh and Teo (2003) [AsiaHedge, EurekaHedge, 1999-March 2003]

The evidence of the impact of fund size and fund fees on performance is completely mixed; the evidence of the impact of fund age on performance is more coherent, suggesting that younger funds do not underperform relative to older funds.

Another strand of the literature analyzes hedge fund abnormal return (alpha), and has also produced a variety of observations and conclusions. Ackermann et al. (1999) find that from 1988 to 1995 hedge funds outperformed mutual funds, but not standard market indices. Liang (1999) also claims that hedge funds offer better risk-return trade-offs compared to mutual funds. Agarwal and Naik (2000) show that hedge funds outperform the market benchmark by 6% – 15% per year. Ibbotson and Chen (2005) find an average alpha of 3.7 percent per year from 1999 till 2004, which is positive and significant. Kosowski et al. (2007) find that on average the hedge fund alpha is positive, but insignificant. At the same time, however, the performance of top funds cannot be explained by pure luck. These funds exhibit positive and significant alphas. Naik et al. (2007) report that during the period from 1995 to 2004 hedge funds generated significant alphas, but that the level of alpha declined substantially over this period. Fung et al. (2008) document that funds of funds showed positive and significant alpha only during one period, between October 1998 and March 2000. Also of note is that funds following different styles seem to have, on average, different alphas. For example, Ibbotson and Chen (2006) obtain the largest alpha estimate for Equity Long Short hedge funds, based on an index regression from 1995 to April 2006.

Different results obtained in the literature are due to differences in performance measures, statistical methodology, databases, time periods, and, last but not least, the highly dynamic nature of hedge funds. Exposure to various macro-factors as well as the influence of micro-level characteristics varies over time and with respect to different strategies. Both time and cross-sectional variation of hedge fund returns (and alphas) cannot be captured by separate time-series or cross-sectional analyses. This paper addresses these problems by using a fixed effect panel regression approach that controls jointly for temporally varying and cross-sectional dependencies of hedge funds. Although the proposed approach does not allow us to find precise estimates of individual fund alphas, it does allow us to rank different groups of hedge funds according to their average alphas and to document the dynamics of the relationship between hedge fund alpha and fund-specific micro-factors such as fund style, size, flows, and fees; this setup also allows us to identify factors with time-stable effects that can be used to better predict the future alpha.

The results indicate that hedge funds declaring different styles may deliver rather different alphas; there is, however, no constantly winning style. The best style during one period does not necessarily remain the best during the subsequent period. At the same time, if the time variation of the average profitability of the hedge funds is taken into consideration, very little incremental difference in the alphas of hedge funds of different styles can be documented. Additionally, I document several stable relations between hedge fund alpha and certain micro-factors. Large hedge funds with high relative fund inflow, charging higher than median management fees, seem to deliver higher alphas. The fund ranking based on these relationships is rather stable over time and for different styles, although the magnitude of the actual alpha shifts varies considerably over time. The relationship between incentive fee and alpha, on the contrary, is rather volatile, and cannot be used for stable hedge fund ranking.

Research Design and Methods

This section first presents the general structure of the models and estimation methodology, and then proceeds with a detailed description of the variables in use.

General Model

The paper uses a panel regression approach with fixed effects that allows one to jointly control for time dynamics as well as for cross-sectional dependencies between hedge funds. Within the class of panel models, one can consider either fixed effect or random effect models. Random effect models require fund-specific effects to be uncorrelated with the factors. We cannot make such an assumption here, since managerial skill is likely to be correlated with flows, assets under management (AuM), and fees. Moreover, if the true model is a random effect model and it is estimated as if it were a fixed effect model, the estimates are still consistent, although they are not efficient. The reverse in not true: estimating the true fixed effect model as a random effect model leads to inconsistent estimates. A fixed effect panel model is therefore chosen for the current study.

Hedge funds often use option-like, non-linear investment strategies (see Fung and Hsieh (1997), Fung and Hsieh (2001), and Agarwal and Naik (2000)). In order to control for this aspect of the returns, the Fung and Hsieh (2004) seven-factor approach is chosen as the base time-series model. The market factors (X_{it}) contain the excess return on the S&P 500 index over the risk-free rate as a proxy for the equity market, the monthly change in the 10-year treasury constant maturity yield as a proxy for the bond market, the difference in the returns on the Wilshire Small Cap 1750 index and Wilshire Large Cap 750 index, and three trend-following option-based factors (bond trend-following factor, currency trend-following factor, and commodity trend-following factor). The trend-following factors were obtained from the web page of David Hsieh[1]. Since each hedge fund can follow a unique investment strategy, fund-specific factor loadings are allowed.

In the time series framework, structural breaks and possible regime shifts also need to be taken into account. In addition to the commonly used two break points framing the internet bubble, I identify two new break points in the data and introduce corresponding time dummies in the regression (D_{τ}^{Time}). The time dummies adjust for the general profitability of the hedge fund industry within each period.

[1] http://faculty.fuqua.duke.edu/~dah7/HFRFData.htm

The use of time period dummies allows us to identify the periods which were profitable for the hedge fund industry as a whole.

In the cross-sectional dimension, fund-specific information is used. First, hedge fund styles are included. $Style_i$ denotes a vector of four components, each indicating a percentage of assets under management invested by fund i within one of four main styles (Equity Long/Short, Directional, Relative Value, and Event Driven). Group dummies for other micro-factors such as fund age (D_{it}^{Age}), fund assets under management (D_{it}^{AuM}), absolute and relative fund flow ($D_{it}^{FlowAbs}$ and $D_{it}^{FlowRel}$), and management and incentive fees (D_{it}^{MFee} and D_{it}^{IFee}) are also used. D_{it}^{Factor} denotes a vector of three dummies $[D_{it,1}^{Factor}, D_{it,2}^{Factor}, D_{it,3}^{Factor}]$ that indicate whether a fund is characterized by a low level of a given factor at a given time, a medium level, or a high level, respectively. The loadings corresponding to style and the group dummies for each micro-factor are restricted to sum to zero. These restrictions allow quantification of the expected changes in the fund alpha conditional on changes in hedge fund age, assets under management, fees, and style. In terms of interpretation, the constant term in the regression characterizes an average baseline alpha of hedge funds. The style, time, age, AuM, flow and fees dummies reflect the deviation from the average alpha of funds belonging to a particular category.

The base model can be then specified as:

$$r_{it} = \alpha + \delta_{it} + X_{it}\beta_i + \varepsilon_{it},$$

$$\delta_{it} = \sum_{\tau=1}^{5} \lambda_\tau D_{t\tau}^{Time} + \left(Style_i, D_{it}^{Age}, D_{it}^{AuM}, D_{it}^{FlowAbs}, D_{it}^{FlowRel}, D_{ti}^{MFee}, D_{ti}^{IFee}\right) \cdot \gamma \quad (1)$$

where

r_{it} is the excess return over the risk-free rate on fund i for period t,

α is a baseline hedge fund alpha,

δ_{it} is the time-varying difference of the alpha of fund i and the baseline alpha level ; this difference is a function of fund-specific micro-factors,

X_{it} is a set of macro-factors,

β_i is a vector of macro-factor loadings specific for each fund,

$D_{t\tau}^{Time}$ is a set of time dummies, taking a value of one if the current time t belongs to one of the five pre-specified periods ,

λ_τ are the loadings on the time dummies, which are constant for all funds,

D_{it}^{Factor} are the vectors of micro-factor dummies,

$Style_i$ is a vector representing the percentage of AuM invested in each of four styles,

γ is a vector of micro-factor loadings, which is constant for all funds,

ε_{it} is an error term.

Getmansky et al. (2004) show that hedge fund returns are often serially correlated up to an order of two, which can be attributed to apparent illiquidity and smoothing of reported returns. In order to control for serial correlation, for each hedge fund i the error term ε_{it} is modeled as an MA(2) process. Equation (1) is estimated using generalized least squares. In the first stage, the OLS regression is estimated and the residuals are obtained. Then the residuals' variance-covariance matrix is estimated under the assumption that the residuals corresponding to each particular hedge fund are serially correlated up to an order two. In the second stage, the factor loadings are re-estimated using the estimated variance-covariance matrix of the residuals. Since the MA(2) residual structure may not completely capture residual heteroscedasticity, Newey-West-corrected standard errors with 12 lags are computed.

Style profitability is likely to vary over time and the relationship between other micro-factors and fund alpha is likely to change both with time and style. These changes are analyzed by augmenting eq. (1) by time-style factors, time-group dummies, and style-group dummies for each of the factors in turn. Identifying the time-varying contribution of different micro-factors to a particular hedge fund's performance is important for analyzing stability of commonly discussed effects such as decreasing return to scale or decline in hedge fund alpha over time, as well as for further investigation of business-cycle effects and predictability of fund alpha.

In carrying out this analysis, a regression similar to eq. (1) is estimated, in which a product of the time dummies and the dummies corresponding to the micro-factors of interest is included. This is then repeated for each combination of interest. For example, in order to estimate the time-variation of style effects, the following regression is estimated.

$$
\begin{aligned}
r_{it} &= \alpha + \delta_{it} + X_{it}\beta_i + \varepsilon_{it}, \\
\delta_{it} &= \sum_{\tau=1}^{5} \lambda_\tau D_{i\tau}^{Time} + \sum_{s=1}^{4}\sum_{\tau=1}^{5} \phi_{\tau s} D_{i\tau}^{Time} Style_{si} + \left(D_{it}^{Age}, D_{it}^{AuM}, D_{it}^{FlowAbs}, D_{it}^{FlowRel}, D_{ti}^{MFee}, D_{ti}^{IFee}\right)\cdot\gamma
\end{aligned}
\tag{2}
$$

where $\phi_{\tau s}$ is a loading on the cross-product of the time-dummy for period and the style factor for style s. It can be interpreted as the incremental alpha of a hedge fund following style s during period .

Construction of Dummy Variables

Time Dummies

In the existing literature, three major periods of evolution in the hedge fund industry are commonly recognized: before the internet bubble, the internet bubble, and after the internet bubble[2]. In this paper, five distinct time periods are identified based on a cross-section of hedge fund volatility and growth of the total AuM. The pre-bubble and post-bubble periods are each additionally divided into two subperiods[3]. Such division allows for better capturing of the time-variation in hedge fund alphas. In order to find the exact breakpoints, I conduct a Chow test based on the regression of the time series of average hedge fund returns using the Fung and Hsieh (2004) seven factor model. For all the chosen break points the null hypothe-

[2] Fung and Hsieh (2004), Fung, Hsieh, Naik and Ramadorai (2008).

[3] The data ends in the middle of 2006, thus the financial crises of 2008 is not covered.

sis of no structural break is rejected at the 1% significance level. This particular choice of the break points assures that the effects of the corresponding time dummies are the most pronounced. At the same time, the results are robust to shifting the break points one month backward or forward. The resulting 5 time periods are listed in Table 2.

Table 2: Time Periods in the Evolution of the Hedge Fund Industry

This table discusses the time periods that correspond to different stages of the evolution of the hedge fund industry. The first column gives the breakpoints, the second column characterizes the cross-section of hedge fund returns and the AuM, and the third column lists corresponding market events.

	Period	Characteristics	Market Events
1	Until Sep. 1997	Moderate cross-section hedge fund return volatility; slow increase in the total AuM.	
2	Oct. 1997 to Sep. 1998	Increasing cross-section return volatility	East Asian currency crisis, Russian Default, LTCM debacle;
3	Oct. 1998 to Mar. 2000	Very high cross-section returns' volatility.	The Internet bubble.
4	Apr. 2000 to Feb. 2005	Decreasing cross-section return volatility, rapid increase in the total AuM.	Economic recession in Europe (2000-2001), in the US (2001-2003); September 11/2001; accounting scandal and bankruptcy of WorldCom (July 2002).
5	March. 2005 to Jun. 2006	Low cross-section return volatility, stable total AuM.	

Age Dummies

The age dummies indicate different sub-periods of the life of each hedge fund:

1. "Young funds" not older than 4 years (28% of funds stop reporting before this age).
2. "Middle-age funds" with age between 5 and 9 years (52% of funds stop reporting within this age interval).
3. "Old funds" with age over 10 years (20% of funds stop reporting within this age interval).

If, for example, during a given month t, a hedge fund's age is between 5 and 9 years, the corresponding age dummy $D_{it,2}^{Age}$ takes a value of 1, and other two age dummies ($D_{it,1}^{Age}$ and $D_{it,3}^{Age}$) take a value of zero.

Asset under Management, Relative and Absolute Flow Dummies

In order to construct the assets under management (AuM) dummies, at each point in time hedge funds are divided into 3 sub-groups according to their AuM:

1. Low AuM group: includes the 30% of all funds having the lowest AuM existing on the date of interest.
2. Middle AuM group: includes the 40% of funds with AuM lying between the 30th and 70th quantiles existing on the date of interest.
3. High AuM group: includes the 30% of funds with the highest AuM of all funds existing on the date of interest.

Note that the critical levels of the AuM, which separate the fund groups, depend on the calendar time. For example, a fund with 100 million in AuM belongs to the high AuM group in 1995, but a fund with the same AuM in 2003 is considered to have only middle AuM.

For the Absolute and Relative Flow dummies, the sub-division into three categories is performed analogously.

In the fund by fund regressions, one cannot simultaneously use variables related to the AuM, and Relative and Absolute Flows since they will be collinear. However, in the panel setting they are not. $10 million in absolute flow can be just a 1% relative flow for a large fund (the dummy of low relative flows takes a value of 1), or a 50% relative flow for a small fund (the dummy for high relative flow takes a value of 1). The empirical correlation coefficients for log(AuM) and absolute and relative flows are, thus, rather small (see Table 3).

Table 3: Correlation Matrix of the Log AuM and Fund Flows

This table reports the empirical correlation coefficient of the logarithm of the asset under management, absolute flow, and relative flow computed for pooled individual hedge funds that report their returns and the AuM during any consecutive 24 months between January 1994 and July 2006.

	log(AuM)	**FlowAbs**	**FlowRel**
log(AuM)	1		
FlowAbs	0.105	1	
FlowRel	0.001	0.035	1

Management and Incentive Fee Dummies

While constructing the management/incentive fee dummies, hedge funds are divided into 3 sub-groups according to the relative level of their management/incentive fee:

1. Low fee group: includes funds with management/incentive fees below the median.
2. Middle fee group: includes funds with management/incentive fees equal to the median.
3. High fee group: includes funds with management/incentive fees above the median.

The median fee is computed relative to all funds existing on the date of interest. The median incentive fee stays constant over the investigation period at the level of

20%. The median management fee increases from 1% in 1994 to 1.5% in 2004 and stays at this level until the end of the investigation period. As a robustness check, the actual fund fees are compared not with the median, but with the average fees of all funds existing on the date of interest. There seems to be a slight upward trend in the average fees of hedge funds, but the results remain qualitatively the same.

The Data

For the current research, the ALTVEST database[4] is used, containing monthly returns, the assets under management, fees and other information for more than 6,800 live and dead hedge funds. Two funds that reported monthly returns over 400% several times are deleted, since these funds do not seem to have reported accurate performance records. I also excluded from the sample 36 defunct funds that report "Duplicate Registration" as a reason for being excluded from the live database. The sample is restricted to those hedge funds that report their returns in US dollars (91% of funds), and only those that have at least 24 consecutive return observations after 1994 are considered. The analysis starts from January 1994, since before this date the majority of databases do not contain any information on defunct funds. Thus, prior to 1994, the database may not be free of survivorship bias. Hedge funds are required to have minimum of 24 consecutive observations in order to assure stability of the results in the time-series dimension. This filtering results in a dataset consisting of 4,767 hedge funds. Additionally, the sample is restricted to those hedge funds continuously reporting their assets under management (AuM), which further restricts the sample to 3,034 funds.

Not all the funds, however, seem to be relevant for investors. Funds of funds, pension funds, insurance companies, and banks are more likely to be interested in hedge funds of relatively large size that are able to absorb large investments. Following Kosowski et a. (2007) only those hedge funds with the assets under management over $20 million are considered. As soon as a fund reaches AuM of $20 million, it is included in the sample and stays in the sample until its liquidation or the end of the investigation period (June, 2006). By excluding the smallest funds, 38% of funds are lost. In terms of the AuM belonging to these funds, however, just around 1% of the total assets under management in the industry is lost, and the current analysis covers by far most of the assets under management of funds reporting to the ALTVEST database. Table 4 illustrates the distribution of hedge funds across different size categories as of May 2005. Around 67% of all funds exceed $20 million in AuM as of May 2005. 98% of the total AuM is controlled by funds managing more than $20 million. Thus, excluding funds holding less than $20 million does not lead to any bias.

[4] The ALTVEST database is provided by Morningstar.

Table 4: Size Distribution of Hedge Funds as of May 2005

This table reports the distribution of hedge funds across different size categories as of May 2005. From the total of 3034 hedge funds that report the AuM, 2146 existed in May 2005. As a measure of size, for each hedge fund the AuM reported on that date is used.

	AuM in $ million							
	Total existing in May 2005	<1	1-10	10-20	20-50	50-100	100-1000	>1000
	All hedge funds							
Number	2146	52	376	250	410	318	638	76
In % of all funds in this category	100%	2.42%	17.52%	11.65%	19.11%	14.82%	29.73%	3.54%
In % of all AuM in this category	100%	0.01%	0.50%	0.97%	3.55%	5.94%	51.71%	37.32%
	Single strategy funds							
Number	1149	37	238	142	227	152	322	16
In % of all funds in this category	100%	3.22%	20.71%	12.36%	19.76%	13.23%	28.02%	1.39%
In % of all AuM in this category	100%	0.02%	0.82%	1.43%	5.07%	7.33%	67.29%	18.06%
	Multi strategy funds							
Number	433	6	84	51	75	60	125	30
In % of all funds in this category	100%	1.39%	19.40%	11.78%	17.32%	13.86%	28.87%	6.93%
In % of all AuM in this category	100%	0.00%	0.43%	0.76%	2.51%	4.27%	38.30%	53.74%
	Funds of funds							
Number	564	9	54	57	108	106	191	30
In % of all funds in this category	100%	1.60%	9.57%	10.11%	19.15%	18.79%	33.87%	5.32%
In % of all AuM in this category	100%	0.00%	0.23%	0.64%	2.70%	5.67%	44.84%	45.92%

After excluding the smallest funds and ensuring that the funds being investigated have at least 24 consecutive observations, the sample consists of 1,873 funds. 988 of them are single strategy funds, 428 are multi strategy funds, and 457 are funds of hedge funds. Since ordinary hedge funds and funds of funds may be subject to different risks, funds of funds are excluded from the analysis. At the same time, both single- and multi-strategy funds are investment vehicles of the same type. Most of them implement various strategies during their life. The multi-strategy funds are to some extent more honest, reporting more information about their actual style than single-strategy funds. Both single- and multi-strategy funds are considered in this analysis. Table 5 summarizes the descriptive statistics of the hedge funds under study.

Table 5: Sample Statistics of Hedge Funds under Study

This table reports the sample statistics of the hedge funds used in the current study. The first row reports the number of funds belonging to single strategy and multi strategy groups. The mean and median returns, return standard deviation, skewness, kurtosis, and the first order autocorrelation of returns are reported for live and dead funds separately as well as for the joint sample. Monthly returns are net of all fees, incentive fees prorated during the year. The last row reports the average life time in months after reaching an AuM of $20 million.

Characteristic	Distribution across funds	Single strategy			Multi strategy		
		All	Live	Dead	All	Live	Dead
Number of funds		988	602	386	428	253	175
Mean return	Average	0.892	1.036	0.668	0.786	0.924	0.587
	STD	0.937	0.845	1.027	0.752	0.521	0.962
Median	Average	0.821	0.954	0.614	0.663	0.853	0.388
	STD	0.902	0.796	1.012	0.978	0.529	1.348
Standard deviation	Average	3.690	3.422	4.108	3.607	2.858	4.689
	STD	3.203	2.781	3.733	4.602	2.331	6.488
Skewness	Average	0.069	0.109	0.005	0.003	-0.117	0.176
	STD	1.107	1.026	1.221	1.399	1.443	1.318
Kurtosis	Average	5.310	5.121	5.604	6.408	6.704	5.980
	STD	5.387	5.243	5.598	9.381	10.845	6.730
1st order autocorrelation	Average	0.143	0.140	0.147	0.139	0.156	0.114
	STD	0.192	0.185	0.202	0.178	0.162	0.197
Average life time in months after reaching AuM of $20 mio		58.172	61.502	52.979	64.11	71.704	53.131

Consistent with common intuition and the descriptive statistics of other widely used databases[5], the live funds tend to have higher mean returns and smaller return standard deviations than dead funds. The difference in mean returns between live and dead funds is significant at the 1% level for single-strategy funds and at the 5% level for multi-strategy funds. The difference in return standard deviation is significant at the 5% level for single-strategy funds and at the 1% level for multi-strategy funds.

[5] Other widely used databases are: TASS (e.g., used by Getmansky, Lo and Makarov (2004), Fung, Hsieh, Naik and Ramadorai (2008)); HFR (Ackermann, McEnally and Ravenscraft (1999), Liang (2000), and Fung, Hsieh, Naik and Ramadorai (2008)); MAR (Ackermann, McEnally and Ravenscraft (1999), and Fung, Hsieh, Naik and Ramadorai (2008)).

Single and multi-strategy funds report their styles by indicating the percentage of AuM invested within the particular style. The following four self-reported styles seem to be the largest in the ALTVEST database[6]: Equity Long/Short (ELS) accounts for 45% of hedge funds under study, Directional excluding ELS accounts for 15%, Relative Value accounts for 27%, and Event Driven accounts for 13%.

In order to have a closer look at the return distribution of hedge funds under consideration, for each hedge fund the Fung and Hsieh (2004) seven-factor model is estimated. The average adjusted R-squared of these models is just 25%. Table 6 reports the average estimated hedge fund alphas, the associated t-statistics, as well as the test results for normality, heteroscedasticity, and first order serial correlation of the residuals.

Table 6: Summary Statistics and Tests of Normality, Heteroscedasticity, and Serial Correlation on Hedge Fund Residuals

This table reports the alpha characteristics and the results of the normality, heteroscedasticity, and the first order serial correlation tests of residuals from the Fung and Hsieh (2004) 7-factor model estimated for each hedge fund separately.

		Mean				Test of normality	Test of heteroscedasticity	Test of first order serial correlation
	Number of funds	Alpha % per month	Alpha t-stat	Residuals' Skewness	Residuals' Kurtosis	Share of funds with Jarque-Bera p<0.1	Share of funds with Breusch-Pagan p<0.1	Share of funds with Ljung-Box p<0.1
Single strategy	988	0.479	1.485	0.129	4.547	0.401	0.329	0.260
Multi Strategy	428	0.413	1.808	0.036	5.194	0.453	0.402	0.248

Among single- and multi-strategy funds, approximately 40% of the associated estimations do not result in normally distributed residuals. The residuals are heteroscedastic for more than 30% of the estimations and serially correlated for approximately 25% of the estimations. Thus, the proposed MA(2) specification for the error term is justified, and the heteroscedasticity and serial correlation correction of the standard errors is essential.

All existing hedge fund databases are subject to several biases. One of the most severe is the self-selection bias. Hedge funds voluntarily decide to report to the database. Poorly performing funds do not report their returns since their managers would prefer to avoid publicity. At the same time, extremely well performing funds also are reluctant to report their performance, since they are likely to be held privately by a group of investors, or simply do not need to attract additional investment. Thus, the self-selection bias has both negative and positive impact on the sample (Ackermann et al. (1999), Liang (2000), and Brown et al. (2001)). The resulting impact of this bias cannot easily be estimated and to the best of my knowledge there is no research that addresses this issue.

[6] Here, a hedge fund is classified as following a particular style if it invests more than 50% of its assets within this style.

The backfilling bias can also be pronounced in the data. Ackermann et al. (1999), Fung and Hsieh (2000), and Ibbotson and Chen (2005) propose to delete the first 12 return observations to control for this bias. Since this paper considers hedge fund's returns only after its assets under management reach the $20 million threshold, for the majority of funds under study, the first year returns are automatically excluded from the analysis. For those funds that turn out to be large from their origination, the first year returns are additionally excluded to control for the backfilling bias.

The ALTVEST database contains information on defunct funds and, thus, the survivorship bias is at least partly ameliorated.

Empirical Results

The following section first discusses the results from the base model (1), and then presents the finer scale analysis of the relation between the various micro-factors and the hedge fund alpha by estimating equations of the form (2) for each micro-factor considered.

Base Model: Baseline Alpha and Micro-Factors

Table 7 reports the baseline alpha and the loadings on the micro-factors' group-dummies estimated using eq. (1). The adjusted R-squared of the regression is 34%.

The results indicate that the baseline alpha is 45 basis points (b.p.) per month and is highly significant. This alpha level is a grand average across all hedge funds with different styles, ages, sizes, and fees computed over twelve and a half years. This average alpha, however, is not stable over time. There are periods during which hedge funds perform poorly, delivering on average an alpha significantly lower than the baseline level. This happens, for example, both before and after the Internet bubble. During the Internet bubble, hedge funds performed much better, delivering on average an alpha that is 38 b.p. per month higher than the baseline level[7]. Among different styles, the ELS funds seem deliver an alpha that is on average 4 b.p. higher than that of other funds. This effect is significant at the 10% level and is consistent with Ibbotson and Chen (2006), who report the highest alpha estimate for Equity Long Short hedge funds based on the index regression from 1995 to April 2006.

[7] The finding is consistent with Fung et al. (2008) who find that funds of hedge funds have positive and significant alpha only during the Internet bubble.

Table 7: Panel Regression with Hedge Fund Micro Factors

This table reports the estimated baseline alpha and the loadings on the micro-factors from the base panel model. The estimation is conducted using hedge funds with AuM larger than $20 million. The first 12 observations for each hedge fund are excluded. The error term for each hedge fund follows an MA(2) process.

Variable		Coefficient	t-statistic
Baseline Alpha		0.449***	9.054
Time	Jan1994-Sep1997	0.068	1.241
	Oct1997-Sep1998	-0.266***	-2.594
	Oct1998-Mar2000	0.384***	4.975
	Apr2000 – Feb2005	-0.162***	-4.244
	Mar2005-Jun2006	-0.025	-0.643
Style	ELS	0.044*	1.716
	Directional	-0.023	-0.687
	Relative Value	0.009	0.331
	Event Driven	-0.030	-0.976
Age	Young	0.018	0.816
	Middle Age	-0.005	-0.203
	Old	-0.014	-0.452
AuM	Low	-0.053**	-1.970
	Middle	0.007	0.364
	High	0.046*	1.901
FlowAbs	Low	-0.051	-1.118
	Middle	0.028	0.923
	High	0.023	0.591
FlowRel	Low	0.007	0.143
	Middle	-0.098***	-3.528
	High	0.091**	2.095
MgmtFee	Below median	-0.083***	-3.825
	Median	-0.023	-0.957
	Above median	0.106***	4.303
IncFee	Below median	-0.026	-0.551
	Median	-0.043	-0.996
	Above median	0.069	0.886
Adjusted R-squared		0.338	

No significant relationship between hedge fund age and alpha can be found within the base model. However, the results provide some evidence of a positive relationship between hedge fund alpha and fund size. Smaller funds seem to have lower alphas than medium size funds, and the largest thirty percent of funds have on average the highest alphas. This effect is also pronounced for relative fund flow. Funds with high relative inflow enjoy significantly higher alpha than funds with moderate or low inflow. At the same time, differences in the absolute flows do not seem to induce any significant deviations from the baseline alpha.

The relationship between management fee and alpha seems to be positive and close to linear. Funds with management fee below the median significantly underperform relative to the funds having the median management fee. And funds with a management fee above the median have alphas which are significantly higher than the baseline level. The incentive fee does not have any explanatory power in terms of hedge fund alpha. The majority of hedge funds in the ALTVEST database require a 20% incentive fee. Thus, the incentive fee level seems to be common across the industry, and it does not seem to have any link to hedge fund quality.

Time and Style Variation of Micro-Factor Effects

This section considers time variation in the micro-factors' effects. It seeks to document whether or not the general ranking of different groups of hedge funds changes across time periods. Equations of type (2) are estimated, in which the products of the time dummies and micro-factor group dummies are added to the regression.

Time Variation of Style Profitability

Table 8 reports the estimated loadings on the time-style factors. Panel A reports the loadings on the time-style variables, if one does not control for the general variability of hedge fund performance and excludes time dummies from the analysis. The results indicate that the average alphas delivered by hedge funds of different styles vary considerably over time. It is not only the absolute values of the style-specific alphas that change over time, but style ranking also changes. During the first period (January 1994 to September 1997), Directional funds clearly underperform, delivering an incremental alpha of -30 b.p. which is significant at the 1% level. Event Driven funds seem to provide the highest alpha during the first and the last of the considered time periods, which is significant at the 10% level. The ELS funds clearly outperform during the internet bubble.[8]

When controlling for the overall time-variation of hedge fund profitability using the time dummies (Panel B of Table 8), one finds less variation in the incremental style-specific alphas. The ELS funds continue to exhibit the highest alpha during the Internet bubble, earning an extra 79 b.p. per month in addition to the baseline level. However, during the other four periods, all styles seem to perform similarly in terms of their incremental alphas. Although for some periods hedge funds of different styles may underperform relative to the baseline level (for example, the Relative Value funds seem to have the lowest alpha during 2 out of 5 periods), these effects are only marginally significant. The only exception is

[8] Superior performance of the ELS funds during the bubble is not surprising. Most of them have long bias and are positively correlated with the market. Through increasing leverage, hedge funds amplify profits on up markets.

Directional funds that underperformed considerably during the Internet bubble relative to the baseline level, which is compensated by the performance of the ELS funds.

Table 8: Time Variation of Style Effects

This table reports the time-varying style components of the total alpha, estimated based on a panel regression of type (2). Panel A presents the results for the specification without pure time dummies. Panel B reports the results for the specification in which the time dummies are also included. For each of the five time periods, the loadings on the styles are required to sum up to zero.

		Panel A		**Panel B**	
	Variable	Coefficient	t-stat	Coefficient	t-stat
Jan1994-Sep1997	ELS	0.077	0.908	0.039	0.353
	Directional	-0.298***	-2.560	-0.096	-0.814
	Relative Value	0.063	0.668	0.007	0.081
	Event Driven	0.158*	1.782	0.050	0.566
Oct1997-Sep1998	ELS	-0.202	-0.954	0.041	0.148
	Directional	0.290	1.007	0.080	0.251
	Relative Value	-0.200	-1.107	-0.317*	-1.793
	Event Driven	0.113	0.522	0.196	0.878
Oct1998-Mar2000	ELS	0.646***	4.116	0.788***	5.059
	Directional	-0.829***	-4.913	-0.702***	-4.378
	Relative Value	-0.048	-0.341	0.031	0.228
	Event Driven	0.230*	1.658	-0.117	-0.872
Apr2000 – Feb2005	ELS	-0.035	-1.026	-0.007	-0.176
	Directional	0.044	1.052	0.027	0.630
	Relative Value	0.050	1.585	0.042	1.291
	Event Driven	-0.059	-1.554	-0.061	-1.558
Mar2005-Jun2006	ELS	-0.042	-1.108	0.040	1.066
	Directional	0.077	1.403	-0.004	-0.065
	Relative Value	-0.114**	-2.164	-0.086*	-1.675
	Event Driven	0.080*	1.701	0.049	1.137
Adjusted R-squared				0.539	

There are two main conclusions to be drawn here. First, superior performance in hedge funds of a particular style in one year does not imply that the funds of this style will also be the best in the future. Second, there are common trends in the hedge fund industry that determine average hedge fund profitability and alpha. If one controls for these common trends and waves, differences in the incremental style alphas become just marginally significant, if at all.[9]

Time and Style Variation of Age Effects

Using the base model and controlling for the backfilling bias, no significant difference in the performance of funds of different ages is documented (Table 7). The results are rather stable over time (Panel A of Table 9). There could be, however, some variation of age influence on the fund alpha across different styles (Panel B of Table 9). Within the ELS and Relative Value styles, young funds seem to outperform, adding 6 b.p. to the baseline alpha. Within the Event Driven style, on the contrary, old funds outperform, delivering an additional 9 b.p. per month. All these effects, however, are significant only at the 10% level. There does not seem to be any pronounced relationship between a fund's age and its alpha.

Time and Style Variation of Size Effects

In order to capture the time variation of size effects, a regression of type (2) is estimated including, first, time-asset under management dummies, and then time-absolute flow dummies and time-relative flow dummies. For all the model specifications, the sum of the time-factor dummies for each of the five time periods is equal to zero. Panel A of Table 10 summarizes the results reporting the values of the loadings for each time-factor dummy variable.

The direction of the AuM effect is fairly stable over time. Hedge funds with large AuM normally outperform funds with low AuM. This is true for all time periods except the Internet Bubble, during which no significant difference in the performance of funds of different sizes can be seen. Moreover, starting from April 2000, the relationship between the AuM and the alpha seems to completely stabilize, for which we see that the smallest funds have the lowest alpha, followed by the middle-sized funds, and the large funds, delivering the highest alpha.

In terms of fund flow influence on hedge fund alpha, after April 2000 no significant relationship between the absolute fund flow and the alpha can be observed, which is consistent with the joint results. Before this period, funds with low absolute flow underperformed, which is consistent with our general finding of an increasing return to scale effect.

The joint results for the baseline model suggest that there is a convex relationship between the relative flow and fund alpha. This pattern is stable for all time periods. Hedge funds with medium relative flows have the lowest alpha, whereas the highest alpha is in most cases delivered by hedge funds enjoying the largest relative flow. Nevertheless, the magnitude of these differences varies widely. If

---

9 Consistent with this finding, during the current financial crises we observe that hedge funds following all styles simultaneously performed poorly. According to the **Credit Suisse/Tremont Hedge Fund Database report, in October 2008 the ELS index dropped by** 7.24%, Global Macro by 4.61%, Fixed Income Arbitrage by 17.75%, Emerging Markets by 15.36%, Convertible Arbitrage by 10.70%, and the Multi-Strategy hedge fund index dropped by 8.09%.

during the Internet Bubble, hedge funds with the largest flow had an alpha on average 1.08% per month higher than the baseline level (significant at the 1% level), in 2005-2006 they deliver only 10 b.p. in addition to the baseline level (significant at the 5% level).

Considering the style variation of size effect, the direction of size effects is relatively stable across all styles (Panel B of Table 10). Larger funds seem to deliver the highest alpha within all styles, except for Directional funds. In terms of the absolute flow influence, hedge funds with low flow have a smaller alpha than hedge funds with medium flow. The winning funds are, however, different across styles. The highest alpha for the ELS and Event Driven funds is delivered by funds with the largest absolute flow, whereas for Directional and Relative Value styles, the largest alpha belonged to funds with medium absolute flow. Directional and Relative Value funds are rather similar in terms of the relative flow impact on their alpha. The relationship seems to be convex; funds with the lowest relative flow deliver the highest alpha, funds with medium flow deliver the lowest alpha, and the alpha of funds with the highest flow is not significantly different from the baseline alpha level.

Table 9: Time and Style Variation of Age Effects

Panel A of this table reports the estimated time-varying loadings on the age dummies, and Panel B reports the estimated style-varying loadings on the age dummies from a panel regression of type (2). For each of the time periods and fund styles, the loadings are restricted to sum up to zero.

	Age	**Coefficient**	**t-stat**
Panel A			
	Young	0.098	1.335
Jan1994-Sep1997	Middle Age	-0.117	-1.483
	Old	0.019	0.203
	Young	0.055	0.354
Oct1997-Sep1998	Middle Age	-0.309**	-1.995
	Old	0.253	1.528
	Young	0.159	1.237
Oct1998-Mar2000	Middle Age	-0.136	-0.959
	Old	-0.023	-0.127
	Young	-0.016	-0.538
Apr2000 – Feb2005	Middle Age	-0.005	-0.150
	Old	0.021	0.486
	Young	0.040	1.213
Mar2005-Jun2006	Middle Age	-0.004	-0.118
	Old	-0.036	-0.899

Adjusted R-squared		0.349	
Panel B			
	Young	0.068*	1.653
ELS	Middle Age	0.002	0.044
	Old	-0.070	-1.414
	Young	-0.014	-0.226
Directional	Middle Age	0.004	0.059
	Old	0.010	0.119
	Young	0.062*	1.717
Relative Value	Middle Age	0.007	0.196
	Old	-0.069	-1.426
	Young	-0.051	-1.105
Event Driven	Middle Age	-0.041	-0.977
	Old	0.092*	1.907
Adjusted R-squared		0.343	

Table 10: Time and Style Variation of Size Effects

Panel A of this table reports the estimated time-varying loadings on the AuM dummies, the absolute flow dummies, and the relative flow dummies from a panel regression of type (2). Panel B reports the estimated style-varying loadings on these factors. For each of the time periods and styles, the loadings are restricted to sum up to zero.

		AuM		Flow Absolute		Flow Relative	
		Coefficient	t-stat	Coefficient	t-stat	Coefficient	t-stat
Panel A							
	Low	-0.042	-0.480	-0.127	-1.271	-0.119	-1.179
Jan1994-Sep1997	Middle	-0.196**	-2.283	0.125*	1.791	-0.228***	-3.418
	High	0.238**	2.413	0.002	0.025	0.347***	3.672
	Low	-0.407**	-2.247	-0.360**	-2.356	-0.159	-1.035
Oct1997-Sep1998	Middle	0.591***	3.866	0.455***	3.088	-0.239*	-1.784
	High	-0.184	-1.061	-0.095	-0.578	0.397**	2.410
	Low	0.157	1.258	-0.314**	-2.470	-0.359***	-2.610
Oct1998-Mar2000	Middle	0.015	0.152	0.127	1.131	-0.719***	-7.003
	High	-0.172	-1.433	0.187	1.332	1.078***	6.709
	Low	-0.150***	-4.317	-0.007	-0.136	-0.018	-0.338
Apr2000 – Feb2005	Middle	-0.029	-1.098	-0.016	-0.477	-0.170***	-5.332
	High	0.179***	6.123	0.022	0.537	0.188***	4.215

	Low	-0.081**	-2.120	0.013	0.247	0.124**	2.305
Mar2005-Jun2006	Middle	-0.076**	-2.405	0.015	0.371	-0.228***	-6.414
	High	0.157***	4.436	-0.028	-0.523	0.104**	2.004
Adjusted R-squared		0.408		0.338		0.381	
Panel B							
	Low	-0.146***	-3.463	-0.199***	-3.490	-0.126**	-1.998
ELS	Middle	0.060*	1.703	0.060	1.461	-0.107**	-1.981
	High	0.086**	2.001	0.138**	2.521	0.233***	3.813
	Low	0.071	1.079	-0.063	-0.801	0.194**	2.438
Directional	Middle	0.102*	1.907	0.111**	1.959	-0.160***	-3.084
	High	-0.173***	-3.150	-0.047	-0.651	-0.034	-0.453
	Low	-0.057	-1.068	-0.045	-0.810	0.151***	2.584
Relative Value	Middle	-0.028	-0.770	0.094**	2.269	-0.129***	-3.454
	High	0.085**	2.323	-0.050	-0.900	-0.022	-0.418
	Low	-0.139**	-2.460	-0.164***	-2.739	0.022	0.327
Event Driven	Middle	-0.007	-0.162	-0.001	-0.020	-0.155***	-3.678
	High	0.146***	3.453	0.165***	3.220	0.133**	2.076
Adjusted R-squared		0.371		0.369		0.533	

Time and Style Variation of Fee Effects

In the joint specification, no significant effect of the incentive fee level on the hedge fund alpha can be documented. The reason seems to be not the absence of the effect, but its high time variation. Panel A of Table 11 reports the time-varying fee effects. During the first of the considered time periods (from January 1994 to August 1997), hedge funds with incentive fees below the median underperformed relative to other funds. Low fee funds delivered an alpha that was 24 b.p. per month lower than the baseline level, whereas funds with the median incentive fee delivered an alpha 16 b.p. per month higher than the baseline level. Both effects are significant at the 5% level. The situation reverted after April 2000. During the last two periods, hedge funds with the median incentive fee underperformed relative to other funds. Moreover, from February 2005 to June 2006 the highest alpha was earned by hedge funds with incentive fee below the median. These funds generated additional 24 b.p. per month, significant at the 1% level. The funds with the median incentive fee, on the contrary, significantly underperformed and had an alpha 37 b.p. lower than the baseline level. In terms of the variation of the incentive fee effect with respect to the reported fund style, little variation can be documented (Panel B of Table 11). For all styles, there is no significant difference in the alphas of funds having different incentive fee levels, with the one exception of the Relative Value funds. For these funds the alpha seems to be positively related to the incentive fee level, and hedge funds charging higher fees than the median incentive fee deliver 14 b.p. on top of the baseline alpha, significant at the 5% level. Hence, the effect of the incentive fee can change dramatically over time. Not only the magnitude of the effect is variable, but also its direction. With respect to fund style, however, very little variation can be observed.

The management fee effect seems to be more stable both over time and fund style. Starting from the Internet Bubble, hedge funds with a management fee below the median delivered a lower alpha than funds having the median- or higher than the median fees. Hedge funds with their fees above the median fee outperform other funds from April 2000 to January 2005, delivering an additional 11 b.p. of monthly alpha, significant at the 1% level. In terms of the style variation, no relationship between management fee and hedge fund alpha can be seen for ELS and other Directional funds. For the Relative Value and Event Driven funds, hedge funds having higher than the median management fee deliver an alpha 10-12 b.p. per month higher than the baseline level.

Table 11: Time-varying Fee Effects

Panel A of this table reports the estimated time-varying loadings on the management and incentive fee dummies from a panel regression of type (2). Panel B reports the estimated style-varying loadings on these factors. For each of the time periods and hedge fund styles, the loadings are restricted to sum up to zero.

		Management Fee		Incentive Fee	
		Coefficient	t-stat	Coefficient	t-stat
Panel A					
	Below median	-0.192	-1.470	-0.244**	-2.453
Jan1994-Aug1997	Median	0.059	0.696	0.161**	2.100
	Above median	0.133	1.501	0.083	0.743
	Below median	0.033	0.121	-0.213	-0.673
Sep1997-Sep1998	Median	0.049	0.286	-0.026	-0.090
	Above median	-0.082	-0.402	0.240	0.449
	Below median	-0.482***	-2.959	-0.153	-0.647
Oct1998-Mar2000	Median	0.290**	2.148	0.241	1.168
	Above median	0.193	1.546	-0.088	-0.236
	Below median	-0.084**	-2.314	-0.024	-0.407
Apr2000 – Jan2005	Median	-0.024	-0.607	-0.089*	-1.701
	Above median	0.108***	3.370	0.113	1.241
	Below median	-0.028	-0.624	0.235***	2.969
Feb2005-Jun2006	Median	0.095**	2.411	-0.369***	-4.857
	Above median	-0.067	-1.121	0.133	1.039

Adjusted R-squared		0.359		0.489	
Panel B					
	Below median	0.076*	1.816	-0.172	-0.877
ELS	Median	-0.078	-1.547	-0.066	-0.349
	Above median	0.002	0.037	0.238	0.636
	Below median	-0.112	-1.512	0.020	0.259
Directional	Median	0.006	0.080	-0.054	-0.749
	Above median	0.107	1.597	0.034	0.268
	Below median	-0.026	-0.577	-0.110*	-1.900
Relative Value	Median	-0.077*	-1.777	-0.028	-0.628
	Above median	0.103***	2.664	0.138**	2.049
	Below median	-0.095**	-2.170	0.187	1.182
Event Driven	Median	-0.024	-0.489	0.006	0.045
	Above median	0.119**	2.124	-0.193	-0.803
Adjusted R-squared		0.409		0.338	

Summarizing these results, ranking hedge funds based on their charged incentive fee does not seem to be very informative. On average, no significant relationship between hedge fund incentive fee and alpha can be found. For different subperiods, however, both positive and negative significant relationships are observed. The incentive fee cannot be treated as a stable predictor of hedge fund alpha. The management fee effect, on the contrary, seems to be more stable. Hedge funds charging higher management fees seem to deliver alphas at least not lower than that delivered by funds charging smaller management fees. This effect is stable across time and fund styles.

Conclusion

The hedge fund industry has been attracting increasing interest of researchers over the last decade. Much effort has been spent on analyzing the determinants of hedge fund alpha. Most studies, however, come to contradictory conclusions with respect to the direction of influence of different micro-factors on hedge fund performance. The inconsistency of these results is driven not only by differences in the used databases and methodologies, but also by the highly dynamic nature of hedge funds themselves. The impact of micro-factors on hedge fund alpha varies over time and with respect to different hedge fund styles. This paper addresses this variation by estimating a fixed effect panel regression, in which micro-factor dummies are included. The loadings on these micro-factors are first kept constant for all funds, then time variation of these loadings is investigated, and finally their variation across styles is considered. The micro-factor loadings quantify the deviation of the alpha of a hedge fund belonging to a particular group, say, a group of hedge funds with high inflows, from the average baseline alpha of the whole industry.

The empirical results indicate that the baseline alpha is 45 b.p. per month and is highly significant. On average during the last twelve years hedge funds have been performing rather well overall. Equity Long/Short funds seem to perform better than other styles, delivering on average an alpha that is 4 b.p. higher than the baseline level. At the same time, style profitability changes noticeably over time, and during different time periods there are different winning styles. It is difficult, however, to use this information on the currently winning style to predict the future development. Superior performance of hedge funds of a particular style within one period does not imply that the funds of this style will also be the best in the future.

Moreover, this paper documents high variation of the average alpha over time. I do not find a negative trend in the average alpha, but rather a succession of periods of high profitability by periods of low profitability and vice versa. The Internet Bubble seems to be a period of high alphas, framed by two periods of alphas lower than the baseline level. Starting from March 2005, the average alpha does not seem to deviate significantly from the baseline level. These common trends in the hedge fund industry determine the average hedge fund alpha. If one controls for these fluctuations, the differences in the incremental alphas of funds of different styles become only marginally significant. Hedge funds of different styles do not seem to be that different in terms of their alphas, if the average profitability level of the industry is taken into consideration.

In terms of the micro-factors' influence on the hedge funds alpha, I do not find any significant relationship between hedge fund age and alpha in the current sample of hedge funds. This absence of relationship is stable across time and fund styles.

The relationship between hedge fund alpha and fund size is found to be positive. This effect is pronounced for the assets under management and seems to be stable over time and across fund styles. The relationship between contemporaneous relative fund flow and fund alpha is convex. Funds with the highest flow tend to have the highest alpha, whereas funds with medium flow tend to have the lowest alpha. Although the fund ranking based on the assets under management or relative fund flow is stable over time, the magnitude of alpha differences between funds of different size/flow groups varies widely. If during the Internet Bubble hedge funds with high flow delivered an alpha of more than 1% per month higher than the baseline level, in 2005-2006 they add only 10 b.p. per month on top of the baseline alpha.

I document a positive relationship between a hedge fund management fees and the corresponding alpha. Hedge funds charging lower than the median management fee tend to deliver the lowest alpha. This effect is stable and pronounced after October 1998. The incentive fee does not seem to have any explanatory power in terms of hedge fund alpha on average, since the effect of the incentive fee is very volatile.

The hedge fund industry is highly dynamic. It seems to generate a positive and significant alpha on average; however, the level of this alpha varies considerably over time. It is difficult to predict the exact absolute alpha level based on hedge fund micro-factors, but it seems to be possible to rank hedge funds using this micro-information. The empirical results suggest that large funds with high relative inflow charging higher than median management fees are likely to deliver a higher alpha than their peers most of time.

References

Ackermann, C., McEnally, R., & Ravenscraft, D. (1999). The Performance of Hedge Funds: Risk, Return, and Incentives. Journal of Finance, 54(3), 833-874.

Agarwal, V., Daniel, N. D., & Naik, N. Y. (2004). Flows, Performance, and Managerial Incentives in Hedge Funds. Working paper. Georgia State University.

Agarwal, V., Daniel, N. D., & Naik, N. Y. (2009). Role of Managerial Incentives and Discretion in Hedge Fund Performance. Journal of Finance, 64(5), 2221 – 2256

Agarwal, V., & Naik, N. Y. (2000). On Taking the 'Alternative' Route: Risks, Rewards, Style and Performance Persistence of Hedge Funds. Journal of Alternative Investments, 2(3), 6-23.

Agarwal, V., & Naik, N. Y. (2000). Generalized Style Analysis of Hedge Funds. Journal of Asset Management, 1(1), 93-109.

Agarwal, V., & Naik, N. Y. (2000). Performance Evaluation of Hedge Funds with Option-Based and Buy-and-Hold Strategies. Working paper: Georgia State University.

Amenc, N., Curtis, S., & Martellini, L. (2003). The Alpha and Omega of Hedge Fund Performance Measurement. Working paper. EDHEC Risk and Asset Management Research Centre.

Brorsen, B. W., & Harri, A. (2004). Performance Persistence and the Source of Returns for Hedge Funds. Applied Financial Economics, 14(3), 131-141.

Brown, S. J., & Goetzmann, W. N. (2003). Hedge Funds with Style. Journal of Portfolio Management, 29(2), 101-112.

Brown, S. J., Goetzmann, W. N., & Liang, B. (2004). Fees on Fees in Funds of Funds. Yale ICF Working paper 02-33.

Brown, S. J., Goetzmann, W. N., & Park, J. (2001). Careers and Survival: Competition and Risk in the Hedge Fund and CTA Industry. Journal of Finance, 56(5), 1869-1886.

De Souza, C., & Gokcan, S. (2003). How Some Hedge Fund Characteristics Impact Performance. AIMA Journal.

Favre, L., Sr., & Ranaldo, A. (2005). How to Price Hedge Funds: From Two- to Four-Moment CAPM. Working paper. EDHEC Risk and Asset Management Research Center.

Fung, W., & Hsieh, D. A. (1997). Empirical Characteristics of Dynamic Trading Strategies: The Case of Hedge Funds. The Review of Financial Studies, 10(2), 275-302.

Fung, W., & Hsieh, D. A. (2000). Performance Characteristics of Hedge Funds and Commodity Funds: Natural vs. Spurious Biases. Journal of Financial and Quantitative Analysis, 35(3), 291-307.

Fung, W., & Hsieh, D. A. (2001). The Risk in Hedge Fund Strategies: Theory and Evidence from Trend Followers. Review of Financial Studies, 14(2), 313-341.

Fung, W., & Hsieh, D. A. (2004). Hedge Fund Benchmarks: A Risk-Based Approach. Financial Analysts Journal, 60(5), 65-80.

Fung, W., Hsieh, D. A., Naik, N. Y., & Ramadorai, T. (2008). Hedge Funds: Performance, Risk and Capital Formation. Journal of Finance, 63(4), 1777-1803.

Getmansky, M. (2005). The Life Cycle of Hedge Funds: Fund Flows, Size and Performance. Working paper: MIT Sloan School of Management.

Getmansky, M., Lo, A. W., & Makarov, I. (2004). An Econometric Model of Serial Correlation and Illiquidity in Hedge Fund Returns. Journal of Financial Economics, 74(3), 529-610.

Goetzmann, W. N., Ingersoll, J. E., Jr., & Ross, S. A. (2003). High-Water Marks and Hedge Fund Management Contracts. Journal of Finance, 58(4), 1685-1717.

Gregoriou, G. N., & Rouah, F. (2003). Large versus small hedge funds: does size affect performance? Journal of Alternative Investment, 5(5), 75-77.

Howell, M. J. (2001). Fund Age and Performance. Journal of Alternative Investments, (Fall 2001).

Ibbotson, R. G., & Chen, P. (2005). Sources of Hedge Fund Returns: Alphas, Betas, and Costs. Yale ICF Working Paper No. 05-17.

Ibbotson, R. G., & Chen, P. (2006). The A,B,Cs of Hedge Funds: Alphas, Betas, and Costs. Yale ICF Working Paper No. 06-10.

Kazemi, H. B., Schneeweiss, T., & Martin, G. (2002). Understanding Hedge Fund Performance: Research Issues Revisited-Part I. Journal of Alternative Investments, 5(3), 6-22.

Koh, F., Koh, W. T., & Teo, M. (2003). Asian Hedge Funds: Return Persistence, Style, and Fund Characteristics. Working paper: Singapore Management University.

Kosowski, R., Naik, N. Y., & Teo, M. (2007). Do Hedge Funds Deliver Alpha? A Bayesian and Bootstrap Analysis. Journal of Financial Economics, 84(1), 229-264.

Kouwenberg, R., & Ziemba, W. T. (2007). Incentives and risk taking in hedge funds. Journal of Banking and Finance, 31(11), 3291-3310.

Liang, B. (1999). On the Performance of Hedge Funds. Financial Analysts Journal, 55(4), 72-85.

Liang, B. (2000). Hedge Funds: The Living and the Dead. Journal of Financial and Quantitative Analysis, 35(3), 309-326.

Naik, N. Y., Ramadorai, T., & Strömqvist, M. (2007). Capacity Constraints and Hedge Fund Strategy Returns. European Financial Management, 13(2), 239-256.

Equilibrium on the Interest Rate Market Analysis

Eva Kvasničková

Dipartimento Studi Economici, Finanziari e Metodi Quantitativi
Tor Vergata University in Rome
Via Columbia 2 - 00133 Roma, Italy.
email: ekvasnickova@gmail.com

Abstract The aim of paper is to analyze the arbitrage existence between interest rates and currency exchange rates during the assumed last three months before global economical crisis (which is considered in many other studies as the last period before global economical crisis where the rate development was still stable unlike during following years). We will discuss the difference between the forward and futures interest rates, called *convexity adjustment*, derive it also explicitly for Ho-Lee model together with appropriate parameter estimates and convert the appropriate futures to forwards. At the end we will provide results comparing implied and real market quotes leading us to reject hypothesis of a significant appearance of arbitrage in this case.

Keywords: Forwards, Futures, Arbitrage, Convexity Adjustment, Interest Rate Models, Eurodollar and Euribor Exchange Rates

1 Convexity Adjustment in No-Arbitrage Interest Rate Model

There are two main types of models; *equilibrium models* and *no-arbitrage models*. In an equilibrium model the initial term structure is an output from the model; in a no-arbitrage model it is an input to the model. Since we want to test the existence of an arbitrage we will consider the no-arbitrage model and compare the implied quotes by the model with the real ones.

These models are considered for pricing of short-term derivatives. They use the observed term structure at the current time as the starting point. Future price evolves in a way which is consistent with this initial price structure and which is arbitrage free. The main advantage of the no-arbitrage models is that they are designed to be exactly consistent with today's term structure. We assume that the term structure depends on only one factor and indicate how the results can be extended to several factors.

Constructing the yield curves, we should calculate discount factors. In many practical applications, an approximation is used when we treat futures as if they were forward. In reality futures rates are greater than corresponding forward and an adjustment is required to convert futures prices to equivalent forward. The arbitrage is to short the future; if rates rise, then margin payments on the future contract

D. Sornette et al. (Eds.), *Market Risk and Financial Markets Modeling*,
DOI 10.1007/978-3-642-27931-7_11,

are received immediately whereas the loss on the forward is not crystallized until later. If rates fall, the converse will happen. The amount by which the futures rate needs to be decreased is called the *convexity adjustment* (CA). It is determined by the market's expectations of future changes in rates, so that different interest rate model imply different convexity adjustment.

Forwards

We assume D_t to be a discount process, given at time t by $D_t = e^{-\int_0^t r_u du}$. The price of a zero-coupon bond paying 1 at time T will then be given by

$$B_t^T = \frac{1}{D_t} \mathrm{E}^Q[D_T|\mathcal{F}_t], \quad 0 \le t \le T, \tag{1.1}$$

where $\mathcal{F}_t$ is a standard filtration process at corresponding time. A **forward contract** is an agreement to pay a predetermined delivery price K at a predetermined delivery date T for the asset whose price at time t is S_t. The **forward price** F or $_S(t, T)$ of this asset at time t is the value of K that makes the forward contract have no-arbitrage price zero at time t. This forward price, denoted for simplicity as For_t^T, satisfies

$$For_t^T = \frac{S_t}{B_t^T}, \quad 0 \le t \le T. \tag{1.2}$$

Suppose that the forward price K is higher than S_t/B_t^T. We could borrow then at time t money in the amount of S_t (by selling short $S_t/B_t^T > S_t$) and buy one asset. At time T we obtain the payoff $K - S_T$, sell the one asset for S_T and pay off our debt, S_t/B_t^T. Consequently, the remaining cash is $K - S_T + S_t - S_t/B_t^T = K - S_t/B_t^T$, an arbitrage. We could do the opposite analogy for K lower than S_t/B_t^T. The forward price can be derived also from the standard pricing formula with risk-neutral measure Q,

$$V_t = \frac{1}{D_t} E^Q[D_T(S_T - K)|\mathcal{F}_t] = S_t - KB_t^T = 0.$$

Futures

The *futures price* is usually defined as $Fut_t^T = E^Q[S_T|\mathcal{F}_t]$. A long position in the futures contract on the interval $[s, t]$ is an agreement to receive the changes in the future price, i.e. $Fut_t^T - Fut_s^T$, as a cash flow. From the definition it can be derived that the futures price is a martingale under Q, satisfying $Fut_T^T = S_T$, and the value of any strategy (futures position) is zero.

Forward-Futures Spread

First, we will assume non-stochastic interest rate. Then $B_t^T = \exp\left(-\int_t^T r_u du\right)$ so the forward price is

$$For_t^T = \frac{S_t}{B_t^T} = \exp\left(\int_t^T r_u du.\right) S_t$$

The futures price in a nonrandom interest rate case is

$$\begin{aligned} Fut_t^T &= E^Q\left[S_T|\mathcal{F}_t\right] \\ &= \exp\left(\int_0^T r_u du\right).E^Q\left[\exp\left(-\int_0^T r_u du\right)S_T|\mathcal{F}_t\right] \\ &= \exp\left(\int_0^T r_u du\right).D_t S_t \\ &= \exp\left(\int_t^T r_u du\right).S_t, \end{aligned} \tag{1.3}$$

so the forward and futures prices agree.

In general, stochastic interest rate case, the forward and futures prices differ from each other. For simplicity, we begin at time zero, the spread is then given by

$$\begin{aligned} For_0^T - Fut_0^T &= \frac{S_0}{B_0^t} - E^Q S_T \\ &= \frac{1}{B_0^T}\left[S_0 - B_0^T.E^Q S_T\right] \\ &= \frac{1}{B_0^T}\left[E^Q[D_T S_T] - E^Q D_T.E^Q S_T\right] \\ &= \frac{1}{B_0^T}.\text{cov}(D_T, S_T) \end{aligned} \tag{1.4}$$

This spread is often called ***convexity adjustment***.

With stochastic interest rates, we demonstrated that the difference between forward and futures price is given by the "local" covariance between the rate of return on the futures contract and the rate of return on a risk-free pure discount bond. We can interpret this result by considering the case when the price of asset *S* is strongly positive correlated with interest rates (as a consequence is then $For_0^T > Fut_0^T$). With increasing *S*, an investor in long futures position makes an immediate gain because of the daily settlement procedure. This gain will tend to be invested in higher rate of interest, since increases in the asset price *S* occur at the same time as increases in interest rate. The converse happens when *S* decreases; the investor will make an immediate loss, which tend to be financed at a lower interest rate. To be not affected in this way by interest rate movements requires to hold a forward contract rather than a futures contract. It follows that a long futures contract will be more attractive in this sense than a long forward contract. Consequently, for *S* strongly positively correlated with interest rates, futures prices tend to be higher than forward prices. Analogous arguments show that futures prices tend to be lower than forward prices when S is strongly negatively correlated with interest rates.

The no-arbitrage model is most often used in empirically testing the pricing of share price index futures contracts. In fact, it is actually a forward, not a futures, pricing model. To apply the model to share price index futures, we assume the equality of forward and futures prices, which is not obviously appropriate assumption. (In particular, if deeper analysis will provide a support for non-zero local covariance (implying a non-zero forward-futures price differential), the use of the no-arbitrage model may be questioned.) This paper will try to analyze the in/appropriateness of assuming the equality of forward and futures prices.

The difference between futures and forward rates is determined by the market's expectations of future changes in rates, so that different interest rate model will lead to different convexity adjustment. Theoretical forward rates are computed from bond prices whereas futures are expected future spot rates computed under risk-neutral measure Q.

CA in Ho-Lee Model

In the simple Ho-Lee model the risk-neutral process for the short rate r_r is given by

$$dr_t = {}_t dt + \ dW_t,$$

the bond price $P(t,T)$ has the form $P(t,T) = A(t,T)e^{-r(T-t)}$, for some deterministic function $A(t,T)$, further described e.g. in Hull [6]. From the Itô's lemma the process followed by the bond price in a risk-neutral world is

$$dP(t,T) = r_t P(t,T)dt - (T-t) \ P(t,T)dW_t.$$

Recalling now $f(t, t_1, t_2) = \frac{1}{t_2-t_1} \ln \frac{P(t,t_1)}{P(t,t_2)}$, we can obtain, using again the Itô's lemma, the process for $f(t, t_1, t_2)$,

$$df(t, t_1, t_2) = \frac{\sigma^2(t_2-t)^2 - \sigma^2(t_1-t)^2}{2(t_2-t_1)} dt + \sigma dW_t. \tag{1.5}$$

The forward rate equals the spot rate at time t_1. Therefore, the expected value of the forward rate at t_1 is the expected value of the spot rate at t_1. Since we consider our model in the traditional risk-neutral world, the expected value of the spot rate is the same as the futures rate. As a consequence, the futures rate is greater than the forward rate by the expected change in the forward rate between times 0 and t_1. This change can be computed easily from (1.5), it is determined by integrating the coefficient of dt between 0 and t_1. It is:

$$\begin{aligned} \int_0^{t_1} \frac{\sigma^2(t_2-t)^2 - \sigma^2(t_1-t)^2}{2(t_2-t_1)} dt &= \frac{\sigma^2}{2} \int_0^{t_1} (t_2 - 2t + t_1)\, dt \\ &= \frac{\sigma^2 t_1 t_2}{2}. \end{aligned} \tag{1.6}$$

As Hull in [6] explains, this convexity adjustment is composed actually from two components:

- The difference between a futures contract that is settled daily and a similar contract that is settled entirely at time t_1.
- The difference between the contract that is settled at time t_1 and a similar contract that is settled at time t_2.

The Ho-Lee model is the simplest interest rate model. This has the advantage that it is analytically tractable, on the other hand, its main disadvantage is that it implies that all rates are equally variable at all times. Other, more complicated models introduced in this work, have various descriptive advantages, such as precious description and avoiding the possibility of negative interest rates, but, unfortunately, they have no analytic tractability. For this reason, we will further focus on the simple Ho-Lee model and we will use it in our calculations.

Our Data Set

In our further analysis we will focus on our selected data set from year 2007 (provided by Bloomberg L.P.), measured between time 08/01/07 and 09/03/07. The reason for selecting the data set from 2007 is that it is commonly considered as the last time-period before crisis appearance where the rate development was still stable unlike during following years - using varying maturities in our further calculations, this aspect will be highly desirable. We dispose of intraday 3-month futures prices quotes on EUR currency (Euribor) as well as on USD currency (Eurodollar-U.S. dollars deposited in commercial banks outside the United States), in 7 different maturities: 19/03/07, 18/06/07, 17/09/07, 17/12/07, 17/03/08, 16/06/08 and 15/09/08. The future prices quotes are stated in terms of a maturity value of 100, so a typical price would be e.g 94.98. Rates are measured during the trading hours every minute and in case that an observation in particular minute is missing, we use the rate from previous minute. (The problem is that bid and ask quotes are not both available throughout the entire sample period in the forward market. The problem is not that data for specific moments are missing, but rather that the market did not report the quotes during entire time.)

As a fair price for the forward quote we set the observed bid price plus one-half the bid-ask spread. (Although this calculation is very rough, for more precise fair price calculations we would need complete traded-volume data set for entire time period and all maturities, which is not available.) This is often referred as a *MID Price* in financial markets. (The main disadvantage of quoting the MID price is that the bid or offer price may be unrealistic and distort the MID price.)

Let us denote the quotes as $FutQuote_{e_i}$ and $FutQuote_{u_j}$ for $i, j = 1, \ldots, 7$, where e, u are the currency indexes (EUR and USD), and i, j the maturity indexes.

For simplicity we will now skip the currency index e, u and the maturity index i, j, since the calculations will be the same for all of them. (These coefficients will be used below only if specially needed and they will be noted in the same form as above.) The futures discrete rates $FutD$ are calculated as $FutD = 1 - \frac{FutQuote}{100}$ and the futures rates with continuous compounding $FutC$ as

$$FutC = \frac{\ln(0.25FutD + 1)}{0.25}$$

for both currencies in all seven maturities. In figures Fig. (1.1) and Fig. (1.2) we plot the Euribor and Eurodollar quotes, as reposted from the market.

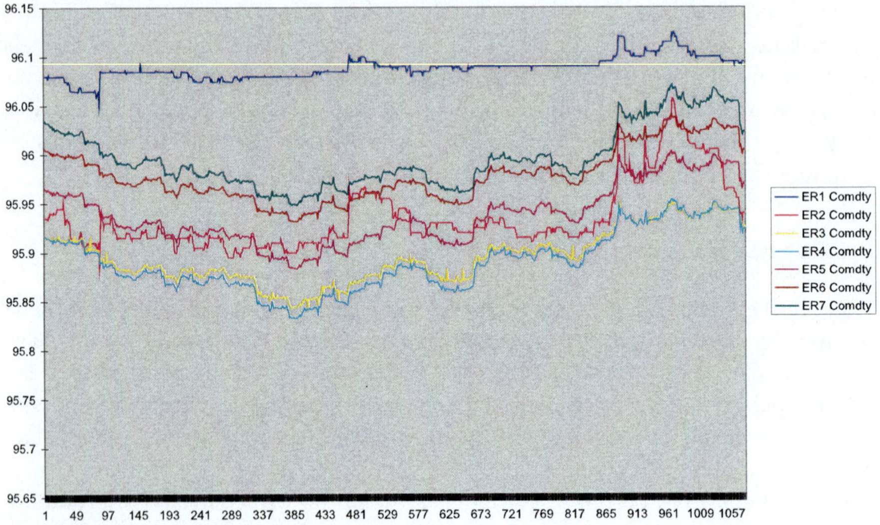

Figure 1.1: Euribor quotes

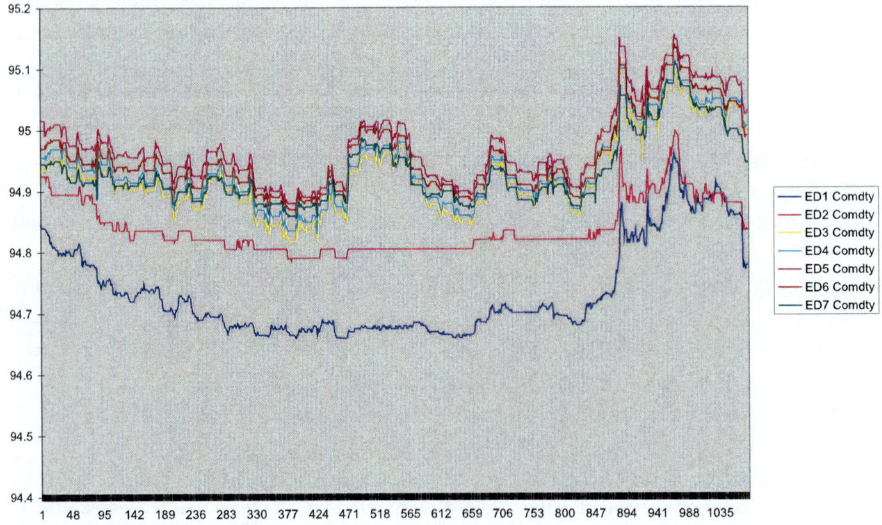

Figure 1.2: Eurodollar quotes

(We plot here the MID price and, because of the extremely large data set, only the hour averages. However, in the calculations the full intraday data set, not the hour average, is used.)

Ho-Lee Model Parameters Estimation

For computing the forward rates we need the convexity adjustment applied on the simplest Ho-Lee model. We denote $FutC_m^d$ as a futures rate in the time moment determined by the day *d* and its minute *m*. In our case we have observations for $D = 45$ whole days ($d = 1, \ldots, D$) and within each day observations for all its M minutes ($m = 1, \ldots, M$). We remove the nontrading days and minutes from our consideration so the resulting time series can be considered as regular (with minute time intervals).

We want to estimate the standard deviation of daily changes of the futures rate and possibly recompute it to annual basis. A model behind our formulas is that the minute sequence of the futures rates is assumed here to form a random walk. (I.e. we assume the changes to have zero expected value, are uncorrelated and homoscedastic. These assumptions are partly based on the results in section 2.2, where we noticed that the forward interest rate in Ho-Lee model is normally distributed.)

Specially $FutC_m^d - FutC_m^{d-1}$, $d = 2, \ldots, D$, $m = 1, \ldots, M$ is a collection of identically distributed random variables with zero mean and finite variance σ_{day}^2. Although these variables are correlated (and so do not form a random sample), the expression

$$\hat{\sigma}_{day}^2 = \frac{\sum_{d=2}^{D} \sum_{m=1}^{M} \left(FutC_m^d - FutC_m^{d-1}\right)^2}{(D-1) \cdot M} \tag{1.7}$$

(sample variance) is an unbiased estimator of σ_{day}^2. The estimate of a standard deviation $\sigma_{day} = \sqrt{\sigma_{day}^2}$ will be obviously $\widehat{\sigma}_{day} = \sqrt{\widehat{\sigma}_{day}^2}$.

Since the annual change of $FutC$ is a sum of individual daily changes through the year, its variance is simply $\sigma_{year}^2 = D_{year} \cdot \sigma_{day}^2$, where D_{year} is the number of (trading) days in one year (in our case is $D_{year} = 260$). Our annual estimators then will obviously be

$$\widehat{\sigma}_{year}^2 = D_{year} \cdot \widehat{\sigma}_{day}^2 \quad \text{and} \quad \widehat{\sigma}_{year} = \sqrt{\widehat{\sigma}_{year}^2}. \tag{1.8}$$

Table 1: Estimated standard deviation of daily changes of the futures rates

Maturity	EUR		USD	
19/03/07	0.97	E-02	1.47	E-02
18/06/07	1.03	E-02	1.31	E-02
17/09/07	1.15	E-02	1.60	E-02
17/12/07	0.85	E-02	1.53	E-02
17/03/08	1.17	E-02	1.61	E-02
16/06/08	1.21	E-02	1.59	E-02
15/09/08	1.13	E-02	1.51	E-02

As already observable from the above table with summarized volatilities, the estimated parameters for the Euribor are slightly below the Eurodollar rates. This can also lead us to brief conclusion that the forward interest rate market during 2007 were more stable-in the daily changes point of view for the EUR currency. (Analyzing this in more detail is not the aim of our paper though. For more details resulting into similar results follow up particular studies of appropriate market volatilities comparatives before global economical crisis.)

After the estimation of the futures rates' standard deviation of daily changes - the only parameter in the Ho-Lee model, we can compute straight-forward the exact amount of Ho-Lee Convexity adjustment, as in (1.6):

$$CA = \frac{1}{2}\sigma^2 t_1 t_2.$$

As we use now the just estimated daily changes standard deviation, the first time variable t_1 is remaining time to appropriate maturity of the contract and the second time variable t_2 will be here simply set as $t_1 + 0.25$, since we work with 3-month futures prices.

In figures Fig. (1.3) and Fig. (1.4) we plot the calculated convexity adjustment for all 7 considered maturities. As already expected from the model analysis before, the exact amount of the adjustment increases with longer maturity. For a fixed maturity, convexity adjustment in Ho-Lee model is decreasing. (Follows directly from the formula (1.6), since closer we are to the moment of expiration, time to maturity t_1 approaches zero.)

Smallest convexity adjustment varies around 0.00001 (0.001%) for the Euribor and 0.00004 (0.004%) for the Eurodollar. Largest adjustment occurs in case of the last maturity and it is 0.000175 (0.0175%) for the Euribor and 0.0004 (0.004%) for the Eurodollar. Even in this largest case, it is not of a big impact for the forward rate consideration. (More significant difference would appear for longer maturities, but usefulness of these calculations for long maturities is questionable.)

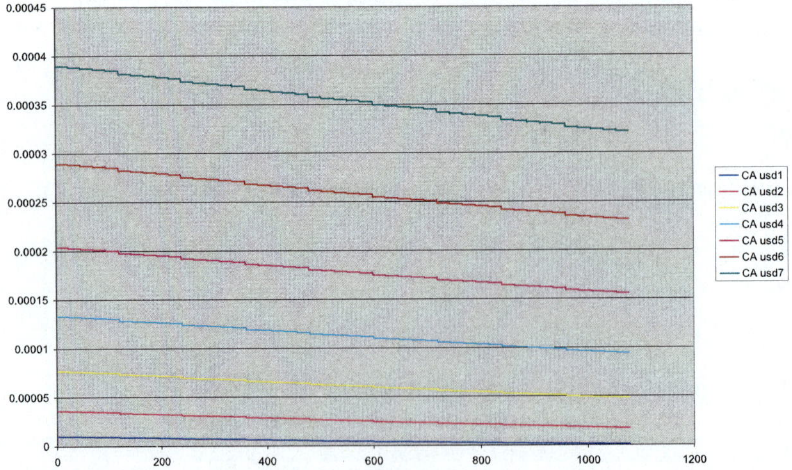

Figure 1.3: Convexity Adjustment for the Eurodollar Futures

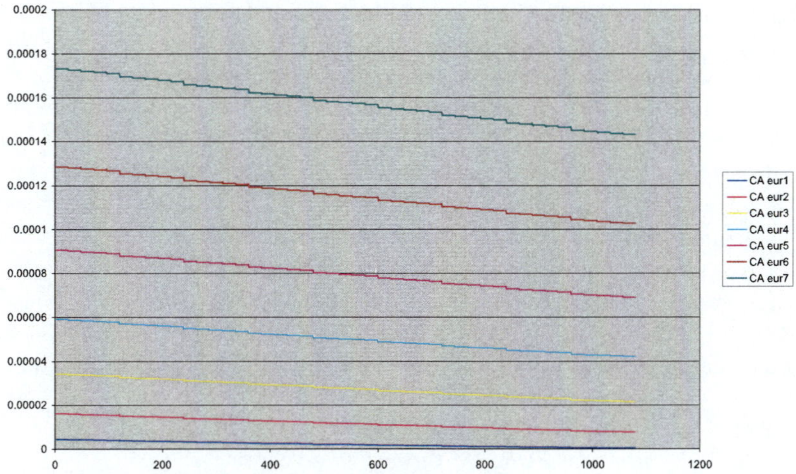

Figure 1.4: Convexity Adjustment for the Euribor Futures

However, most of calculations on the real market simply assumes that the forward and futures prices are equal, or use the same parameters in calculations for all maturities. For example, Hull in [6] recommends to use = 0.015, which is very close to our deviation estimates for USD futures prices model.

Implied Forward Rates

Eurodollar futures reflect market expectations of forward 3-month rates. An implied forward rate indicates approximately where short-term rates may be expected to be sometime in the future. The forward rates for both currencies and all seven maturities can be now easily obtained from futures rates reduced by the convexity adjustment calculated above:

$$For_{e_i} = FutC_{e_i} - CA_{e_i}, i = 1, ..., 7, \tag{1.9}$$

$$For_{u_j} = FutC_{u_j} - CA_{u_j}, j = 1, ..., 7. \tag{1.10}$$

We will use these in the following chapter in order to arrive to possible arbitrage existence between interest rates (the Euribor and Eurodollar futures quotes) and currency exchange rates (corresponding currency forwards).

2 Arbitrage Analysis

Currency Forwards

Considering now the most common definition of arbitrage - as a process with positive probability of gain and zero probability of lose - we will construct the arbitrage possibilities using our Euribor and Eurodollar rates and appropriate currency forward rates. A currency forward contract is defined on the market as forward contract in the forex market that locks in the price at which an entity can buy or sell a currency on a future date. Also often referred as "outright forward currency transaction", "forward outright" or "FX forward". In our further calculations we will denote it as F *or* FX , which will mean the Euro FX futures. This rate assesses the relative value of the U.S. dollar compared to the euro, provides a way to manage risks associated with currency rate fluctuations in the FX markets and to take advantage of profit opportunities stemming from changes in those rates.

Since we are analyzing the futures interest rates measured between days 08/01/07 and 09/03/07 with maturities from 19/03/07 until 15/09/08, for the arbitrage construction we will use the corresponding forward exchanges rates: the spot rate, 1 week, 1-, 2-, 3-, 4-, 5-, 6-, 9-, 12-, 15-, 18- month and 2-year rate. These are often labeled on market as *EUR Curncy* (spot rate), *EUR1W Curncy* (one week rate), ..., *EUR2Y Curncy* or *EUR24M Curncy* (two year rate).

Currency forward rate for 21 months is not quoted and we will have to approximate it by interpolation using the *15M, 18M, 21M* and *24M Curncy* rates. Let x be the forward change between 18 and 21, and y the change between 21 and 24. Then

$$x + y = EUR24M\ Curncy - EUR18M\ Curncy.$$

Furthermore, we assume that the trend of the currency forward will remain the same across the time and so that

$$x/y = (EUR18M\ Curncy - EUR15M\ Curncy)\ /x.$$

Putting both equations together we get the quadratic equation (here with short notation), of which solution gives us approximated *EUR21M Curncy* rate:

$$x^2 + x\,(18M - 15M) - (18M - 15M)\,(24M - 18M) = 0$$

Now, after obtaining the *EUR21M Curncy*, we can perform the full linear interpolation between these currency forwards (according to the relevant maturity) in order to obtain the approximate forward rate for every trading day considered in our analysis. Nevertheless, the currency forward computation presented here might be in some cases very vague and not explaining the real market behaviour. In general though, it should be sufficient for our further calculations, as it takes into consideration the main estimative currency forward trend.

Construction of the Arbitrage

The main idea of our arbitrage consideration is comparing the two possibilities: having one EUR unit we can first exchange it to the USD using forward exchanges rates and then deposit it with the forward dollar interest rate. Or, as a second case, we can start with deposition using the forward euro interest rate and then exchange it to USD currency using the matching forward exchanges rates. At the end of these both we should arrive to the same amount of USD.

Since we already have performed all calculations needed to obtain the appropriate forward dollar/euro interest rates and the forward exchanges rates are derived directly from the data, the 2-step-arbitrage considered above can be now easily computed.

Let us assume now we start with one EUR unit at time 0. We move to time t within the first step (exchange or deposit as first) and arrive to the second step (deposition after exchange or exchange after deposition) at time T.

We denote here the corresponding exchange rates as $F\ or\ FX\ (t)$, $F\ or\ FX\ (t)$.

In case of no arbitrage appearance we have:

$$ForFX(t) \cdot e^{For_u(t).(T-t)} = e^{For_e(t).(T-t)} \cdot ForFX(T), \tag{2.1}$$

or

$$For_e(t) = For_u(t) + \frac{1}{0.25} \ln \left(\frac{ForFX(t)}{ForFX(T)} \right), \tag{2.2}$$

since we work with 3-month futures prices and so $T - t = 0.25$.

Futures Quotes vs. Implied Quotes

Using the results just derived in previous section, we will present the arbitrage as a difference between the real market Euribor quotes and Euribor quotes calculated using the exchange rates from above. More precisely, after computing the implied forward rate for EUR as in (2.2) we can next obtain the implied EUR futures interest rate (by addition of a convexity adjustment, already calculated in previous chapter). Finally, we will compare the implied Euribor quotes with the real ones, observed from the market.

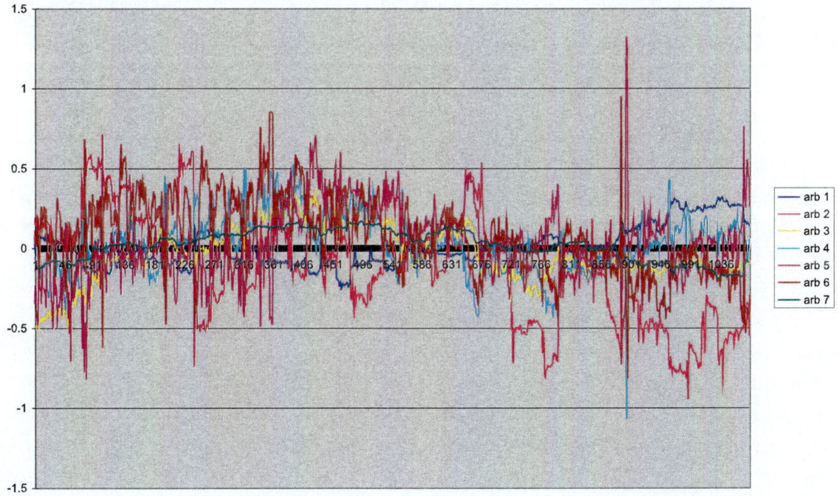

Figure 2.1: The difference between the real market Euribor quotes and implied Euribor quotes (in bps)

In Fig. (2.1) we plot the difference between calculated EUR currency futures quotes and those observed from the market. It is plotted here in the common price fluctuation units - *basis points (bps)*, which means we multiplied the computed difference by 100. The exact results are presented in the table below. The most striking fact is the small sample mean of the arbitrage. For two maturities the sample mean is negative, which indicate that the market quotes are below the implied, calculated ones. In the rest of the cases, sample mean is positive, but still very close to zero. However, on the second contract we can notice, how misleading this might be. Sample mean of arbitrage is in this case negative (and larger than for other contract), but the median value is positive.

Table 2: Futures Quotes vs. Implied Quotes

Maturity	Sample Mean	Mean Standard Error	Median
19/03/07	0.00654	0.00368	-0.01669
18/06/07	-0.10107	0.01053	0.05179
17/09/07	-0.03733	0.00528	-0.06815
17/12/07	0.03386	0.00545	0.03529
17/03/08	0.03067	0.00690	0.00897
16/06/08	0.06887	0.00719	0.05593
15/09/08	0.01909	0.00279	0.02755
	Sample Variance	Max	Min
	0.01466	0.32335	-0.25452
	0.11989	0.64867	-0.94135
	0.03013	0.36850	-0.49857
	0.03216	0.52581	-1.04880
	0.05145	1.30983	-0.82011
	0.05589	0.94792	-0.80177
	0.00839	0.16775	-0.19173

Trying to test the data for the zero-hypothesis makes no moderate statistical sense, since most of considerable hypotheses would be strongly rejected according to the high number of observation. Therefore, simple look at the pictures plotting the arbitrage will make more sense this time.

Figure (2.2) plots the calculated arbitrage possibilities for the contract in different maturities. (Denoted here on this figure as *arb*1, ..., *arb*7.) In some moments, the amount of the arbitrage exceeds 1 basis point in both negative and positive sense. Most of the time they oscillate in a narrow range around the zero value.

However, for some certain moments of time, the trend for some maturities seems to be strongly biased in negative or positive direction. This may be caused by imperfect estimation of the appropriate currency forwards in our previous calculations.

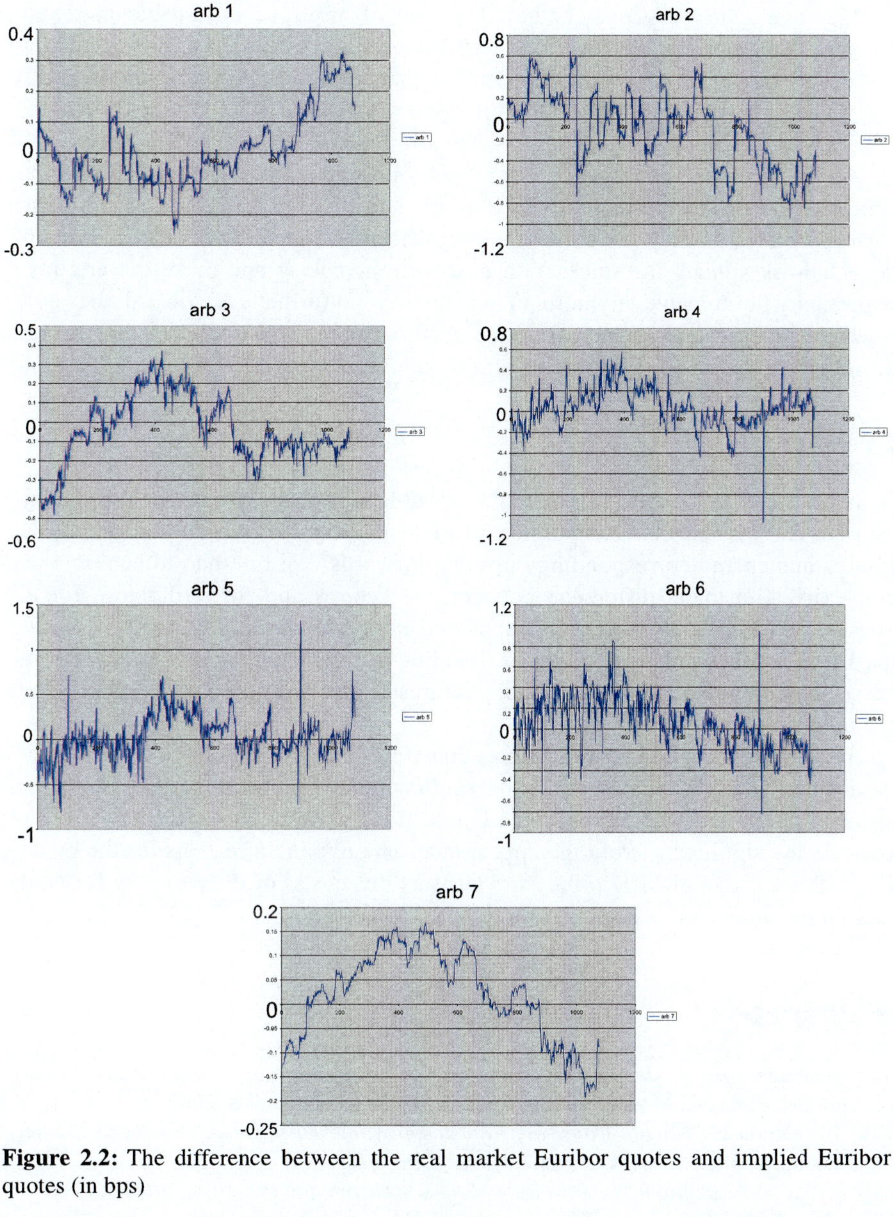

Figure 2.2: The difference between the real market Euribor quotes and implied Euribor quotes (in bps)

Furthermore, not all rates which we used here, were recorded at a same time instant. We had to achieve the appropriate data by assuming the rates not to change dramatically at the specific moment. This might have also caused some bias though. (Since all the rates are not recorded at the same time instants, some random variation between them can be observed. This random error, though, will not bias the results.)

Moreover, the question whether this kind of arbitrage is tradable in reality remains as major. First reason is that we have used the MID prices for our calculations. This might occur as a problem in case that the bid-ask spread is too large. (If e.g. the ask quote is too high, the arbitrageur would find it impossible to make a profit, even if here appears existence of an arbitrage in our analysis.)

Another reason, and maybe even more important, is the transaction costs appearance. For the futures rates the costs are relatively small, but in case of the currency forwards they are sometimes significantly higher. Specially, in cases of large bid-ask spread, the transaction costs are increasing and make the arbitrage opportunity not tradable anymore. (There are several further analytical studies considering the transaction costs within the profit/arbitrage construction – done so far, most of which results are summarized right above.)

Overview

In this paper we had a closer look to the possible arbitrage existence between interest rates and currency exchange rates. More concretely, the Euribor and Eurodollar futures quotes and corresponding currency forwards. We first had to compute the convexity adjustment-difference between the futures and forward rates. For all considered seven maturities it has appeared in a very small amount, anyway, we used it in order to calculate the corresponding futures interest rate. We have compared the computed (implied) Euribor futures quotes with the data reported from the market.

The difference – considered here as constructed arbitrage – has shown up in all cases fairly small, oscillating around zero. In couple of moments we have observed stronger deviation from zero or even biased trend as well. However, this does not indicate the significant arbitrage appearance. The two main reasons for the resulting bias are usage of MID prices and transactions costs for the currency forwards and futures interest rates.

Bibliography

[1] Benhamou E.: *A Martingale Result for Convexity Adjustment in the Black Pricing Model,* Financial Markets Group, London School of Economics, 2000.
[2] Benhamou E.: *Pricing Convexity Adjustment with Wiener Chaos,* Financial Markets Group, London School of Economics, 2000.
[3] Brigo D., Mercurio F.: *Interest Rate Models – Theory and Practice,* Springer, 2006.
[4] Cornell, B., Reinganum M.: *Forward and Futures Prices: Evidence from Foreign Exchange Markets,* Journal of Finance, 36, December 1981, 1035-45.
[5] French K.: *A Comparison of Futures and Forward Prices,* Journal of Financial Economics, 12, November 1983, 311-42 .
[6] Hull J.C.: *Options, Futures and Other Derivatives,* Third edition, Prentice Hall, 1997.
[7] James J., Webber N.: *Interest Rate Modelling,* John Wiley & Sons LTD, 2000.
[8] Jílek J.: *Finan ní a komoditní deriváty v praxi,* Grada, Praha, 2005.

[9] Melicherčík I., Olšarová L., Úradníček V.: *Kapitoly z finan nej matematiky,* Epos, Bratislava, 2005.

[10] Park H.Y., Chen A.H.: *Differences between Futures and Forward Prices: A Further Investigation of Marking to Market Effects,* Journal of Futures Markets, 5, February 1985, 77-88.

[11] Piterbarg V., Renedo M.: *Eurodollar Futures Convexity Adjustments in Stochastic Volatility Models,* Working Paper, Bank of America, February 04, 2004.

[12] Sandmann K., Sondermann D. *A Note on the Stability of Lognormal Interest Rate Models and the Pricing of Futures,* Mathematical Finance 7, 119-128, 1997.

[13] Šeli . N.: *An Examination of the Convexity Adjustment Technique in the the Pricing of Constant Maturity Swaps,* Advanced Mathematics of Finance Honours Project, 2003.

[14] Shreve S.E.: *Stochastic Calculus for Finance II-Continuous Time Models,* Springer Finance, 2004.

[15] Steele J.M.: *Stochastic Calculus and Financial Applications,* Applications of Mathematics, Springer, 2001.

[16] Vaillant N.: *Convexity Adjustments between Futures and Forward Rates Using a Martingale Approach*, Probability Tutorials, 1999.

Term Structure Models

Victor Lapshin

National Research University Higher School of Economics, Moscow, Russia.
email: victor.lapshin@gmail.com

Abstract The paper is an overview from scratch of the term structure modeling field. We present a brief review of the problem of modeling the term structure of interest rates. We start with informal problem formulation, and then, via different formalizations, we arrive at several different term structure models. We propose a new classification of term structure models based on the nature of a priori assumptions employed. We also illustrate the difference between snapshot and dynamic models, present arguments in favor of and against the approaches discussed and also point out some difficulties arising while using and combining such methods.

Keywords: yield curve modeling, term structure, interest rates.

JEL classification: G12

Introduction

Interest rates continue to be an important driving factor for many financial and economical applications. In what follows, we abstain from discussing their importance and the need for mathematical modeling of such an entity, instead concentrating on transparent exposition and key examples.

There are many good surveys of interest rates modeling in the literature. There are good general financial economics textbooks like Panjer, (2001) or Cochrane, (2005) and some very comprehensive specialized surveys like James, (2000), Rebonato, (2002) or Brigo, (2006) with thousands of references therein. The present paper does not present any new results; neither does it claim to be a thorough review of all relevant literature. Instead it very quickly guides the reader from the very foundation of interest rates modeling to advanced topics such as the Heath-Jarrow-Morton framework. The topics covered are considered by the author sufficient for a novice reader to rightfully state that she "has heard of interest rate modeling".

Interest Rates

Consider a bank's deposit conditions. Some bank A may offer a 4% annual yield for a deposit for up to 6 months, 5% annual yield for a deposit for a term from 6 months and 1 day to 1 year, 5.5% annual yield for a term from 1 year and 1 day to

D. Sornette et al. (Eds.), *Market Risk and Financial Markets Modeling*,
DOI 10.1007/978-3-642-27931-7_12, © Springer-Verlag Berlin Heidelberg 2012

2 years and 6% for a deposit for more than 2 years. The yield (in %) clearly depends on the term of the investment. Typically, the longer the term, the higher the yield, thus encouraging longer investments. The dependence of the yield on the term is called the term structure of interest rates. Note that even though the word "yield" is typically employed in context of earning the money (from an investment, for example) and "interest rates" usually refers to money losses (say, via paying interest on a loan), we shall employ the two interchangeably, thus ignoring the difference between borrowing the money and lending it. Of course, it requires somewhat "ideal" conditions, which we shall explicitly state later.

The word "yield" may denote different entities depending on what type of yield it is. Namely, the yield may be: simple; compounded (annually, semiannually, quarterly, monthly… etc); continuously compounded.

While being any of the above, the yield may be also expressed in terms of: per annum, per period (for compounded yield), "pure" or gross percentage.

While the yield may be almost any combination of type and term, the yield calculation usually employs one of the following day counting conventions: 30 days in a month, 360 days in a year (30/360); 30 days in a month, 365 days in a year (30/365); actual number of days in a month, 365 days in a year (Act/365); actual numbers of days in a month and in a year (Act/Act)… etc.

For example, $100 invested on 01 Jan 2000 under "5% yield" will become at 01 Jan 2001:

- $105.148 if it is 5% per annum compounded semiannually under Act/360.
- $121.551 if it is just 5% compounded quarterly.
- $105.142 if it is 5% per annum continuously compounded under Act/365.
- $105.014 if it is 5% per annum under Act/365.
- $105.000 if it is simply 5% gross.

The values quoted above refer to what is called the wealth factor. The wealth factor *w(t)* is what becomes of a unit sum invested for the term *t*. A very close notion is the discount factor. The discount factor *d(t)* is the sum we need to invest now in order to receive a unit sum in time *t*. Clearly,

$$d(t) = \frac{1}{w(t)} .$$

Wealth and discount factors depend on whether we lend or borrow money, on taxation, on counterparty's and our own credit risk, on embedded options and many other details. Nevertheless, both provide a sound basis for comparison of yields given that the terms are equivalent. Still, if the investment promises more than one future cash flow we need a means of comparing it to a similar investment with a possibly different cash flow. Let us describe our basic assumptions about the *Present Value* of a promised cash flow:

1. Only promised cash flows matter. No ratings, embedded options etc.
2. All promised cash flows will happen. No credit risk or randomness of any kind.
3. The Present Value (PV) is unique.

4. The PV is additive: PV(A and B) = PV(A) + PV(B) for any portfolios A and B.
5. No trading restrictions and absolute liquidity: PV(-A) = -PV(A). Taking a short position yields exactly as much as it would cost to take a corresponding long position.
6. No taxation or transactional costs.

Within these assumptions[1] the present value of an instrument promising N cash flows F_i, $i = 1, \ldots, N$ at times t_i, $i = 1, \ldots, N$ is

$$\sum_{i=1}^{N} F_i d(t_i) ,$$

where *d(t)* is the discount function: the PV of a unit cash flow promised in time *t*. Now if we suppose that the PV is exactly the opportunity cost and if we have an ideal market where one can invest any positive or negative amount of money for any term (fractional, irrational, etc.), that is one on which bonds with all face values and all maturities are traded, then *d(t)* may be considered as the current price of a bond with unit face value and time *t* to maturity.

Note that the discount function *d(t)* and the term structure of interest rates *r(t)* (also called the [zero-coupon] [spot] yield curve) are in one-to-one correspondence once we fix the compounding and the day count convention. Throughout the rest of the article we employ continuous compounding with yield expressed per annum which implies $d(t) = e^{-r(t)t}$. This is just a convenience agreement since continuous compounding is easier to deal with from the mathematical point of view.

The Problem

The problem of term structure modeling is to describe the current discount function given observed bond prices and bond descriptions (promised cash flows). The task being very simple for special cases, it becomes increasingly hard to accomplish within more realistic frameworks.

The simplest case arises when all bonds are discount bonds (promising one cash flow) and have one price observed without error; the prices are believed to be equal to the present values of these bonds. Then the price P_k of a bond with notional value N_k and redemption due in time t_k is $P_k = N_k d(t_k)$ and one easily acquires discount factors from these equations.

For the case of coupon-bearing bonds, it is assumed that the cash flow times t_k are common for all bonds. If it is not the case, zero cash flows may be introduced where necessary. Then the price of a bond promising N cash flows is determined from $P_k = \sum_{i=1}^{N} F_{i,k} d(t_i)$. This is a system of linear algebraic equations with respect

[1] Note that this is not exactly the case. One also needs mild technical assumptions to prohibit linear but non-continuous PVs. Measurability or positivity of PV would suffice, as well as continuity.

to the discount factors. Unfortunately the system is usually underdetermined since the number of equations is equal to the number of bonds and the number of variables is equal to the total number of cash flows; and every bond provides one or more cash flow. Moreover, we may desire discount function values in intermediate points.

The lack of available data (recall that the system is underdetermined) forces one to employ a priori assumptions. Different a priori assumptions lead to different problem formulations and, in general, to different results. We propose to separate all such methods into two classes.

Parametric methods presuppose some fixed parametric form of the discount function, which leaves us with the problem of estimating the unknown parameters from the observed data. Since the number of parameters may be arbitrary low, the problem is usually overdetermined and the parameters are estimated using least squares or some estimation other technique.

Spline methods assume that the true discount function (or zero-coupon yield curve or equivalent) possesses some extreme property. This is usually interpreted as having maximal smoothness over some class of acceptable functions. The solution is usually a spline of some form, which gave the name to this class of methods. For example, it is well known that the condition of minimal potential energy results in the curve being a common cubic spline.

Note that if we postulate a spline nature of the discount function and estimate its coefficients via some numerical technique, then the method thus obtained is a parametric method, not a spline one, because instead of an extreme property we simply assume the specific parametric form (which turns out to be of spline form, but that is not relevant.

In what follows we present several methods of estimating the term structure of interest rates, together with additional assumptions needed to justify (if possible) the use of the technique in question.

Bootstrapping

This method is usually attributed to Fama, (1987). The simplest method of obtaining discount factors from coupon bond prices requires either a very special data set or an unrealistic assumption. It falls into the parametric subclass of yield curve models and the chosen parametric form is piecewise constant yield $r(t)$. The algorithm is very simple.

1. Chose from the dataset the bond with the shortest time to maturity T_1.
2. Supposing constant zero-coupon yield on $[0, T_1]$ find the value of the yield r_0 which makes the computed price of the shortest bond equal to its observed price via solving the following equation with respect to r_0:

$$P_1 = \sum_{i=1}^{N_1} F_{1,i} e^{-t_i r_0}$$

3. Find the bond with the next shortest time to maturity T_{k+1}.
4. Given yield curve for $0 < t < T_k$ and supposing constant yield r_k for the terms from T_k to T_{k+1} find the value of r_k which makes the computed price of the bond in question equal to its observed price.
5. Repeat steps 3 – 4 until the last bond.

Advantages of the bootstrapping method:

- It is very simple.
- It is reasonably fast: one has to solve one simple nonlinear equation for every bond in the dataset.
- It exactly replicates the observed bond prices.

The disadvantages are somewhat more numerous:

- It produces discontinuous interest rates.
- It exactly replicates the observed bond prices.
- It may fail (produce negative interest rates for large terms).
- The resulting interest rates may have no economic sense for large terms.

The ability to exactly replicate the observed prices may be viewed as an advantage, but generally we admit that the prices are subject to random variations independent from any possible reasonable influencing factors.

The assumption about the yield being constant between maturities of bonds is surely not realistic. However, there is one very important special case arising if the dataset is specially chosen so that the shortest bond has no coupons, the second shortest pays only one coupon exactly at the redemption of the shortest bond, the third shortest pays only twice, in times of redemption of the two shorter, etc. In this case, the above procedure is just an algebraic solution of a system of linear equations for discount factors.

Spot Forward Rates

The following methods chose not to model the discount curve or the yield curve (like bootstrapping), but the spot forward rate curve. The spot forward rate *f(t)* for term *t* is the value of the spot yield *r(0)* which we may fix today for the time *t* in future in a sort of a forward contract.

The intuition behind the spot forward rate is the interest rate density. Observe the equation which relates the discount curve, the zero-coupon spot yield curve and the spot forward rate curve in the case of continuous compounding.

$$d(t) = e^{-r(t)t} = e^{-\int_0^t f(x)dx}$$

The yearly interest rate is thus nothing else but the averaged spot forward rate over the whole time span: $r(t) = \frac{1}{t}\int_0^t f(x)dx$.

The Nelson-Siegel Method

This model was proposed by Nelson and Siegel, (1987). It is a parametric method with respect to the spot forward rate curve. Assume that the spot forward rate has the form

$$f(t)=\beta_0+\left(\beta_1+\beta_2\frac{t}{\tau}\right)e^{-\frac{t}{\tau}},$$

where $\beta_0,\beta_1,\beta_2,\tau$ are the unknown parameters. The parameter β_0 determines the long rate (the yield for infinite term). β_1 sets the short rate (the yield for infinitesimal term). β_2,τ determine the hump: its magnitude and location on the spot forward rate curve.

Now $d(t_i)=d_i(\beta_0,\beta_1,\beta_2,\tau)$, and we need at least 4 bonds to estimate all parameters. If the number of bonds is greater than 4, one may use a nonlinear least squares estimation.

$$\sum_{k=1}^{N}\left(P_k-\sum_{i=0}^{n}F_{i,k}d_i(\beta_0,\beta_1,\beta_2,\tau)\right)^2\to\min_{\beta_0,\beta_1,\beta_2,\tau}$$

This corresponds to the assumption that the prices are observed with Gaussian errors, which is not a bad way to cope with the stochastic nature of prices.

Due to its simplicity, the Nelson-Siegel model has seen a vast number of modifications and upgrades, of which the most famous is the Svensson model [Svensson, 1994]. It simply adds the second hump to the forward rate curve with the help of two more parameters.

$$f(t)=\beta_0+\left(\beta_1+\beta_2\frac{t}{\tau}\right)e^{-\frac{t}{\tau}}+\beta_3\frac{t}{\tau_2}e^{-\frac{t}{\tau_2}}$$

with the discount function determined from it as usual. When intersecting, two humps may produce much more variable forward rate curve shapes (and subsequently yield curve shapes).

Advantages of the Nelson-Siegel model:

- It is relatively simple.
- It is relatively fast: the objective function in the least squares minimization is only 4-dimensional and 3 of 4 variables enter linearly in *f(t)* and therefore exponentially in *d(t)*.
- It produces sensible yield curve shapes.
- It is easily extended.

The disadvantages are as follows:

- The chosen parametric form admits negative spot forward rates for certain parameter values.

- The precise parametric form of the spot forward rate curve doesn't have sufficient economic intuition behind it.
- The set of possible yield curve shapes is too small: the model is not flexible enough.
- The inter-temporal correlations (correlations between yields for different terms to maturity) are fixed due to fixed parametric form.
- It is incapable of reflecting complicated term structures of interest rates: they will inevitably be smoothed out since the only possible term structures within the chosen parametric form are very smooth and regular.

Sinusoidal-Exponential Splines

This method was proposed by Smirnov and Zakharov, (2003), and further developed by Lapshin, (2009). The object of modeling is still the spot forward rate $f(t)$ and it falls into the category of spline methods.

In order to ensure the positivity of the spot forward rates we let $f(t) = g^2(t)$ for some unknown function $g(\cdot)$. The optimal function $g(t)$ is supposed to satisfy the maximal smoothness condition given its values for all cash flow times:

$$\int_0^{T_{\max}} [g'(x)]^2 dx \to \min_{g(\cdot)} .$$

The bond prices are supposed to be the present values (PVs) with independent Gaussian errors, with standard deviation equal to half of the bid-ask spread:

$$P_k = \sum_{i=0}^{n} F_{i,k} d(t_k) + \varepsilon_k w_k$$

where

$$w_k = \frac{Ask_k - Bid_k}{2}, \quad \varepsilon_k \sim N(0,1)$$

Now the task of determining the term structure of interest rates is reduced to the following mathematical problem. Find a function g with $g' \in L_2[0, T_{\max}]$ such that

$$\sum_{k=1}^{N} \frac{1}{w_k^2} \left(P_k - \sum_{i=0}^{n} F_{i,k} \exp\left(-\int_{x=0}^{t_k} g^2(x) dx \right) \right)^2 \to \min .$$

$$\int_0^{T_{\max}} [g'(x)]^2 dx \to \min$$

It is a multiple criteria optimization problem and the simplest method of solving it is via assigning relative weights to both criteria. It corresponds to the Tikhonov regularization concept, see Tikhonov, (1977). With the relative weight assigned to the smoothness criterion (this weight is called the regularization parameter) the problem becomes

$$\sum_{k=1}^{N}\frac{1}{w_k^2}\left(P_k-\sum_{i=0}^{n}F_{i,k}\exp\left(-\int_{x=0}^{t_k}g^2(x)dx\right)\right)^2+\alpha\int_0^{T_{\max}}\left[g'(x)\right]^2dx\to\min .$$

It may easily be solved via calculus of variations or optimal control techniques to obtain the following solution.

$$g(t)=\begin{cases}C_1\exp\left\{\sqrt{\lambda_i}\,(t-t_{i-1})\right\}+C_2\exp\left\{\sqrt{\lambda_i}\,(t_i-t)\right\} & ,\lambda_i>0\\ C_1\sin\left\{\sqrt{-\lambda_i}\,(t-t_{i-1})\right\}+C_2\cos\left\{\sqrt{-\lambda_i}\,(t_i-t)\right\} & ,\lambda_i<0,\\ C_1(t-t_{i-1})+C_2 & ,\lambda_i=0\end{cases}$$

for $t\in[t_{i-1},t_i],\;\; g(t_i-0)=g(t_i+0),\;\; g'(t_i-0)=g'(t_i+0),$

where the coefficients $C_{1,2}^{i},\lambda_i,\; i=1,\dots,n$ have to be determined via nonlinear optimization. So the solution, as the name suggests, is really a sinusoidal-exponential spline with 3 parameters per spline segment and with one segment per every cash flow time moment (coinciding times of cash flows do not produce additional segments).

The advantages of the sinusoidal-exponential splines.

- Non-negative spot forward rates.
- Liquidity consideration: the bid-ask spread is employed as a proxy of liquidity thus assigning more weight to prices of more liquid bonds.
- Flexible smoothness/precision interplay via adjusting the regularization parameter.
- The spline nature allows one to capture various yield curve shapes.

The disadvantages follow.

- The algebraic formulae for *r(t)* and *d(t)* are very sophisticated and difficult to understand and do algebra and calculus with. Computer algebra systems are needed in order to correctly implement minimization procedures requiring analytical derivatives of the objective function.
- The transversality conditions imply $g'(0) = g'(T_{max}) = 0$. This is realistic on the long end (Dybviget al. (1996) show that the forward rate curve must have a limit as *t* becomes infinitely large), but is completely nonsense at the short end.
- The nonlinear optimization problem required to fit the model to the data has large dimensionality (usually 600 – 1000 variables). The solution may be slow.

Temporal Issues

All methods described above are so-called snapshot methods. They deal with a snapshot of the market; that is all prices are believed to correspond to the same instant. If in fact the prices are observed at different times, the underlying discount function might have changed between observations. So in order to use the information collected at different times we have to build a model of the discount function (or the yield curve / forward rate curve) dynamics in time. The model in question should of course be of stochastic nature since the market movements are generally believed to be stochastic.

A connected problem arises on an illiquid market when some bonds may just not be traded during some trading days. Negligence of this issue while sticking to the snapshot methods may result in a somewhat unpleasant result. Consider four zero-coupon bonds which are traded on the market as shown in Figure 1. Then one may easily show that the zero-coupon yield curve should smoothly connect the points (time to maturity; yield to maturity). But suppose that for the next day the yield curve didn't change, instead the shortest bond was not traded at all. Every sensible yield curve fitting method would now give completely different picture (see Figure 2). We now see that on illiquid markets one is forced to use data from more than one time instant.

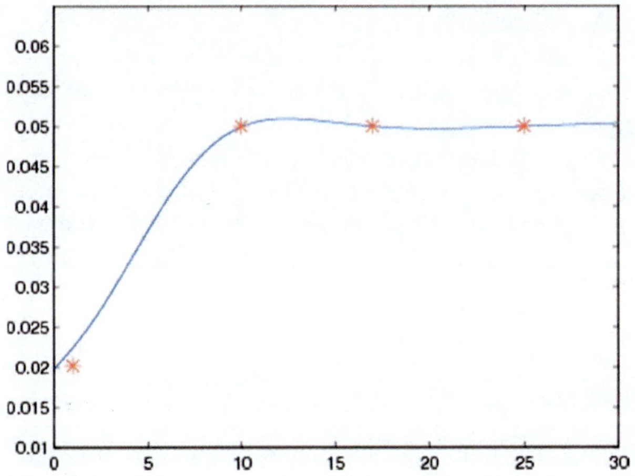

Fig. 1: 4 bonds traded

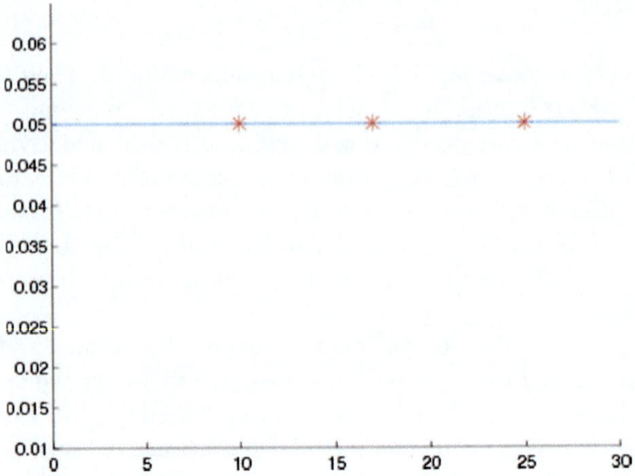

Fig. 2: Just one bond is missing

Snapshot models exhibit various advantages:

- They are simple, fast and analytically tractable.
- They work with snapshot data. There are applications when this is all we have and a snapshot method would ideally suit our needs.

But the drawbacks are sufficiently severe:

- The results are unstable in time for illiquid markets (see Figures 1 and 2).
- The results are meaningless on the short and/or long ends if no bonds of corresponding maturities are traded.
- They require a full set of data to get sensible results.
- They are unfit for derivatives pricing because of their static nature; and the dynamic extensions tend to admit arbitrage opportunities (consult Filipovic, (1999) for a proof that a dynamic Nelson-Siegel model will always allow arbitrage).

Stochastic Models

We need a way to use dynamic information for inference. That is, to describe dependence between the discount function (or yield curves etc.) in different time moments. But a description of the dynamics of interest rates must describe the stochastic dynamics of an infinite number of interest rates (one for each term), and is thus a very complex object. There are several approaches to this problem. One may either employ “higher maths” to describe the stochastic dynamics of an infinite-dimensional variable (term structure) or simplify the problem. In what follows we give a brief sketch of both approaches.

Simplified Dynamic Models

Instead of modeling an infinite number of interest rates, we chose to work with only a small subset of key parameters, thus making the model 1-2-3-dimensional instead of infinite-dimensional. The most common choices for modeling parameters are:

- instantaneous (spot) interest rate;
- spot and long (for infinite term) rates;
- benchmark yields for several key terms;
- several general factors;
- …etc.

Given the stochastic dynamics, the whole yield curve may be derived from it (even if the stochastic dynamics is specified only for the spot rate). This is because the current spot forward rate should be related to the expected future spot rate – a value which is computable from the given dynamics. The exact formulae depend on a specific issue which is called market price of risk or risk-aversion. We may compute current prices as expected future prices only if investors are risk-neutral. Otherwise minor corrections to the formulae are needed in order to account for invertors' risk-aversion. Details may be found in any textbook, such as Panjer, (2001) or Hull, (2009).

The simplest, and at the same time the most common, simple stochastic interest rate models include the Vasicek, (1977) (Vašíček, pronounced "Washeeczech") model and the Cox-Ingersoll-Ross (CIR) (Cox et al., (1985) model. Both models describe the dynamics of the spot rate as a diffusion stochastic process. Vašíček proposed the simplest mean-reverting process: Ornstein-Uhlenbeck $dr_t = k(\theta - r_t)dt + \sigma dW_t$. The rates are Gaussian in this setting, which eases calculations. But the Gaussian distribution allows negative rates. The CIR model deals with the negativity problem at the cost of functional simplicity. The spot rate is modeled as a square root process $dr_t = k(\theta - r_t)dt + \sigma\sqrt{r_t}dW_t$, and the implied distribution for rates is a non-central $\bullet^2$ distribution.

Simple dynamic models tend to produce poor yield curve shapes. This is pardonable since these models were not designed for such applications, but nevertheless, if one is in need of a dynamic model **and** of a suitable yield curve model, more advanced methods should be employed.

Advantages of simple dynamic models:

- They are simple. They are dynamic.
- They are sometimes analytically tractable, which facilitates computations a lot.
- They allow for simple tree-based simulation calculations.
- Parameter inference for these models is relatively simple.

Among disadvantages are:

- Incompatibility with snapshot yield curve fitting methods and unrealistic implied snapshot yield curve shapes.
- Unrealistic behavior of modeled variables.
- Lack of flexibility due to extreme simplicity.

Summing the things up, simple dynamic models are used primarily because they are simple and not because they really do model anything.

Another option is to model the entire set of interest rates via so-called whole yield curve models. Heath et al., (1992) proposed a framework which was improved by Brace et al., (1997). Since then, various approaches within the framework have appeared with more or less success. However, discussion of these (more advanced) approaches is beyond the scope of the present paper which was planned as an introduction.

Conclusion

Term structure models arise from the same need, but due to different formalizations of the task there exist a variety of models, from very simple to very complicated. Some models are used because they are simple, others because they require just the data which is available. And some models are not used at all, only written about, because they either are too sophisticated to correctly implement and infer parameter values from data or don't offer substantial improvement over simpler and coarser models.

References

Brace, A., Gatarek, D., & Musiela, M. (1997). The market model of interest rate dynamics. Mathematical Finance. 7(2). 127 – 155.

Brigo, D., & Mercurio, F. (2006). Interest Rate Models – Theory and Practice: With Smile, Inflation and Credit. Berlin, Germany: Springer Finance.

Cochrane, J.H. (2001). Asset Pricing. Princeton, USA: Princeton University press.

Cox, J.C., Ingersoll Jr, J.E., & Ross, S.A. (1985). A theory of the term structure of interest rates. Econometrica. 53(2. 385 – 407.

Dybvig, P.H., Ingersoll Jr, J.E., & Ross, S.A. (1996). Long forward and zero-coupon rates can never fall. Journal of Business. 69(1). 1 – 25.

Fama, E.F., & Bliss, R.R. (1987). The Information in Long-Maturity Forward Rates. The American Economic Review. 77(4). 680 – 692.

Filipovic, D. (1999). A Note on the Nelson-Siegel Family. Mathematical finance. 9(4). 349 – 359.

Heath, D., Jarrow, R., & Morton, A. (1992). Bond pricing and the term structure of interest rates: A new methodology for contingent claims valuation. Econometrica. 60(1). 77 – 105.

Hull, J. (2009). Options, futures and other derivatives. Prentice Hall.

James, J., & Webber, N. (2000). Interest rate modeling: financial engineering. West Sussex, UK: Wiley.

Lapshin, V.A. (2009). Determining the term structure of interest rates. Moscow University Computational Mathematics and Cybernetics. 33(4). 206 – 213.

Nelson, C.R., & Siegel, A.F. (1987). Parsimonious modeling of yield curves. Journal of Business. 60(4). 473 – 489.

Panjer, H.H. et al. (2001). Financial Economics with applications to investments, insurance and pensions. Schaumburg, Illinois, USA: The Actuarial Foundation.

Rebonato, R. (2006). Modern Pricing of Interest-Rate Derivatives. Princeton, USA: Princeton University Press.

Smirnov, S.N. & Zakharov, A.V. (2003). A Liquidity-Based Robust Spline Fitting of Spot Yield Curve Providing Positive Forward Rates. EBC Working Paper.

Svensson, L.E.O. (1994). Estimating and Interpreting Forward Interest Rates: Sweden 1992-1994. NBER Working paper 4871.

Tikhonov, A.N & Arsenin, V.Y. (1977) Solution of ill-posed problems. Washington, USA: V.H. Winston and Sons.

Vasicek, O. (1977). An equilibrium characterization of the term structure. Journal of Financial Economics. 5(2). 177 – 188.

Current Trends in Prudential Regulation of Market Risk: From Basel I to Basel III

Alexey Lobanov

REA Research Risk Management Group, Non-Commercial Partnership, and PRMIA Russia Steering Committee, Moscow, Russia

Abstract The recent financial crisis has again evoked interest in regulation of bank risks in general and of market risks in particular. Heavy losses on trading portfolios incurred by some of the largest banks have elicited deficiencies in their internal models and processes for managing market risks. The magnitude of losses and the volume of government-sponsored bailouts have raised doubts about the effectiveness of regulatory approaches proposed by the Basel Committee on Banking Supervision in the mid-1990s and later incorporated into Basel II. These drawbacks were the main reason underlying the revision of the market risk capital regulation passed on by the Basel Committee in 2009 and laid the first building block in the 2010 reform package known as Basel III. The Basel capital requirements for market risks are discussed in the paper. The latest modifications to the internal models approach are shown to significantly increase minimum capital requirements for market risk and hence undermine its incentive-compatible design.

Keywords: Capital Requirements, Market Risk, Basel II, Internal Models Approach, Stressed VaR.

JEL classification: G21, G32

Introduction

As long as the expected loss due to market risk is generally not covered by specific provisions or fully hedged, capital is required to cover losses in excess of expected return including P&L from hedging (Lobanov, 2009).

When estimating the required capital from an internal, or economic, perspective, a bank pursues two distinct yet conflicting objectives. On the one hand, it strives to maximize its return on equity (ROE) or reach a target ROE given the portfolio size and structure. On the other hand, it needs to be solvent at a specified confidence level consistent with its risk appetite. The first of the two goals can be reached by reducing the level of capital relative to the bank's debt, while the most straightforward way of achieving the second goal is a contrary action, i.e. a decrease in leverage. The economic capital is therefore a trade-off between these opposite targets.

D. Sornette et al. (Eds.), *Market Risk and Financial Markets Modeling*,
DOI 10.1007/978-3-642-27931-7_13, © Springer-Verlag Berlin Heidelberg 2012

However, it is not as clear which motivation is right for a regulator imposing capital requirements. For instance, the minimum capital adequacy ratio may be set to make sure that the bank is solvent in normal times, i.e. has enough capital to absorb an abnormally long series of 'normal-size' losses. The regulator could also be interested in ensuring that the bank remains solvent after a severe one-off firm-specific loss, such as incurred by Barings in 1995 or Societe General in 2007 due to rogue traders. The supervisory authority would definitely like to avoid a situation in which it would need to recapitalize banks during or after a severe financial crisis, as was the case with UBS or RBS in 2008.[1] Ultimately, the regulator may prefer that banks hold a capital cushion against not only their 'standalone' risks but also (a portion of) systemic risk, i.e. an unexpected build-up of losses propagated through interlinkages of financial institutions. Clearly, each of the above goals implies different minimum capital requirements for banks.

Basel Approaches to Setting Capital Requirements for Market Risk

The Basel Capital Accord from 1988 was aimed at credit risk and did not take market risk into account. Market risk was only marginally recognized as a magnifier of credit risk, e.g. as reflected in the risk weight of 100% for FX-denominated claims on central governments or in add-ons for calculating the credit-equivalent amounts of derivatives. In 1993, the Basel Committee proposed a standardized approach to the treatment of market risk, followed by an internal-models approach in 1995. Both the approaches were released in the 1996 Amendment to the Basel Capital Accord to incorporate market risk, implemented in G-10 member countries by 1998, and incorporated into Basel II with some minor alterations in 2006.

Under the standardized approach, banks must reserve capital against interest rate risk and equity risk in the trading book (both calculated as the sum of general market risk and idiosyncratic 'name' risk) plus currency risk and commodity risk across the bank. While interest rate risk in the banking book was left out of this framework, equity risk in the banking book is accounted for either through deductions from total capital (for non-consolidated equity holdings in subsidiaries) or through credit risk capital charge (by applying a 100% risk weight to other equity investments). The risks are aggregated by simple summing to arrive at the total capital requirement.

Being a 'one-size-fits-all' framework, the standardized approach has been a simple but crude shortcut to estimate the regulatory capital. One of its main drawbacks is that it does not allow banks to recognize non-perfect correlations inside and across risk types on a portfolio level which leads to overestimation of capital requirements for low-risk (e.g. hedged) portfolios.

The internal models approach was devised to overcome most of the shortcomings of the standardized approach. It was the first time banks were offered the pos-

[1] In all cases, it is in the interest of the government to minimize the spending of public funds to bail out banks, even if this aid must be repaid.

sibility to calculate regulatory capital using their own estimates of market risk, subject to certain minimum qualitative and quantitative requirements. Under the internal models approach, market risk capital charge is a function of the bank's internal VaR estimates:

$$MRC = \max \; m \cdot \frac{1}{60}\sum_{i=1}^{60} VaR_{t-i},\ VaR_{t-1} \ . \qquad (1)$$

where m is a supervisory multiplier subject to the minimum value of 3 (for VaR-models deemed adequate based on backtesting results).

The historical observation period for estimating volatilities, correlations and other input parameters must be at least 250 trading days. The bank must perform backtesting of its VaR-model at least quarterly and, in case of inadequacy, adjust the value of the multiplier m.

If the specific risk of interest rate and equity positions in the trading book is not fully captured by their VaR-models, banks must calculate it using standardized methodology and add it to the VaR-based capital charge as a surcharge. To properly reflect specific risk, the model must meet the following criteria (Basel 2006):

- explain the historical price variation in the portfolio (e.g. has an in-sample R^2 of 90%[2]);
- capture concentrations in the portfolio (magnitude and changes in composition);
- be robust to an adverse environment (e.g. through using a full-cycle historical observation period, simulation, or worst-case scenario analysis);
- capture name-related basis risk (the differences between similar but not identical positions not attributable to the general market risk);
- capture event risk (e.g. migration risk for debt, mergers/takeovers for equity);
- be validated through backtesting.

Event risk beyond the 99% confidence level and 10-day holding period not captured by the model must be factored in, e.g. through stress testing, while market liquidity risk must be reflected through scenario analysis and conservative proxies.

The regulatory multiplier m was widely debated in the academic and professional communities. Many have viewed it as a means to combat 'objective' model risk arising from the estimation error due to the high confidence level. However, the high minimum value of the multiplier could indicate that the Basel Committee intended to also mitigate 'subjective' model risk. In other words, the multiplier could be meant to serve as a penalty imposed to counterbalance incentives to underestimate VaR and thus minimize regulatory capital.

Here it should be noted that such multipliers have long been used in the industry to calculate economic capital. For instance, a multiplier could have been calibrated

[2] Apparently, the required goodness-of-fit pertains to the total variation of returns caused by both general and specific market risk. Regression models with a high in-sample R^2 are generally overfitted (i.e. have too many degrees of freedom) and, as a result, have low out-of-sample predictive power.

as a long-run historical average ratio of stress-test results to average VaR (Monet, 2001). In this case, it would have served to build a capital cushion to absorb losses caused by sharp market movements at the onset of a financial crisis. Other possible interpretations of the multiplier include an implicit capital requirement for market liquidity risk or a 'penalty' for a missing or ineffective corrective action of bank's management to reduce its exposure to market risk.[3]

The multiplier's minimum value of 3 has also come under criticism. Kupiec and O'Brien (1997) in their pre-commitment approach argue that the multiplier is redundant and capital should be set equal to an bank's own loss projection, such as VaR. Lucas (1998) shows that the current minimum value of the multiplier is too low and the add-ons applied to it for models from the 'yellow' zone are not effective to curb the bank's incentives to 'game' the regulator. As a result, the bank is likely to significantly underestimate its VaR figures reported to the regulator for capital adequacy purposes. He suggests using a steeper step-wise penalty function for setting the appropriate value of the multiplier so that its highest value would be more than twice as high as proposed by the Basel Committee (i.e. 8–10 instead of 4). According to internal estimates of J.P. Morgan (Monet, 2001), the multiplier in the real world should be about 12 for some portfolios.

The internal models approach had a truly revolutionary meaning for the industry in that banks were not demanded to have any specific model type for calculating VaR. However, the banks are required to use the same model not only for calculating regulatory capital but also for other internal tasks including limit setting for market risk. Under this approach, banks also must conduct regular stress testing of their portfolios and report the results to the regulator.

The internal models approach looks very appealing for banks but is not free from deficiencies, of which perhaps the most important one is a strong incentive for banks to play down their risk and capital numbers. Given the information asymmetry between the bank and the regulator, the latter has only limited ability to detect and prevent model-related abuses (e.g. the use of multiple models for reporting and internal purposes). For riskier portfolios, a more accurate risk estimate automatically translates into a higher capital charge compared to the standardized approach. This helps explain why most banks preferred to stay with the standardized approach.[4] At the same time, there is some evidence that banks working under the internal models approach may be using overly conservative models, apparently to avoid regulatory interference (Jeffery, 2006).

The design of the internal models approach is not flawless either. One of its shortcomings is that the Basel add-ons to the multiplier for 'yellow-zone' models might be too conservative, as banks may quickly improve their VaR models after backtesting.[5] Another weakness lies in the requirement to compare daily VaR num-

---

[3] For instance, the trading desk's stop-loss limits may be missing or too lax.

[4] See, e.g., Holtdorf et al. (2004).

[5] Live testing of VaR models could ameliorate this problem; however, it is not allowed by the Basel Committee for capital adequacy purposes. One approach to live testing is proposed by Lobanov and Kainova (2005).

bers with both actual P&L (the so-called 'dirty' backtesting) and theoretical P&L ('clean' backtesting)[6] which may lead to controversial conclusions about the model accuracy.

It is worth noting that a simplified version of the standardized approach was already introduced by the Central Bank of Russia in 1999 in its Regulation 89-P (Bank of Russia, 1999). In 2007 it was superseded by Regulation 313-P (Bank of Russia, 2007) which differs from Regulation 89-P only in some details.

While the Central Bank of Russia has not attempted to introduce the internal models approach over the past ten years, the Federal Securities Commission, the regulator of the securities market in Russia, considered implementing a modified version of this approach in 2001. The approach was intended for all non-bank professional market participants that would have to assess daily the adequacy of available funds based on the VaR of their trading books. The most important modifications of the Basel framework concerned the holding period for calculating VaR (20 days for non-listed securities), the capital multiplier (only three possible values were proposed: 3 for adequate models, 4 for 'conditionally adequate' models and 5 for inadequate models), and the backtesting of the internal models (authorized third parties could perform the backtesting besides the regulator; if the financial institution would like to waive the backtesting, its minimum available funds were set equal to the book value of positions).[7]

Market Risk Regulation under Basel III

The global financial crisis of 2007/08 has had a strong impact on the implementation of Basel II in the developed countries. As the inadequacy of both the above regulatory approaches have become apparent, the Basel Committee (2009) had to make significant adjustments including higher capital charges for a specific interest rate risk of securitized assets under the standardized approach and the introduction of 'stressed VaR' as an additional charge in the internal models approach. In the following discussion, we will briefly examine the latter amendment.

Starting from 2011, the capital requirement for market risk must be calculated in the following way:

$$\begin{aligned} MRC &= \max\left(m_c \cdot \frac{1}{60}\sum_{i=1}^{60} VaR_{t-i},\ VaR_{t-1} \right) + \max\left(m_s \cdot \frac{1}{60}\sum_{i=1}^{60} SVaR_{t-i},\ SVaR_{t-1} \right) = \\ &= \max\left(m_c \cdot VaR_{avg}, VaR_{t-1}\right) + \max\left(m_s \cdot SVaR_{avg},\ SVaR_{t-1}\right), \end{aligned} \quad (2)$$

[6] Theoretical P&L is calculated for a static portfolio as a result of changes in market prices of its constituent positions over the trading day, while actual P&L is the true P&L booked by the bank which can be 'contaminated' by intraday trades and fees earned by the brokers.

[7] Market participants would have to supplement VaR calculations with regular stress testing of proprietary and client portfolios over a set of scenarios specified by the Federal Securities Commission.

where *SVaR* denotes the stressed *VaR*, m_c and m_s are regulatory multipliers, each subject to the absolute minimum of 3.

Assuming that the average values of *VaR* and *SVaR* multiplied by m_c and m_s respectively are higher than the previous day's estimates of *VaR* and *SVaR*, expression (2) can be reduced to:

$$MRC = m_c \cdot VaR_{avg} + m_s \cdot SVaR_{avg}. \tag{3}$$

A stressed VaR must be calculated by the bank at least weekly using the same model and input parameters as the 'normal' VaR (i.e. 99% confidence level and 10-day holding period). The only difference lies in the sample of historical data: The stressed VaR is calculated over the continuous 12-month period of significant financial turbulence. The Basel Committee recommends using a yearly period related to the most recent crisis of 2007/08. However, the regulator may permit a bank to use another time frame more relevant for its portfolio. Backtesting is not applied to stressed VaR for obvious reasons.

As in Basel II, the bank's VaR model must account for the specific risk of interest rate and equity instruments in the trading book. For interest rate instruments in the trading book that are subject to the specific risk capital requirement, the bank must also have a methodology to reserve capital against so-called 'incremental' risk, which encompasses default risk and rating migration risk not reflected in its VaR-model (Basel Committee, 2009)[8]. Incremental risk can be accounted for in the internal model or calculated separately as a surcharge under the standardized approach, if the bank's internal model does not capture incremental risk. In either case, the bank must ensure that the incremental risk estimate for a position in the trading book is not less than would be required against credit risk of this position in the banking book under the internal ratings-based approach. However, the Basel Committee no longer demands that banks capture the risk of low-probability, high-severity events beyond the 10-day holding period and 99% confidence level.

The incorporation of stressed VaR into the regulatory formula (2) reflects the industry trends that have long manifested themselves in internal methodologies for allocating economic capital developed by large dealer banks. For instance, J. P. Morgan calculated in the early 2000s its economic capital for market risk (EC) in the following way (Monet, 2001):[9]

$$EC = K \cdot Risk\ Index, \tag{4}$$

$$Risk\ Index = 50\% \cdot M \cdot VaR(1\ day,\ 99\%) + 50\% \cdot Stress\,Loss\ , \tag{5}$$

---

[8] Default risk and rating migration risk are removed from the definition of specific risk to avoid double-counting.

[9] J. P. Morgan (see Monet, 2001) reported that the Risk Index was about 1.2 annual standard deviations of revenue (varied by business).

where K denotes a capital multiplier applied to Risk Index (it was set equal to 2 for portfolios managed to an index and to 4 for other portfolios);

M is a multiplier set for each business based on a long run historical ratio of stress test to VaR;

Stress Loss is a historical or hypothetical estimate of extreme monthly losses based roughly on the worst month in the previous 15 years.

The second term in formula (2), reflecting the contribution of stressed VaR to the capital requirement, can be viewed as analogous to the Stress Loss parameter in J. P. Morgan's methodology (5). The major difference between them is that the Stress Loss in the Risk Index is estimated through stress testing, i.e. scenario analysis, while the Basel Committee requires obtaining a stressed VaR by means of the bank's VaR-model. The Basel Committee (2009) does not prescribe any specific ways of calculating the stressed VaR, yet suggests applying e.g. 'antithetic' scenarios or absolute rather than relative volatilities.

Admittedly, the idea of using VaR-models for stress testing is also not entirely novel. Best (1999) proposed stressing VaR for variance-covariance or Monte-Carlo based models by varying volatilities and/or correlations as their input parameters. It should be noted, however, that the covariance, or delta-normal, method for calculating VaR and, to a lesser extent, its higher-order modifications including delta-gamma and delta-gamma-vega are based on linear approximations of price changes to (infinitely) small increments of risk factors (so-called 'deltas'). For options and other instruments with non-linear payoff functions, the approximation error grows with the increase in changes of underlying risk factors. Since stress testing by definition presumes extreme jumps of risk factor values, the usage of such models requires estimating the linear sensitivity of position prices to such large changes or, alternatively, stressing only a correlation matrix rather than a covariance matrix.

The purpose of the multiplier m_S from the Basel formula (2) is unclear, as scaling up stress losses does not meet any of the possible interpretations of a capital multiplier considered above. While applying the first multiplier (m_C) could be justified by the need to hold capital against unexpected losses caused by a sharp increase in volatility, we cannot help observing that the second multiplier (m_S) has been introduced only to enhance the minimum capital requirement. To show this, notice that the average SVaR at any given time for a given portfolio will almost always be at least as high as the average portfolio VaR. This allows formula (3) to be rearranged as follows:

$$MRC = m_c \cdot VaR_{avg} + m_s \cdot (VaR_{avg} + SVaR_{avg} - VaR_{avg}) = (m_c + m_s) \cdot VaR_{avg} + m_s \cdot (SVaR_{avg} - VaR_{avg}). \quad (6)$$

Recalling the minimum value of 3 for each of the multipliers, it is straightforward to see that market risk must now be covered with bank capital *at least* sixfold compared with the minimum ratio of three in Basel II before the 2009 revisions. As the Basel Committee allows banks to scale up their daily VaR figures to 10-day holding period by multiplying them by the square root of 10, the minimum capital will be about 19 times higher than the average daily VaR. It can be easily shown that formula (6), combined with capital charges for specific and incremental risks, may yield a capital requirement in excess of the market value of the position,[10] which obviously does not make economic sense. It should be noted that the Basel Committee (2009) has not bounded the minimum capital requirement for market risk with the market value of the position similar to the cap imposed for credit risk (Basel Committee, 2006).

Surprisingly, the overhaul of the internal models approach has not been extended to the equity risk in the banking book, i.e. to non-consolidated equity holdings subject to credit risk capital charge. Under one of the possible approaches to treating this risk, the so-called 'internal models method', banks may set the regulatory capital for these investments equal to a 99% VaR measure calculated for the difference of the equity's quarterly returns and a risk-free rate estimated over a long-term observation period (Basel Committee 2006).

An Example of Calculating a Market Risk Capital Charge for a Portfolio of Russian Stocks

Let us consider an illustrative example of calculating capital charges for equity risk in compliance with the version of the standardized framework used by the Central Bank of Russia (Bank of Russia, 2007) and the internal models approach before and after the 2009 revisions[11]. A sample trading portfolio consists of liquid Russian stocks from the MICEX10 Index, in which position sizes are inversely proportional to the prices of the respective stocks (see Table 1).

All calculations were conducted as of 30th December, 2010 based on MICEX closing prices. VaR numbers were obtained using three different methodologies: historical simulation, Monte Carlo simulation, and a variance-covariance approach. For the latter two models, a conservative assumption of a zero expected return was made. All the VaR-models were found adequate based on backtesting results and, as they qualified for the 'green zone', both the capital multipliers were set equal to their minimum values of three.[12]

Under the standardized approach, the minimum capital requirement for equity risk is 12% of the portfolio value. When turning to the internal models approach, the capital charge is significantly higher and ranges from 38.1% for Monte Carlo simulation to 42.2% for historical simulation. Adding scaled stressed VaR under Basel III leads to almost doubling of the regulatory capital and varies from 85.2%

[10] The capital requirement will exceed the market value of the position if the average 10-day VaR is at least 1/6=0.167 of the position value. For the one-day VaR, this threshold is met already at VaR equal to 1/19=0.053 of the position value. Such volatility is not infrequently observed in practice, especially in emerging markets. Given the second positive term in formula (6), the threshold levels of VaR at which market risk capital surpasses the position value are in fact even lower.

[11] See formulas (1) and (2) above.

[12] Model backtesting, VaR and capital calculations in this example were conducted using *Prognoz. Market Risk* software. The author thanks Sergey Ivliev (Prognoz) for sharing the data and computation results.

for Monte Carlo simulation to 89.4% for historical simulation (see Table 1 for details).

Table 1: An example of calculating market risk capital under different approaches

Instrument	Position size, # of shares	Market value, RUB	Market risk capital (MRC) before 2009 Basel II revisions, %[1]			Stressed VaR, %
			Monte Carlo simulation	Historical simulation	Variance-covariance	
AK Transneft (pref)	26	982,670.00	69.51	63.23	69.15	23.03
VTB	9,900,990	999,999.99	46.56	56.90	47.24	20.37
NorNickel GMK	140	1,003,100.00	39.16	31.67	39.01	16.98
Gazprom	51,680	1,000,008.00	39.39	37.08	39.56	25.43
LUKOIL	574	999,908.00	37.50	36.70	37.41	24.75
Rosneft	4,569	999,925.65	46.72	50.44	46.49	17.28
RusGidro	606,428	999,999.77	45.77	47.45	46.54	15.19
Sberbank	9,599	1,000,023.82	47.73	46.35	47.93	20.19
Sberbank (pref)	13,316	1,000,031.60	49.59	48.13	49.48	26.52
Severstal	1,924	1,000,191.40	57.88	47.41	56.83	14.94
Portfolio	MRC under Basel II[1]	9,985,858.23	38.13	42.23	38.34	
	MRC under Basel III[2]		85.26	89.35	85.47	15.71

[1] By formula (1) with $m = 3$.
[2] By formula (2) with $m_c = m_s = 3$.

Conclusion

The modifications of the internal models approach introduced by the Basel Committee in 2009 bring about a significant increase in minimum regulatory capital for market risk due to a stressed VaR add-on. Although some banks have long reserved economic capital against a loss that might be incurred during a market crisis, they mostly used scenario-based stress testing to size up such a loss. The Basel Committee requires obtaining this estimate with the same VaR-models banks use under normal market conditions. This might potentially entail significant approximation errors for non-linear positions if large price shocks are modeled using a linear approximation to changes of risk factors. The multiplier applied to translate a stressed VaR into the regulatory capital lacks a clear economic explanation. Moreover, under some plausible conditions, it can produce a capital requirement that exceeds the market value of the portfolio.

Some tentative calculations performed for a portfolio of liquid Russian stocks indicate that the new Basel III rules lead to more than a doubling of regulatory capital compared to the original 1996 version of internal models approach. Unlike Volcker Rule (U.S. Congress, 2010) that restricts proprietary derivatives trading and equity investments of U.S. banks, Basel III makes banks increasingly cover market risk of their portfolios with their own funds. Unsurprisingly, the internal models approach may lose its incentive-compatible design for banks that are currently using it and become even less attractive for banks working under the standardized approach.

References

Bank Rossii (2007) O Poryadke Rascheta Kreditnymi Organizatsiyami Velichiny Rynochnogo Riska [Bank of Russia (2007) On the Procedure of Calculating the Value of Market Risk by Credit Institutions] Vestnik Banka Rossii 68 (1012)

Bank Rossii (1999) O Poryadke Rascheta Kreditnymi Organizatsiyami Razmera Rynochnykh Riskov [Bank of Russia (1999) On the Procedure of Calculating the Size of Market Risks by Credit Institutions] Vestnik Banka Rossii, 60 (404): 27–42

Basel Committee on Banking Supervision (1988) International Convergence of Capital Measurement and Capital Standards. Basle, July, updated to 1997, April

Basel Committee on Banking Supervision (2006) International Convergence of Capital Measurement and Capital Standards: A Revised Framework. Comprehensive Version. Basel 2006 June

Basel Committee on Banking Supervision (2009) Revisions to the Basel II Market Risk Framework. Basel 2009 July

Best P (2000) Stress Testing. In Lore M, Borodovsky L (eds.) The Professional's Handbook of Financial Risk Management. Oxford Butterworth-Heinemann, 2000, pp. 233-260

Holtdorf C, Muck M, Rudolf M (2004) The New Basel Capital Accord. In Frenkel M, Hommel U, Rudolf M (eds.) Risk Management: Challenge and Opportunity, 2nd edn. Berlin: Springer Verlag, pp. 79–98

Kupiec PH, O'Brien JM (1997) The Pre-Commitment Approach: Using Incentives to Set Market Risk Capital Requirements. FRB Finance and Economics Discussion Series No. 14, Board of Governors of the Federal Reserve System

Jeffery C (2006) Taking Exception. Risk 2006 (August): 36–39

Lobanov AA (2009) Integrirovanny Risk-Menedzment na Urovne Predpriyatiya [Integrated Enterprise-Wide Risk Management] In Entsiklopediya Finansovogo Risk-Menedzhmenta, 4-e izd. [Encyclopedia of Financial Risk Management, 4th edn.] Moscow Alpina Business Books, Chapter 8, pp. 575–701

Lobanov A, Kainova E (2005) Sravnitel'ny Analiz Metodov Rascheta VaR-Limitov Uchtom Model'nogo Riska na Primere Rossiskogo Rynka Aktsi [Methods for Setting VaR Limits with an Adjustment for Model Risk on the Russian Stock Market: A Comparative Study] Upravlenie finansovymi riskami, 2005, 1: 44–55

Lucas A (1998) Testing Backtesting: An Evaluation of the Basle Guidelines for Backtesting Internal Risk Management Models of Banks. Research memorandum 1998-I, Vrije Universiteit Amsterdam

Monet C (2001) JP Morgan Chase's Economic Capital Framework. Presentation to GARP 2nd Global Risk Management Convention. JPMorgan, New York, Marriott WTC

Rattaggi ML (2000) International Regulatory Requirements for Risk Management (1988–1998). In Lore M, Borodovsky L (eds.) The Professional's Handbook of Financial Risk Management. Oxford Butterworth-Heinemann, pp. 690–739

U.S. Congress (2010) Dodd-Frank Wall Street Reform and Consumer Protection Act. Washington, 2010 July 21 Section 619 Available via Internet: http://www.gpo.gov/fdsys/pkg/BILLS-111hr4173ENR/pdf/BILLS-111hr4173ENR.pdf Accessed 26 Feb 2011

Belarusian Banking System: Market Risk Factors

Svetlana Malykhina

Member of Risk Management Committee of Belarusian Banks Association, Minsk, Republic of Belarus. email: s.malykhina@mail.by

Abstract The need for effective risk management in order to minimize the negative impact of risk factors on the activities of the bank, which would meet the current demands of the developing domestic financial market and would be consistent with international standards, is now in a leading position in the system of management of the bank. Therefore, a key objective of market risk management in banks of the Republic of Belarus is to identify the factors of occurrence of these risks and limit their negative impact on capital and the bank's activities with the help of various tools within the risk management strategy selected by the bank.

Keywords: Market Risk, Risk Factors, Risk Management, Risk Strategy, Internal Control

JEL classification: G21, G32

Introduction

For a comprehensive analysis of factors affecting everything from the sustainability of the banking system of Belarus to the market risks in a developing economy as a whole, as well as the subsequent choice of the adequate management strategies at the level of the individual bank, the following main categories of the influencing factors are distinguished, with an account of their manageability:

- external factors (global economic, political, regulatory) – uncontrollable;
- internal factors of a systemic nature (intra-country and economic, political and regulatory intra-sectoral) – relatively uncontrollable, i.e. possible indirect impact of banks on individual factors; and
- internal factors of an individual nature (financial condition and risk management at individual banks, their behavior in the market) – controlled, i.e. possible transformation of the individual factors in the internal factors of a systemic nature.

Market Risk Factors Analysis

The external factors affecting the susceptibility of banks to market risks primarily include the following global factors affecting the stability of the banking sector as a

D. Sornette et al. (Eds.), *Market Risk and Financial Markets Modeling*,
DOI 10.1007/978-3-642-27931-7_14,

whole, as well as the formation of regulatory requirements and recommendations for the organization of the risk management systems (including market risks) at banks:

- ***The level of social and economic development of Belarus, movement towards the integration the Belarusian economy into the world economy.*** Important real steps in this direction were the assignment of a number of ratings of international social and economic development to the Republic of Belarus, such as "Doing Business" (58-th place in the world), as well as the credit ratings of Moody's Investors Service and Standard & Poors. This contributed to increasing the investment attractiveness of the country for all investors, made it possible for the banks (including those without external credit ratings) to borrow resources at lower interest rates, and opened up the prospect of obtaining credit ratings for companies. Also, the assigned country rating allowed the issue in 2010-2011 of the first Belarusian Eurobonds, totaling USD 1.8 billion. These had a maturity of not less than 5 years, were listed on the Luxembourg Stock Exchange, and were originally assigned ratings similar to the sovereign ratings of Belarus – B1 (Moody's) / B + (Standard & Poors). The initial yield, which was determined including political risks, increased from 9% at issue to 12% in March (Figure 1), meaning a noticeable rise in the cost of new external borrowing through the placement of Eurobonds;

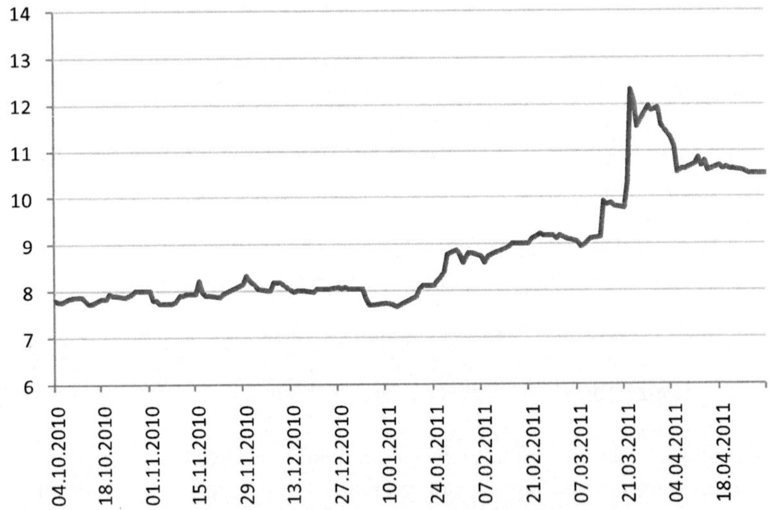

Fig. 1: The Dynamics of Yield of Belarusian Eurobonds placed in January 2011 (%)

- ***Impact of the global financial crisis of 2008-2010,*** which manifested itself as a drop in the rate of economic development of the main economic partners (out of 160 trading partners, the share of Russia and EU countries account for 40%), restricted the access of the Belarusian banks and their customers to external funding under ordinary conditions, reducing the foreign trade turnover, causing a fall in the volume and an increase in terms of hard currency of the proceeds of banks' customers from export;

- ***Economic sanctions imposed by the U.S.*** against the largest Belarusian companies-exporters (state concern Belneftekhim, Lakokraska, Belorusneft, Polotsk-Steklovolokno) for political reasons, which block the flow of payments and foreign exchange earnings, thereby increasing the level of currency risk of banks. To reduce the risks, the enterprise diversified markets for their products, but there is no doubt that the sanctions psychologically adversely affect the plans of potential foreign investors with respect to Belarus;
- ***The state of the Belarusian-Russian relations,*** which, in particular, are manifested in the form of an increase in the percentage of Russian investments in the total foreign investments in the country (from 30% in 2008 up to 70% in 2009.), a rise in energy prices and "dairy", "sugar" and other trade wars. These conditions destabilize the financial condition of Belarusian enterprises and banks that serve them, including major Russian subsidiaries (OJSC BPS-Bank, Belvnesheconombank, Belgazprombank, CJSC VTB Bank (Belarus), CJSC Alfa-Bank, OJSC Moscow-Minsk Bank, CJSC Belrosbank);
- ***Unifying management methods and techniques by banks and supervision at the global level,*** primarily through the efforts of the Basel Committee on Banking Supervision. Since 2005 in the Republic of Belarus,single basic (thesimplest) approaches are set for all banks for the calculation of regulatory capital to cover credit, market (interest, stock, currency, commodity) and operational risks in accordance with Basel II. Since 2009, the banks have been allowed to calculate the operational risk using the standardized approach SA (depending upon the banks' readiness, under validation of the National bank);
- ***Increase in responsiveness of international organizations and regulators developing management standards and recommendations.*** The Republic of Belarus, when it is connected by one degree or another to the economies of other countries, is interested in establishing common rules in the banking field. In view of that, the National Bank, since the release of Basel II, monitors documents of the Basel Committee on Banking Supervision on a regular basis, as well as analysing them for possible use in the national banking legislation, taking into account the peculiarities of our banking system. There has already been issued a number of guidance documents on management of operational, credit, interest rate and liquidity risk, on the risks associated with outsourcing in financial services, on conducting stress testing, on the organization of corporate governance and on internal auditing activities. Currently, the proposed standards for capital and liquidity in Basel III are under consideration.

The internal factors of a systemic nature that affect the susceptibility of banks to market risks include:

- ***Problems associated with meeting the budget deficit,*** a negative balance of trade which amounted to USD 7425.6 million at the beginning of 2011, such as the need to return the growing external debt (10% of GDP), the solution of which will depend on the state's ability to provide resource support to banks;

- ***The formation of the financial market*** – to raise its level, the Ministry of Finance has developed a concept which gives an idea of trends in the development of existing market players (banks, insurance companies, the organization of the securities market infrastructure), targets the emergence and development of new organizations, mainly non-bank financial institutions, and provides for creation of a system of monitoring and thus prevention of crisis in the financial market;
- ***The formation of the securities market*** – for its development the Program of Corporate Securities Market Development was adopted in 2008-2010. The main goal of the Program was to create the necessary conditions for the emergence of a holistic, liquid, transparent and efficient securities market as part of the financial market, integrated into the global securities market and attracting investments. Almost everything that was planned in the Program has been implemented: reversal of golden share, reduced taxes on income from securities (with the decision to refer the issues of costs to the cost), conducted a step-by-step removal of restrictions on the disposal of shares under moratorium that were introduced in 1998. A secondary circulation began to develop; emissions of corporate bonds increased (from BYR 300 bln. to more than BYR 10 trln.), as well as the number of issuers (from 7 to more than 150) and the number of non-bank issuers and the share of their bonds in the total emissions (from 5% to 15%). The new tools, such as commercial papers and paperless mortgages appeared in the securities market, and in two banks funds of bank management were created. The new Development Program for 2011-2015 is strategic in nature and is aimed at the introduction of new instruments to the securities market, the formation of investors, and preparation of the law on investment funds (collective investors of long-term resources);
- ***Development of the Belarusian Currency and Stock Exchange,*** which is responsible for the organization, provision and development of securities markets of all kinds in terms of the procedures and mechanisms for the listing, trading, provision of depository services, and by performing clearing of exchange transactions involving securities and providing information services to investors in the Republic of Belarus. The Currency and Stock Exchange is a universal one (it trades in currency, securities and derivatives thereof), its infrastructure is adequate to the scope and nature of operations in the financial market of the country. Interaction with members is organized in three sections. Under the Currency Market Section the daily trades in foreign currencies are performed (the major currencies – the U.S. dollar, the Euro, the Russian ruble); the total volume of all types of currencies in 2009 amounted to BYR 39.4 trln. Today the FX rates formed on the basis of trades are included in the category of core indicators of the Forex market. The Stock Market Section is staffed by two sectors – government securities and securities of the National Bank of Belarus, as well as corporate securities. The total volume of stock trades in securities of all types in 2009 amounted to more than BYR 42 trln., with OTC – BYR 4.7 trln. Under the Futures Market Section, fixed-term financial instruments have been traded since 2004 (futures contracts on FX rates and interest rates on the government securities market);

- ***Institutional imbalance in the financial sector.*** In 2009, 96.8% of total assets were accounted for by banks (as of January 1, 2011, there are 31 banks operating), 3.2% by insurance companies. In this market there are no financial institutions such as pension funds, mutual and other investment funds, venture capital, factoring and other companies. This is limiting the ability of domestic investment, diversification and hedging of risks;
- ***Dominance of the money market of short-term funds,*** subjected to severe fluctuations in the case of movement of speculative capital and to the absence of a long-term capital market;
- ***Readiness of banks to enter the international financial capital markets,*** the realization of which will sharply increase the level of market risk, and will require a mandatory organization of market risk management (or a correcting of the existing one). According to foreign analysts, the country has gone from almost complete obscurity of foreign investment to the favorable climate of being recognized by the World Bank;
- ***Assignment of credit ratings by international rating agencies to a number of banks,*** which has made it possible for the banks to borrow resources at lower interest rates. As of January 1, 2010, the three leading agencies assigned ratings to the ten largest Belarusian banks, but in early 2011, they were all reduced, which means an increased cost of resources for these banks and increases in the interest rate risk;
- ***Growth of foreign investments in the banking sector –*** in 2009, the share of nonresidents in the aggregate authorized fund of the sector reached 27.3% (due to the sale of JSC BPS-Bank to the Savings Bank of Russia), and the number of banks controlled by foreign capital rose to 23, which means that getting access to the cheaper resources of foreign investors directly affects the interest policy of the Belarusian banks, and increases competition in the market of banking services;
- ***State domination in the banking sector*** (still more than 80% of the statutory fund). During 2009, the Herfindahl-Hirschman Index grew to 0.2366 in terms of assets and 0.2247 in terms of capital, which indicates the presence of the risk of concentration and limitation of the level of internal competition between banks, and increases the desire to develop a market of alternative market-based instruments;
- ***Participation of banks in the financing of priority public programs*** that significantly reduces their profitability and provokes non-market approaches to managing interest rate risk;
- ***A significant proportion of foreign exchange component in the assets and liabilities*** (42.0% and 30.7% respectively on January 1, 2010), significant increases in the open FX position (ratio of total foreign exchange position to the bank's regulatory capital increasedfrom 8.7% to 11.7% in 2009), increasing dollarization of the economy (share of foreign-exchange component in the broad money supply in 2009 increased by 12 percentage points), all of which are a significant source of foreign exchange risk. One reason for realization of this risk is the currency devaluation by 20%, conducted on January 2, 2009. This also adversely

affected the repayment of foreign currency loans, including retail, whose volume in 2008 increased by 87.4%, and caused a raise in the level of credit risk. To reduce these risks for both banks and the households in a period of financial instability, the National Bank first suspended the issuance of foreign exchange loans to individuals, and then fully prohibited them;

- ***Inflation and devaluation expectations*** associated with both the impact of the global financial crisis, and with the fears based on historical examples of the recent past, which destabilize the national currency, increase the volatility in the FX market and are a source of foreign exchange risk. In particular, such expectations are changing the preferences of the population with respect to currency savings. Thus, in 2009, the balances of households' funds in the national currency in bank accounts grew by only 3.6% in nominal terms while foreign currency deposits grew by 83.4% in the BYR equivalent, and by 40.9% in the USD equivalent, which increases the banks' short currency position. In February-March 2011, devaluation expectations intensified once again, forcing the National Bank, jointly with the Government of the Republic of Belarus, to take a series of urgent temporary measures in order to maintain and increase gold reserves, as well as creating conditions to encourage the export activities of enterprises and reduce currency risk;
- ***Changes in legislation, including banking*** – amendments to regulations relating to the legal acts of the Belarusian banks and the establishment of prudential requirements to them, are made almost every year (as planned) and more often (on special occasions, including under pressure of some large banks); changes in tax and customs regulations also have significant impact on banks.

The internal factors of individual character, affecting the susceptibility of banks to market risks, include the following factors that are common to the majority of banks in the Republic of Belarus:

- ***The structure and size of the bank's position, subject to market risks,*** which depend on the nature and scale of the transactions of the individual bank, the amount and stability of the trade, investment, and commodity portfolios, the income by foreign exchange, and the maturity mismatch of assets and liabilities etc.;
- ***The bank's strategy with respect to market risk,*** which is particularly reflected in the definition of risk appetite and subsequent monitoring of its value, or in a lack of strategy that generates a stochastic style of market risk management. For example, the level of currency risk is influenced by such strategic factors, such as the effectiveness of hedging foreign exchange positions (narrowing of position's maturity gap, hedging income, use of financial instruments such as futures and options), and the discrepancy in volume and timing between the positions of foreign and local currency, which is a chronic problem for Belarusian banks. Thus, on October 1, 2010, in the banking sector, the share of foreign exchange component in the clients' deposits was 40.1% (USD 7,157.0 million), whereas in the credits it was 27.3% (USD 7,427.9 million);

- ***Complication of management organization as a natural consequence of more complex activities of banks.*** This process has generally an objective character that is associated with the development of business of the banks' customers and the economy as a whole and access to international capital markets. However, the Belarusian banks should guard against the temptation to complicate their work, carrying out operations with poorly examined or doubtful derivatives and other financial instruments, including using borrowed funds, which could trigger a sharp increase in the level of risk due to the unwillingness of banks to manage them;
- ***Optimization of the banks' organizational structure.*** Currently in the Republic of Belarus several trends of structural transformations can be traced, which are due either to the strategy of foreign owners of Belarusian banks or to the other banks' desire to follow the best in their opinion management decisions, namely: the transformation of affiliates (branches) of the largest banks into structural units (CBU, RCC, additional offices, etc.) that have no self-balance; the opening of numerous remote locations for the sale of credit products directly from the point of sale of credit products (typical of retail banks); a banks' merger in order to meet capital requirements or for other subjective reasons, which, however, have a single character. These structural changes involve changes in the systems of risk management and internal controls and the formulation of a new task – to achieve the ultimate objective of the structural transformation of the bank, which usually is the optimization of business processes and the reduction of costs of the bank;
- ***Foreign top-managers accession to the Belarusian banks.*** A natural consequence of the influx of foreign investment in the banks of Belarus became the influx of foreign top-managers that sometimes even do not speak Russian, not to mention Belarusian, sent by the owners to implement the management systems adopted in the parent bank, and to implement what is called on-site control. In practice, the difference in mentalities, lack of understanding of local conditions and their unsuitability to the infused model of bank management often gives rise to conflicts of interest between such "Vikings" and local managers at the bank in the process of adjusting the current system of internal control and risk management to the new demands of the owners. This directly affects the quality of bank management in general;
- ***Lack of effective organization of corporate governance, risk management and internal controls in banks*** leads to some banks not being able to ensure the correct positioning in the market, including in international financial capital markets (where compliance with the best corporate governance standards is a mandatory requirement). This is needed to form strong mutually beneficial relations with customers and investors, comply with legislation and local acts, to maintain acceptable level of accepted risks and capital to cover them, as well as the proper level of business reputation and competitiveness;
- ***Inadequate level of automated systems of risk management*** in general and, primarily, in the management of market risks, which is almost impossible to measure without an automated information management system. The National Bank

developed the Concept of Automated Risk Management of Banking Activities in the Republic of Belarus (ARMS), which contains a number of basic requirements for an Automated Risk Management System, regardless of its developer (the bank, the parent bank, an IT company, the National Bank): adaptation to the requirements of legislation of the Republic of Belarus, regulatory legal acts of the National Bank, recommendations on risk management methodology for their assessment, internal controls, corporate governance; integration of all data sources into a single database, integration with internal accounting and operating automated systems of the bank; providing information processing and conduct calculations to assess, monitor and control risks (credit, operational, market, liquidity risk); implementation of modern methods of analyzing bank activity; presentation of information in the form of reporting and online analytical processing based on multidimensional data models; meeting international safety standards.

Use of Market Risk Factors

Based on the identified quantitative factors affecting market risk capital and bank activity, the degree of each risk (low – medium – high) can be determined based on qualitative factors – the quality of risk management (good – satisfactory – unsatisfactory), andthe extent to which quality control determines the level of risk (low – medium – high). The proposed scale is quite simple and versatile and can be used to assess the level of any market risk. Depending on the degree of controllability of the factors, the bank chooses the risk strategy and, accordingly, risk management tools (Table 1).

Table 1: Market Risk Management Strategy Selection

	Factors Category	Degree of Manageability	Selected Strategy
	External Global	Uncontrolled	Acceptance
			Acceptance
	Internal Systemic	Relatively uncontrolled	Control
			Avoidance
Market Risk Factors			Acceptance
			Control
	Internal Individual		Avoidance
		Controlled	Insurance
			Diversification

It is also advisable to use the identified influence factors in determining the risk appetite and the optimal level of market risk in the bank, the rationale for setting limits (constraints), as well as to select the shock parameters for stress tests.

Conclusion

The current stage of development of the banking system of Belarus is characterized by its gradual steady integration into the global banking system, its attraction of foreign investment and the development of the stock and currency market as well as the new markets for our country: derivatives, precious metals and stones at banks, which will inevitably lead to the emergence of market risks, as well as strengthening their impact on capital and the stability of the banks. The identification of these risk factors is necessary to create an effective management system that ensures the maintenance of market risk at an optimal level determined by the bank in order to minimize the potentially significant losses caused by the market risks.

References

Basel Committee on Banking Supervision. International Convergence of Capital Measurements and Capital Standards. A Revised Framework. Comprehensive Version. Basel 2006 June

Kallaur P.V. (2007). Razvitije risk-menedzhmenta v bankakh [Risk Management Development in Banks] Bankovskij Vestnik 31 (396)

Malykhina S. (2010). Sovremennyje metody otsenki (izmerenija) rynochnykh riskov [Modern Methods of Market Risks' Assessment (Measurement)] Bankovskij Vestnik 10 (483), 13 (486)

Malykhina S. (2010). Risk-menedzhment skvoz prizmu korporativnogo upravlenija [Risk Management in the Light of Corporate Governance] Bankovskij Vestnik 25 (498)

Natsionalny Bank Respubliki Belarus (2006). Instruktsija o normativakh bezopasnogo funktsionirovanija bankov i nebankovskikh kreditno-finansovykh organizatsij [National Bank of the Republic of Belarus (2006) Instructions on the requirements to secure functioning for financial institutions banks and non-bank credit and financial institutions]

Natsionalny Bank Respubliki Belarus (2009). Finansovaja stabilnost Resbubliki Belarus/Analiticheskoje Obozrenije [National Bank of the Republic of Belarus (2009) Financial Stability of the Republic of Belarus/Analitical Review]

Natsionalny Bank Respubliki Belarus, Sovet Ministrov Respubliki Belarus (2008). Programma razvitija rynka korporativnykh tsennykh bumag na 2008-2010 gody [National Bank of the Republic of Belarus, Council of Ministers of the Republic of Belarus (2008) Program of the corporate securities market development for 2008-2010 years]

Portret Belorusskoj valjutno-fondovoj birzhy (2011). [Belarusian Currency Stock Exchange Portrait]

The Psychological Aspects of Human Interactions Through Trading and Risk Management Process

Polina Mikhailova

Psychotherapist, trainings developer, Moscow, Russia.
email: polina-derivatives@yandex.ru

Abstract The "Copernican Revolution" in psychology performed by Sigmund Freud brought bright light to the phenomenon that a human being's behaviour is strongly driven by forces of his/her unconscious. Risk management is no doubt a discipline that is extremely affected by human unconscious-driven decisions. Here the author proposes a theoretical psychological approach based on a personal 10-year practice as a market risk manager in top Russian banks, an investment company and the MICEX Derivatives department. Ideologically and instrumentally, this approach uses such theories and concepts as transactional analysis (ego state model, transactions and scripts), fixation, psychological defence etc. To verify the applicability of the main concepts, the author performs a psychological study. Its results illustrate that a risk manager strongly shifts to formal, criticizing self-style in professional interactions with a trader, and emphasize the keen importance of increasing risk managers' self-awareness. Moreover, the author provides an ideological framework with practical recommendations for the risk manager, trader and risk manager's professional society. It includes various psychological tests for traders, a comprehensive investigation of the trader's unconscious personal life script (by synthesizing the statistical and psychological methods), and "Know Yourself " as the new principle (the building block of enterprise-wide risk management). A risk manager should be brightly conscious of his/her inner scenarios driving his/her reactions in decision-making. Otherwise risk management itself is under the high risk of becoming financial industry brake.

Keywords: Psychology, Interaction, Self-Awareness, Loss, Script

JEL classification: A12, C18, D74, G32

Introduction

Risk management is the discipline that is intended to do the best to cope with risk. And the very "risk" is no doubt the psychological phenomenon. It is represented in human consciousness as uncertainty, which acts as the "black screen", driving the human being to make personal projections upon it (according to Freudian psychoanalytical concepts).

Moreover, if the source of risk is identified as "human behaviour and all mistakes that could originate from it" (subset of operational risk), or if risk manage-

D. Sornette et al. (Eds.), *Market Risk and Financial Markets Modeling*,
DOI 10.1007/978-3-642-27931-7_15, © Springer-Verlag Berlin Heidelberg 2012

ment is a process of interaction between human beings (as it is in corporate life), the role of understanding unconscious psychological forces becomes vital for risk management efficacy.

How can we manage uncertainty if we are not aware of our own inner unconscious fantasies, or projections of them? And more, how can we help other people, say, in the trading and investment department, manage their (even not our own!) risks in this situation (speaking more precisely, we as risk managers pretend not only to help, but also to teach and to lead others in coping with risks)?

Certainly, no person (perhaps excluding those who have reached enlightenment), is free of his/her unconscious forces. Nevertheless, there is the very good example of a broad professional society that is intended to help other people manage their lives notwithstanding those restrictions of the human mind. We mean psychotherapy. Its philosophy, connected with its practical structure, is built very wisely, requiring the psychotherapy professionals to go through their own thorough psychotherapy first, before they even begin to practice, and providing them with a supervision mechanism during all professional life, which effectively helps them become more conscious in situations with clients. There is no stop, no final point of excellence where even a world famous therapist can rest in a "know-everything" air.

Indeed, it seems to be very sensible to take a look at the related psychotherapy industry (no kidding – because of its analogous orientation to "coping with people's manifestations"). One doesn't need to become a therapist himself/herself, and there is no need to go through a ten-year personal psychoanalysis in order to apply the basic principles of psychotherapy in risk management. It is possible to take some of its useful and flexible tools, such as basic concepts of transactional analysis, for instance.

Characteristic Transactions Between Risk Manager and Trader

Transactional analysis (TA) is the theory of Eric Berne (1964), a Canadian-born psychiatrist, who himself studied psychoanalysis under Dr. Paul Federn, an early, important follower of Sigmund Freud. The ego state model (Parent-Adult-Child) is one of the most widely spread ideas that TA is known for – and sometimes, it is erroneously called a primitive, "simplified version of psychoanalysis". But transactional analysis' plainness is deceptive: TA is a deep integrative approach to the theory of psychology and psychotherapy, and, due to its structural simplicity, is flexible and effective.

According to TA, people manifest themselves in real life (behave, feel, and think) through three ego states: Parent, Adult and Child (fig.1).

In the **Parent** ego state people display themselves in an unconscious imitation of how their parents (or authority figures) acted in the person's childhood (or, more precisely, how people perceived the activities of those figures).

In the **Adult** ego state people are devoted to an objective appraisal of reality – dealing with reason and rationality, gathering information, solving problems, drawing conclusions. It is a bit like a computer processing information (though it is not deprived of some specific emotions – feeling "structural beauty" of a theorem, masterpiece or abstract idea, or "strictly genital" sexual feelings).

In the **Child** ego state people behave, feel and think like they did in childhood. The Child is the source of emotions, creation, spontaneity and intimacy, risk taking, jocosity, flirt, "romantic" sexual feelings – and on the other side, compliance and servility or rebelliousness.

There are subdivisions[1] within Parent and Child ego states: **Nurturing Parent** (caring, permission-giving, protecting) or **Controlling Parent** (comparing to family norms, social traditions and moral ideals), and **Adapted Child** or **Natural (Free) Child**.

Natural Child behaves freely, naturally, without limitations (in this ego state a person smiles, runs, shouts, laughs when he or she joyful, and cries when he or she wants to cry). **Adapted Child** behaves in response to parents, important figures or society, and is, in-turn, subdivided into **Positive Child** (who does his/her best to execute all he/she wants, to fulfil all those requirements) and **Negative Child** (who reacts in strictly opposite way[2] – "not to perform" anything he/she wants).

As one can see, Parent and Child ego state are, at least in the beginning, inherited by the person (from his/her real childhood). Further, all ego states develop and become more complex.

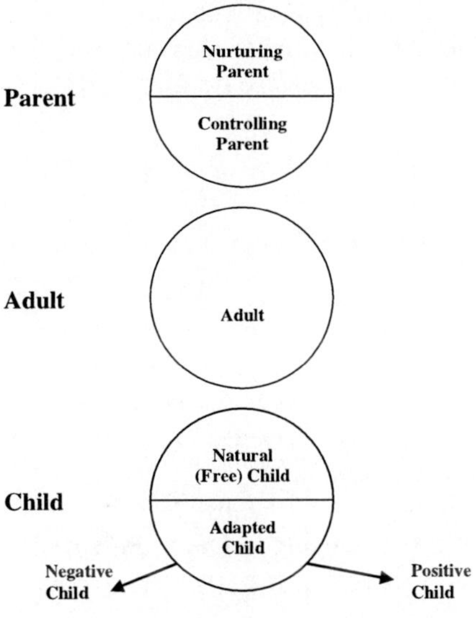

Fig. 1: Ego state model

[1] This is one of available structures of Parent and Child. Some authors subdivide Child into three separate parts – Adapted Child, Free Child and Little Professor; some include two parts into Nurturing Parent, Controlling Parent and Natural Child – "negative" and "positive".

[2] There is a tricky moment: Negative Child's reactions are not free. They are the same way stipulated by the outer environment, its' rules, assessments, opinions. They are in some amount automatic. So, if one behaves in the way «they won't make me do that! » (a «teenager's» character) it is not the manifest of real mental freedom, it is nearly the same mental or emotional bound as Positive Child shows! That is why Negative child is the equal part of Adapted Child.

But how do ego states manifest themselves in usual life? As most of us know, people frequently can be in dialog with themselves, "speaking voices" into their heads[3]. Good news is that it is not a kind of schizophrenia (hopefully, in most cases). It is the very common way the inner dialog is structured: by the contact of different ego states with each other. More broadly, the interaction of inner ego states organizes people's decision-making and behaviour.

The important feature is that there is no "right" or "correct" or "healthy" or "best" ego-state! Each ego state performs its function. We can only talk about more or less adequate human behaviour, which in terms of TA corresponds to more or less adequate switching of ego-state in a real situation. This can be illustrated through the concept of the transaction.

Transaction is the unit of each human interaction. It consists of *stimulus* and *response***.** Stimulus is sent when the first person *contacts* the second person from *one's own ego state* to *some ego state of the second person***.** A response appears when the second person "*replies*" *from his/her own ego state* to *some ego state of the first person.*

Those ego states can be the same or can differ. During the transaction, it is possible to use 1 to 4 ego states (one or two producing the stimulus and one or two forming the response).

If the response is completely parallel to stimulus (e.g. Child-Parent response is given to Parent-Child stimulus), the transaction is called **complementary**. Let us provide two simple examples (see also fig.2).

Example 1:
Stimulus: "Have you noticed at which level the Dow Jones fixed yesterday?" (Adult to Adult)

Response: "Yes, it was a 0.5% drop." (Adult to Adult)

Example 2:
Stimulus: "I am waiting for my daily report from your department!" (Parent to Child)

Response 1: "Excuse me, Mr. James, just a second! It is not my fault; it was a delay from the back office!" (Positive Child to Parent).

Another variant of response:

Response 2 (abruptly): "I have heaps of work, so I will not bring it not before I finish my previous report" (Negative Child to Parent).

3 For instance, some part of me speaks to me: "I want to sleep! I hate finishing this paper!" and forces my body to bed. It is my Negative Child. (But on the other side it can be my Natural Child, and it is really a question as to what ego state is turned on). And my Controlling Parent replies without compassion: "You must!" As the final result, you read this article.

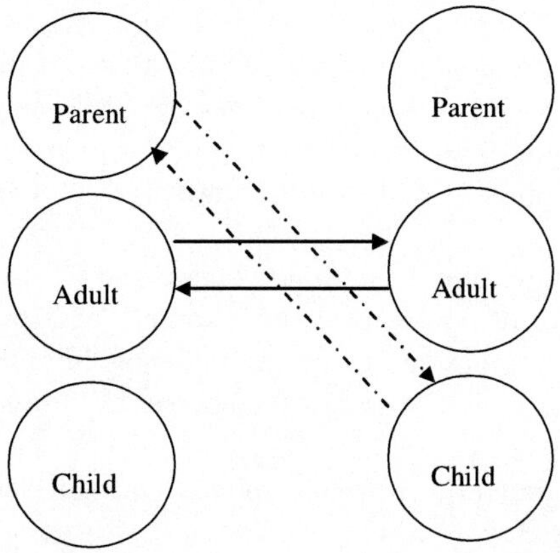

Fig. 2: Complementary transactions. Solid line – example 1, dotted line – example 2

As you can see, communications like this are (at least locally) psychologically balanced.

However, a wide variety of communication failures can be described by a **crossed transaction**: when response is *sent* from an*other ego state than that from which the stimulus was received*, or when a response *addresses another ego state than that from which the stimulus was sent* (or even *both* of these miscommunications, as it is shown at fig.3). Crossed transaction can be the basis for enormous number of conflicts.

Example 3:
Stimulus: "Have you noticed at which level Dow Jones fixed yesterday?" (Adult to Adult)

Response: "It's none of your business!" (Child to Parent)

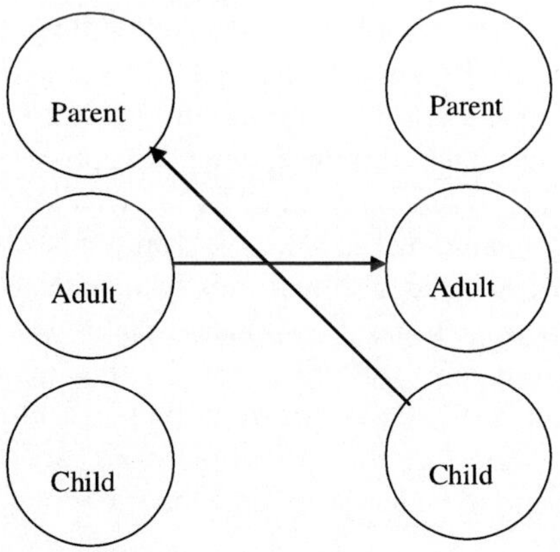

Fig. 3: Crossed transaction (example 3)

Back from theory to our interactions in financial world. Risk management consists of comprehensive information processing and analysis, which implies a strong Adult ego state presence. The results of risk management analysis must be the subject of regular presentations to other departments, as a part of a broad business process, which presupposes Adult–Adult transactions between parties (in both directions).

Though not pretending to make a broad generalization, it is worth noting that a characteristic position of a risk manager may sound peevish, for example, "those traders only want to gain more and more and they absolutely don't care about risk they take!" Risk managers often manifest themselves as "judging" persons, in an "I – know" manner.

No wonder that the trader quite often responds symmetrically, for example "you know nothing about the Real Market, you academic worm!"

The bad news is that this kind of interaction shows no sign of that "ideal" complete four-ego-states Adult-Adult transaction. This characteristic stimulus is that of Controlling Parent to Child! And small wonder that it gets quite natural response – from Negative Child to Controlling Parent. Overall, the transaction looks like aggressive fencing (as is shown in fig.2, example 2, response 2).

An even more lamentable case arises when the risk manager behaves in an honest Adult-Adult manner, but the trader, who get accustomed to the "all-risk managers'" judging position responds nearly automatically from Negative Child to Controlling Parent , building up the crossed transaction (see fig.3).

We further illustrate this behavioural hypothesis by research data.

"Life Script of Loss" Written by Trader in Early Childhood: Discovery

According to TA, each person can have his/her personal **script**. A script is a life plan, in its structure and contours it is analogous to a little personal Myth. A person begins writing his/her own life script in early childhood, and although it is revised throughout life, the script is almost complete by his/her teens. In early age, the script is decisional, i.e. chosen in response to the perception of the world (mostly of parents or other influential figures) and in order to make sense of living.

Though in the early beginning the script was our choice, for the grown-up person it is nearly completely unconscious, mostly outside awareness. Only some markers – strangely repetitive occasions, situation patterns – can implicitly show us that our life is partly "guided by mysterious force"and is out of our control.

The interesting point is that the script structure is directly programmed by person in early childhood, almost in the sense of the word "script" not as a "scenario", but as a "computer program"! That gives us an extra hope that some cases can be found programmatically.

Script can be positive, "a script of a winner", but unfortunately, most human scripts are destructive. It may sound like "I am not worthy", "I am not good enough to be wealthy", "It is immoral to make a big profit", "I can get some money, but I must pay for it by something else". A life script might include "not to gain any profit", or "not to gain easily", "to lose several times before winning once" and so on. These patterns can be found in trader's performance, in the way he/she reacts in similar market conditions, personally significant dates, life marks etc.

Let us consider several cases when a trader's "loss script" can be "turned on".

- The pattern **"to have large unrealized profit and to lose it in one moment"**, when a position becomes very profitable, but is not closed for a long time. And after the price at last goes in a negative direction, it is "suddenly" fixed close to zero profit point, as if the trader "waited" for the moment when nearly all unrealized profit at last expires. In terms of TA, it is the script reward of Tantalus, the mythological hero who cannot eat or drink, though infinite amount of delicious food and beverages are always besides him. In this case, the "realized P&L[4] to integral unrealized P&L" ratio for the given period must be sufficiently small, which can be considered a *script marker.*
- The symmetrical case of **«quick panic sell»**, when the market price of a «just open» position goes (for short time) in negative direction. That forces the trader to close the position as soon as possible. But then price quickly draws back and moves to profitable region, because it was only a small technical dropdown. (This will be discussed in some more details later, after «Fixations»).
- **Person-specific repetitive P&L patterns** (not seasonal or due to market correlation). It is purely statistical work to find P&L patterns that do not correlate with market indices and are not seasonal. If such patterns are found, the risk manager may search for correlations with personally significant dates (birthday, birthdays of relatives, dates of marriage or divorce, etc.), or government, professional and religious holidays. If no explanation is found, it could be that the dates or periods have a very personal meaning – and the risk manager's job is not to dig into the details, just to provide the trader with an interesting information feed.

To discover an underlying scenario is a purely psychological problem. But to determine those repetitive patterns could be a statistical or purely programmatic task, in which the risk manager is powerful.

Practice of Managing a "Script of Loss": Rewriting. Disassembling[5]

Script deciphering is very delicate work, which can in some circumstances be painful even under the guidance of experienced psychotherapist. A risk manager can do little with a trader's script directly. He or she only can, with a sincere, sympathetic and researcher's manner, go to the trader and, show him or her well illustrated results of P&L research.

---

[4] P&L is used as the abbreviation for "profit and loss"

[5] Let us repeat that "script" can be understood as a "scenario" and as a "program code". Just as scenario can be rewritten, the program code can be disassembled (deciphered).

If it is done well, in a polite and friendly way, it is possible that trader will hear his or her brother's (or sister's) voice saying something new about his/her own trading strategy. Further, they can go together through this quest of finding reasons for these "bad" patterns, or it can be enough for trader to make some conclusion alone.

And further, the trader's "script of loss" could in this way be uncovered (by the risk manager, trader and psychotherapist) and re-programmed (by psychotherapist only).

But the first obvious problem is that **it is impossible to force a trader** to go into **psychotherapy**. There are no psychological, ethical and legal circumstances for that. Psychotherapy is performed from the Adult position, not from the Child (trader) who is told to do it by the Controlling Parent (risk manager).

Second, deep psychotherapy, especially psychoanalysis, is a significantly long process.

It sounds reasonable to find the **balance** between a **"classic psychoanalytical"** and **practical "coaching"** approach. One good idea is to perform group **training** with the slogan something like "*to improve your own trading performance*". In this case, a person goes to training not to *heal* himself or herself from some psychological pathology, but to *improve* his/her performance. The training format is relatively "psychologically safe", and is much more rapid than personal psychotherapy.

Trader's Stress Profile, "Anal Fixation" Trading Style and Problem Gambling (Ludomania)

A trader is human, and may act "extremely human" in risky occasions. These extreme "peak" decisions could be a visible part of a long-term repetitive behaviour pattern originating from the inner personal life script (though in this paper the script analysis is oriented mostly at a quiet market).

Yet another way to foresee how a trader might behave in stressful situations is by studying the **psychological defence** mechanism.

Defence is an unconscious psychological process invoked to cope with reality. McWilliams (1994) subdivides these defences into primary and secondary. Some more detailed classifications are possible – for example, into pathological, immature, neurotic and mature defences.

Although mature defences are of a high adaptive function for a person, the more primitive a defence is, the more it acts to distort reality.

In this paper, the author brings examples of defences from various classifications, in which they might be called immature, **primitive defences**. In this context, *primitive isolation* (infantile reaction to stress by falling asleep), infantile illusion of *omnipotent control* (resulting in insidiousness, excessive risk taking and "stepping over" other people), *retreat into fantasy* (to resolve conflict), *passive aggression* (resulting in procrastination), *somatisation* (pain, illness, and anxiety), *projection* as a *primitive form of paranoia* (severe prejudice and vigilance) and *acting out* are worth noting.

Dominating defences are brought into play especially in stressful occasions. In this way, the kind of defence that dominates is very important information about trader. Knowing his/her defences, one is able to suggest how he or she will react in a situation of local (enterprise-wide) or global (worldwide) financial crisis.

A reasonable hypothesis is that if primitive defences dominate, it is a sign for the risk manager that this person could be not very adequate when crisis comes.

There are special tests, questionnaires available for psychoanalysts, which can show what kind of defence is dominating. Some of them could be realized as software, though those standard tests need to be adapted for a business situation. These tests can be made part of an all-over psychological test (e.g. when a new trader is passing an interview). This way a **trader's stress profile** can be built.

Another noticeable moment of trading style concerns fixations. Psychoanalysis states that humans may form a **psychological fixation** due to receiving traumatic experience during some psychosexual stage of development. There can be fixations at oral (from birth to 1 year), anal (1-3 years), phallic (3-6 years), latency and genital phases.

It may not seem very obvious, but **anal fixation** is especially interesting in terms of finance. It is the stage of active separation of personality from the rest of the world, but this separation is not completed yet. A traumatic experience at that stage may concern events when a little child sees something that came out of him/her, and feels it as a part of himself/herself. But parents may call "it" dirty, this way **de-valuing** the very little person – because the child concludes that personally he/she (not that part coming out of him/her) is dirty, bad.

Therefore anal fixation has much to do with concept of "**value**", and partially **money**. If the grown-up person tends to retain money (not to buy securities at a good moment) or to get rid of it (to sell securities in unvafourable moment), perhaps he or she had problems at this stage.

Knowing (for instance, by tests) that a person has a fixation at the anal stage may predict a style of trading strategy.

Going back to the before-mentioned "quick panic sell" loss script. This can be interpreted in terms of anal fixation. It is the stage dedicated to both bladder and bowel elimination, and if trader tends to quickly "wash away" a position, in may be said that he or she has problems to (both metaphorically and verbatim) "hold liquidity".

But the question is – what can be done about this? At the first stage, this is a risk to identify, but not to eliminate. Risk management, in cooperation with higher management, will be aware of the risks associated with these people, and taking into account their possible behaviour, will be able to develop special personal anti-crisis procedures for these traders.

The specific, and of greatest importance, case is **ludomania**, or **problem** (in severe cases – pathological) **gambling**. In some classifications it is an addiction (similar to chemical, as some studies indicate); in some it is an impulse control disorder (like kleptomania, pyromania). Such a person turns to third parties or performs illegal acts in order to obtain money, lying in order to hide the extent of gambling (according to DSM-IV (2000)). If this person is a trader, it is no doubt a very high danger for the organisation.

It is a great question whether early screening of ludomaniac person is possible. But author suppose that one important characteristic symptom, which sounds like **"trying to win back losses with more gambling"**, can also be found out programmatically, by analyzing consequent deals in line with their realized P&L.

Risk Manager's Psychological Profile: From Personal Life to Professional Interactions

After providing such a comprehensive analysis framework for the trader's personality, let us glance back to the risk manager. Being among the professional society, the author had the chance to study the ego state structure of risk managers. An objective appraisal is essential in order to prove the above-mentioned theses regarding characteristic transactions.

For the ego structure definition, a popular "word choice" questionnaire was used. In completing it, the person implicitly gave a self-estimate of his/her ego state activity (in terms of the "psychical energy" present in each of five ego states – Controlling Parent, Nurturing Parent, Adult, Natural Child and Adapted Child). This test reflects the «ego state profile» of a person[6] – i.e. points out how much each ego state is present in real life, how is it active, and how the person manifests it.

It is worth mentioning that this test cannot be "diagnostic", because there is no «good» ego state and no «ideal» ego state profile. But its results can be symptomatic, giving information to think about.

There were two tests taken – the first concerning "common life", and the second, some time later, after brightly pretending (modelling in mind) a realistic professional situation when the risk manager should defend his/her professional opinion against a trader (who actively opposes risk manager, willing to make an important deal which is "inappropriate in terms of risk") and the Credit or Asset and Liability Management Committee.

The test was taken by 48 persons who participated in Perm Winter School 2011, aged from 19 to 60 (11 men, 32 women, 5 anonymous). The percentage of "classical" industry risk manager professionals was not high, though a broad variety of close specializations were present – academic researchers, students, Ph.D. students, regulatory authorities and so on. The mean age (through those who mentioned it) was 26 years.

For each personal test, the peaks were taken, i.e. those ego states that showed maximum or minimum activity. The ego state that showed the maximum activity is

[6] Following some potential objections that this test does not show some metric of real social behaviour, but reflects only the inner state, the author emphasizes the following. First, real-time behavioural measuring is very complicated (if ever possible), and must be held over a long time in order to get a broad distribution of ego state manifestations, not just the one ego state which is present for one short period when all others are dormant. (It is especially complicated for the specific case of a 'risk manager in a professional situation', because of the objective difficulty in re-creating a series of these situations). Second, as it is mentioned further, a precise inner sense of emotional state and its appraisal are essential for self-awareness.

the dominating state, and the ego state that showed minimum activity is the most suppressed one for the person.

For each ego state, the total number of times it was a maximum or minimum value was calculated over the whole sample[7]. On the graphs (fig. 4) there is shown the total quantity of persons for whom Controlling Parent (or Nurturing Parent, and so on) is dominating (the raw "max") and is suppressed (the raw "min").

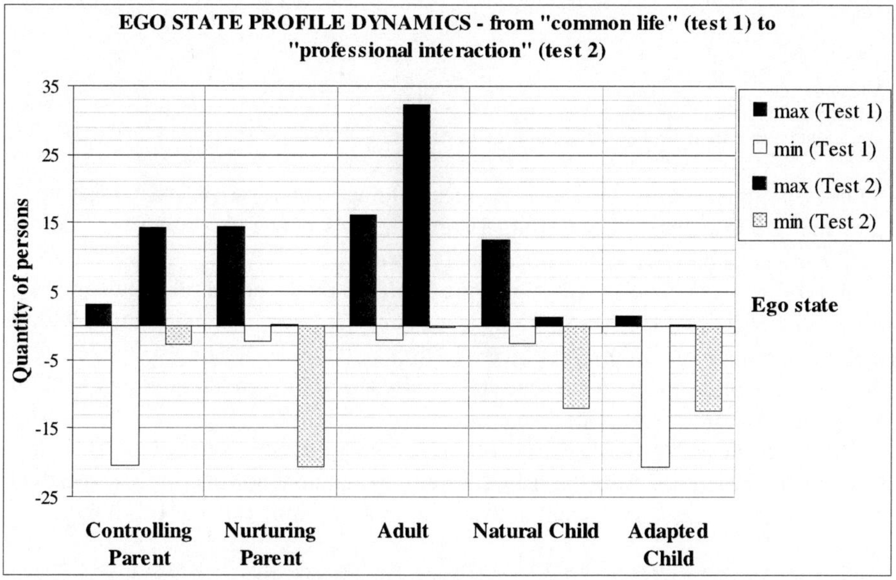

Fig. 4: Risk managers' society ego state profile dynamics. (Quantity of suppressed ego states is presented by negative numbers for the sake of graph's intelligibility)

Pleasingly, the test did not show that Controlling Parent strictly dominates over Adult in personal life (fig.4). The "Common life" ego state profile looks quite balanced: there is no obvious peak – the maximum is in Adult, but Nurturing Parent and Natural Child keep abreast of it. Controlling Parent is, surprisingly, suppressed (little maximums and many minimums). So is Adapted Child (do risk managers seem to be very adaptive?)

[7] In some observations, it was impossible to unambiguously define a minimum or maximum ego state (because two or more ego states showed an equal level of energy), so each of these ego states was counted as a peak, but the quantity was divided into normalizing coefficient (the number of "equal energy" ego states).

Table 1: Ego state profiles (Test 1 – "common life", Test 2 – "professional interaction")

Ego state	Quantity of persons			
	max (Test 1)	min (Test 1)	max (Test 2)	min (Test 2)
Controlling Parent	3,2	20,4	14,2	2,9
Nurturing Parent	14,5	2,4	0,2	20,5
Adult	16,2	2,2	32,2	0,2
Natural Child	12,5	2,5	1,2	12,0
Adapted Child	1,5	20,5	0,2	12,4

* Fractional numbers reflect the fact that for some persons several ego states were equally active

But the second test shows dramatic changes: interaction with a trader **strongly** activates the risk manager's Controlling Parent! It rises nearly 4,5 times (!), almost completely vanishing from the suppressed position.

Not bad news is that the Adult increases about 2 times, and there is no suppression in this ego state. It is the obvious leader now. It looks like negotiation with a trader requires the maximum presence of Adult skills.

Adapted Child sharply decreased its activity (even though already very little in Test 1), but became "not so suppressed".

But speaking of Nurturing Parent and Natural Child, who were very well manifested in "common life" profile, brings a quite lamentable outline: in this case they almost completely vanished from activity and both became the leaders of suppression.

Table 2: Ego state profile dynamics (from Test1 to Test2)

	Max change, %	Comment	Min change, %	Comment
Controlling Parent	343,8%	Rose 4,5 times and became the second leader of activity	-85,9%	Nearly vanished from suppression
Nurturing Parent	-98,6%	Vanished from activity	767,6%	Became the leader of suppression
Adult	98,8%	Rose 2 times and became the obvious leader of activity	-90,9%	*
Natural Child	-90,4%	Vanished from activity	375,0%	Became the second leader of suppression
Adapted Child	-87,0%	Vanished from activity	-39,8%	**

* We can say that Adult vanished from suppression, but it nearly wasn't suppressed even in the Test 1

** Adapted Child decreased its suppression, but its decrease was not very noticeable

We can supplement these results with another view and way of measurement – the mean/median value for activity (energy) of each ego state taken over all observations. Mean and median values showed to be very close to each other, so only mean value is presented on the graph (fig.5, table 3). Values are measured in % of the maximum possible in the test.

With this measurement there are also dramatic changes in Nurturing Parent and Natural Child – their energy is decreased about 2 times! Adapted Child is also suppressed. But Controlling Parent increases to 20%, and Adult to 10%.

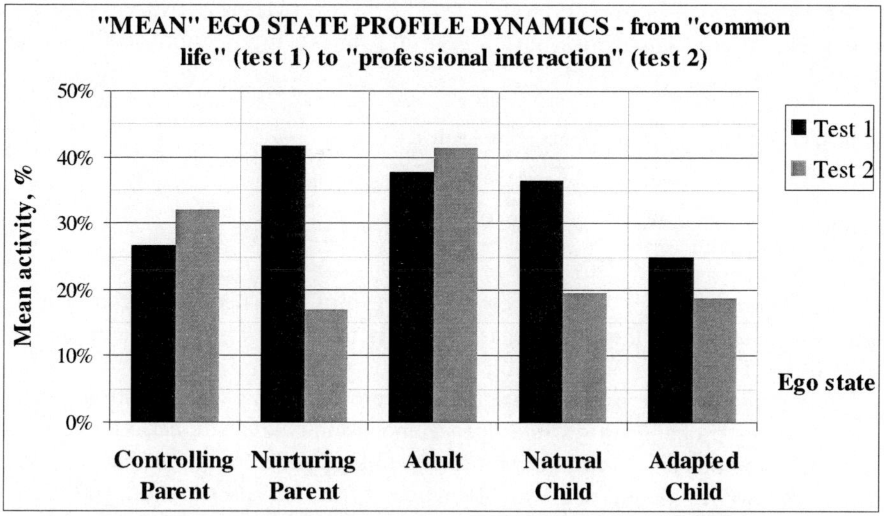

Fig. 5: Mean ego state energy dynamics

Table 3: Mean ego state energy dynamics

Mean energy	Test 1	Test 2	Relative Change (% from initial)
Controlling Parent	27%	32%	20%
Nurturing Parent	42%	17%	-59%
Adult	38%	41%	10%
Natural Child	37%	19%	-47%
Adapted Child	25%	19%	-25%

"Soul Blindness" – the Source of Risk Inside the Risk Manager?

As a result, the ego states that are responsible for freedom, pleasure, and caring for somebody are dramatically suppressed. On the one side, that is not a surprise – it is a business situation. But this result is a point to think about – in terms of "what is the price for that?"

On the other side, Natural Child is not only responsible for joy and carefreeness, but also it is the source of creativity. This way, by decreasing its activity, we reduce our creative mind!

And Nurturing Parent, who deals with the slogan «*how to help somebody do what he/she needs without restricting my own needs*», who is the source of real partnership, is also fully out of energy – what partnership between the risk manager and trader is possible after that?

The other significant fact is that not only the activity of Natural Child and Nurturing Parent, but also the overall mean energy (average activity of all ego states) is dramatically decreased (table 4). This means that the activation of Controlling Parent and Adult does not compensate for the suppression of other ego states!

Table 4: Overall mean ego state energy dynamics

	Test 1	Test 2	Relative Change (% from initial)
Energy	34%	26%	-25%

Psychical energy, like physical, does not just expire "nowhere" – it can change form and location. So the question is: where is this "missing" psychical energy located?

Since we reduce the overall conscious and pre-conscious manifestation of our ego, its energy probably flows into deeper unconscious layers. One hypothesis is that it can become conserved in our inner psychological defences' mechanism. But when psychological defences are highly active, it is a stressful situation, and in the long term it can be psychologically dangerous.

All these findings necessitate the increasing of personal awareness for risk managers. We need to be brightly conscious of our current ego states, and of transactions we take part in. Otherwise, we stay in a "judging" position, lose contact with ourselves (and then quickly lose contact with the trader), and have great difficulty in learning (in a broad sense) – because a *Parent doesn't learn* – it only *knows everything*[8]! Further, we should get in touch with our own scripts, psychological fixations and defences, as all these mechanisms force us into behaviour that is out of our awareness, and can then lead to unexpected results in communication and business.

"Know Yourself" must be the new principle for the risk manager.

[8] Including "knowing future" – because a very characteristic phrase of the Parent ego state sounds like "Be careful! You will break this cup now!" (It is said supposedly to prevent accident, but it implies that Parent intrinsically knows what will exactly happen with another person in the near future)

Four Pillars: New Industry Infrastructure

To summarize, all these findings and ideas can be shaped into a 4-pillar infrastructure.

While *Know Yourself* seems to be the essential part of inner culture and can be practiced by a person independently, there are some things that can not be performed alone. A great impact on psychological studies can be brought by interchange between financial organizations that will perform their investigations in the fields listed in paragraphs 1-2 below, by creating a pool of research.

1. Risk manager: knowledge about the trader
   - Crisis: trader's stress profile (discovering dominating psychological defences)
   - Trading style of retaining/getting rid of cash or asset (discovering anal fixation if present)
   - Ludomania (trading book and P&L analysis for screening)
   - Risk manager: in intercourse with trader
   - Quiet market: trader's "life script of loss" (statistical analysis of P&L and partnership in research)
2. Risk manager: personally
   - *"Know Yourself"*: personal awareness (ego state structure, transactions, dominating defences, fixations, script)
   - Building "Adult – Adult" relationships with the trader
3. Risk managers' society
   - Develop investigations (trader's ego-structure, defences, fixations)
   - Build a summary psychological risk profile of the trader
   - Develop group trainings for the purpose of deprogramming "scripts of loss"

Conclusion

Among what psychology can propose for risk management needs, the author recommends building a personal "**stress profile**" for the trader (based on the mechanism of psychological questionnaires for dominating defences, fixations and relevant personal characteristics) in order to foresee his/her potential behaviour in critical situations, to analyze trading strategy for the purpose of discovering specific negative P&L patterns (probably originating from unconscious "**life script of loss**"), and to provide "screening" for the detection of a potential **ludomaniac**. This is the first step (concerning the "risk identification" stage). Further, it can be recommended in some circumstances to analyze the test results in partnership with the trader, with perfect tactfulness tending to find key personal information together, or, in other circumstances (to help the trader implicitly find keys to personal unconscious patterns) by participation in intriguing "improve-your-performance" **group training** sessions specially developed for this purpose. In some cases the good choice could be "to do nothing" (with the trader directly), only taking this risk source in account and building a "crisis plan" for it, and creating an appropriate reserve.

This is the one, most obvious, side of a psychological approach to risk management: answering the question "*what else can we do with this trader*?" It meets the needs of risk **identification, analysis** and the process of **control.**

But the unpleasant surprise for us, risk managers, is that nothing positive can be really done with another human's soul if it has not been already performed by the very originator with himself/herself. The results of the conducted ego state structure study have shown the **characteristic switching** of risk manager's more or less **harmonious "relationships with world"** to a **much more stressed, formal, criticizing self-style** when brought into a situation of tight professional contact with trader. Most risk managers, though staying in the activated Adult ego state and keeping their objective analytical skills strong and active (and in this way providing risk management's functioning on the **acceptable** level for some **short-term** perspective), highly rouse their Controlling Parent ego state and dramatically suppress the Natural Child and Nurturing Parent ego states. The Natural Child's suppression leads to the **extinction** of the risk manager's **creative mind** and **ability to learn**, and that can **hamper the progress** of risk management **in the middle term**. An active Controlling Parent together with a suppressed Nurturing Parent provoke trading departments to become totally resisting, protesting, and hinder their opportunity to get the useful information and experience from risk management. Thus, **in** the **long term**, the **risk management** itself **risks** becoming the "**brake of the business**"!

This way, professional society should take a look at building a serious humanistic component into the enterprise-wide risk management process. "**Know Yourself**" can be proposed as the **new principle** for the risk manager. The good news is that it is not obligatory to go through serious psychotherapy, though it no doubt can guide a human being to heights. Personal awareness can take origin in simple self-questioning: "*what do I feel right now?*", "*which ego state am I in now?*" The next step can be "*what transaction are we in?*" (with a trader or in personal life) and – much more demanding – "*what Game do we play?*"[9] Even simply, these steps can be of great efficacy.

The concept of "Know Yourself", though sounding quite sharp and unexpected to a "finance man/woman" (quite odd, sooth to say), is nevertheless completely inside the swiftly growing trend of an "environment-friendly" or **"feminine" approach to business**. This approach is **opposed** to our "seemingly-obvious" **patriarchal** way of life (see e.g. European single currency "architect" B.Lietaer (2003) for reference). Here, the "Know yourself" principle, due to its clarity and "**paradigm shift**" (from "masculine" to "feminine") can be the breakthrough idea of business structure evolution.

---

[9] The concept of Game is beyond the scope of this article and is recommended for further reading (Berne, 1964).

Appendix I. Psychological Research Methodology

In this research we used the method of reflected subjectness by V.Petrovskiy (Petrovskiy, 1985). The method consists in the comparison of individual manifestations of the individual A in real or imaginary presence of the individual (or situation) B, that allows to find out how B "lives" in A (how is B reflected, presented in A).

In our experiment the interviewee was told to describe himself or herself twice, using the same questionnaire, containing the personality traits corresponding to different ego states (words, characteristic facial expressions, intonations, attitudes, describing the ego states). In the first case, the individual assesses himself in the "neutral" situation (i.e. outside the real or imaginary interaction with another person or situation), in the second case - in a situation with a significant other (or in some particular situations).

Comparing the frequencies of traits attributed to himself or herself in the first and second situation, the experimenter concludes about the impact of significant other person on the examinee.

Finally, one can exclude an indication of the situation and talk strictly about the impact of the individual B on the individual A.

In this work, the questionnaire was guided with the preface:

Please check the words, intonation, etc., that are most typical for you. Please decide spontaneously.

Test number 2 is very similar to test number 1, so perform it after some time (from 15 minutes to an hour).

Now imagine yourself at a Credit Committee, or Assets and Liabilities Committee, where you have to "fight" - you need to defend your position in a fairly tough situation. Trading division actively wants to open a big limit on "very bad" bank, or aggressively offers "risk-free" scheme with the derivative instruments, which in case of risk event will lead to huge losses, or is going to take absolutely illiquid securities as the collateral for the doubtful deal, arguing by the large discount and "reliability" of the counterparty.

Then, when you felt yourself "inside" this situation, act the same way as in the previous test: Please check the words, intonation, etc., that are most typical for you. Please decide spontaneously.

Do not look at the previous test - this will contribute to the accuracy of the results.

QUESTIONNAIRE «WORD CHOICE»:

Disclaimer: the original version of the questionnaire is probably developed in English, but its origin and author(s) unfortunately are not known to the author of the article. This is the reverse translation from Russian version of the questionnaire and can not be correctly used for the sake of psychological interviews and researches.

WORDS				
Never	Good	A Reasonable	Fine	I Can't
Be Sure To	Nice	How	Fun	I Hope
You Need To	Love you	What	Want To	I'll Try To
Must	Magnificently	Why	Don't want to	Thank You
Bad	Soft	Where	I'm Afraid	I beg your pardon
Always	Poor baby	The Result Of The	Shine	Sorry
Wrong	Don't worry	Practical	Fantastic	Had to
Funny	Let me	Another possibility	Mine	After you
Make	Be careful	Number Of	The Secret Of	I Can wait
Don't do	Don't forget to	That is why	Riddle	Only Me
Correctly		Rationale	Hey, listen	
INTONATION				
Critical	Loving	Quiet	Free	Weak
Condescending	Cheery	Credible	Excited	Stubborn
Magistral	Warm	Inquiring	Loud	Capricious
Mocking	Comforting	Calm	Hurried	Ingratiating
Indulgent	Sympathetic	Without emotion	Cheerful	Apologetic
Ordering	Supporting	Business		Complaining
Important				
FACIAL EXPRESSION				
"What you deserve"	Open	Reflection	Relaxed	Suppressed
Haughty	Encouraging	Active	Spontaneous	Sad
Demanding	Grin	Considerate	Flirting	Helpless
Harsh	Cheering	Sincere	Surprised	Rigid
Warning	Comforting	Interested	Mercurial	Worried
Critical		Impersonal	Expressive	
Alienated				

ATTITUDE				
Assessing	Understanding	Open	Curiosity	Adaptation
Condemning	Care	Logical	Uncertainty	The modest agreement
Moralizing	Sympathy	Neutral	Enthusiasm	Flexible
Magistral	Generous	Without prejudice	Brokenness	Timidity
Omniscient	Courteous	Inquisitiveness		Rebellious
				Doubt
				Complaint

References

American Psychiatric Association. (2000). Diagnostic and statistical manual of mental disorders, Fourth Edition, Text Revision: DSM-IV-TR. Washington, DC: American Psychiatric Publishing, Inc.

Berne, E. (1964). Games People Play – The Basic Hand Book of Transactional Analysis. New York: Ballantine Books

Lietaer, B. (2003). A world in balance. Reflections, the journal of the Society for Organizational Learning at MIT (SOL), volume 4, number 4.

McWilliams, N. (1994). Psychoanalytic diagnosis: Understanding personality structure in the clinical process. New York: The Guilford Press.

Petrovskiy V. (1985). Printsyp otrazhennoj subjektnosti v psikhologicheskom issledovanii lichnosti. Voprosy Psykhollogii, vol.1. (The Principle Of Reflected Subjectness In The Psychological Study Of Personality, Questions of Psychology).

Options: Risk Reducing or Creating?

Marianna Morozova

Institute of Economics and Industrial Engineering, Siberian Branch of RAS, Novosibirsk, Russia. email: morozova.marianna@gmail.com

Abstract The question connected with the main function of options, i.e. risk hedging, alternatively raises a contradictory version of the question, i.e. creating risk. These pieces of question statement are connected with the investigation of effectiveness of the derivative market and in particular the mechanisms of option pricing. The Russian option market is presented by the only one segment of Russian Trading System called Futures and Options on RTS — FORTS. In this paper we propose a method to calculate options fair prices based on risk-neutral pricing and show the degree of market effectiveness in the sense of whether the arbitrage opportunities tend to drive the market to an arbitrage-free equilibrium or not. The dynamics of the underlying assets' log returns is described as an infinitely divisible Levy processes and mean-correcting Monte-Carlo simulation of risk-neutral market trajectories is applied to calculate option fair prices. An empirical study of more than 250 future options on AO Gazprom and AO Sberbank stocks and the RTS Index is realized. Results show a systematical ineffectiveness of the Russian option market in the sense that option prices allow long running arbitrage with no demand reaction, leading to price adjustment as would be expected.

Keywords: option pricing, fair price, Levy processes, risk-neutral valuation, arbitrage opportunities, effective option market

JEL classification: C0, G0, G13, G12, G14

Introduction

Although options are generally considered a tool for financial market risk hedging, they may create additional risks themselves. The dynamics of log returns of underlying assets follow distributions differing from the normal distribution, which option pricing on the basis of the Black-Sholes Option Pricing Model (OPM) is based on. Thus, options are estimated incorrectly and can`t be priced fairly (i.e. arbitrage-free). This leads to risk arbitrage including liquidity risk, model risk and other environment risks. However, arbitrage opportunities in risky markets represent investment strategies that with positive probability lead to positive profits, not exposed to any risk of loss. At the same time, the long-running existence of such opportunities is considered as market inefficiency, meaning that some of the traded assets are priced irrationally, while in effective markets the opportunities appear as

D. Sornette et al. (Eds.), *Market Risk and Financial Markets Modeling*,
DOI 10.1007/978-3-642-27931-7_16,

fast as they disappear under the continuous pressure of demand-supply driving forces, which make market prices converge to an arbitrage-free level. Therefore, arbitrage is considered herein as a criterion of option pricing effectiveness verification.

The most developed markets are often assumed to be dynamically arbitrage-free, i.e. the arbitrage opportunities are rather hard to find and if such an opportunity would show up, it would generate a large demand, prices would adjust, and the opportunity would disappear. The absence of arbitrage opportunities is a key assumption in the option pricing models. A common problem in developed derivatives markets analysis is then to calibrate the real market prices of derivatives to a theoretical parametric law (e.g. a pricing rule given by a risk-neutral martingale market measure) to explain the stylized facts of market prices dynamics, understand pricing mechanisms, develop and analyze hedging strategies etc.

Two main clues of FORTS ineffectiveness are served as the research motivation. Unfortunately, when a developing market (such as the one in Russia) is at hand, its effectiveness and functionality is not obvious, if considered possible at all. The only derivative market in Russia where options are traded (FORTS) has a very short history (in comparison with the World derivative market, which is about 4 times older). Though its principal task is to implement a wide range of financial instruments allowing market participants to hedge effectively, the set of contract types available at FORTS is limited, and trades usually have poor activity, resulting in continued low liquidity and unfair prices. This reasoning lead to the first clue of FORTS option prices ineffectiveness.

The second clue of FORTS option prices ineffectiveness is supported by simple analysis of the derivatives trade results and the trading mechanism set by the RTS itself. Theoretical option prices based on the Black-Sholes OPM with dynamically-updated implied volatility of the underlying asset log returns are published by the market-maker in an on-line manner during the whole life-time of each option, and market prices are bounded in the dynamic corridor around the theoretical Black-Sholes (BS) option price. However, BS prices are fair only for the case of complete markets. FORTS is clearly not complete (as log returns are not Normal). But as practice shows, the actual market prices tend to remain close to these theoretical prices. Therefore, the trades are usually most active when the contracts are soon to expire, with the market prices remaining close to the theoretical Black-Sholes prices, but not close enough to keep call-put parity. Thus, the market systematically allows for arbitrage with no further price-adjustment.

The low liquidity of the Russian option market, as well as the fact that market option prices are based on the false assumption of arbitrage-free market, indicates that the market option prices cannot be considered fair prices. The problem of calibrating the market models still remains. Therefore, the main goal of this paper is a verification of option pricing effectiveness on FORTS. Here we propose a method of calibrating risk-neutral pricing rules to the underlying assets market in order to calculate fair prices for traded options. First, the dynamics of the underlying assets' log returns are described as infinitely divisible Levy processes, to estimate risk-neutral measures of the underlying market. Then, applying a mean-correcting

Monte-Carlo simulation of risk-neutral market trajectories, the corresponding risk-neutral (i.e. arbitrage-free) option prices are calculated and compared to the market ones showing the degree of market effectiveness in the sense of whether the arbitrage opportunities tend to drive the market to an arbitrage-free equilibrium or not.

Research Methodology

The research algorithm framework consists of three problems:

1) proposing reasonable models for the price behavior of the underlying assets and calibrating them statistically;
2) developing the fair option prices estimation method for illiquid markets, such as the Russian option market;
3) calculating corresponding fair prices for a vast variety of present options and comparing them to the market ones.

In this paper a series of more than 250 future options on AO Gazprom and AO Sberbank stocks and the RTS Index is analyzed. The corresponding data samples of underlying assets' prices include the daily close of American call option prices for the period between January 2007 and April 2010 (from approximately 40 to more than 360 points). Data samples for underlying assets include the daily close of future prices for the period between December 2006 and February 2010. To improve the representative properties of the results, data from a vast period of time are analyzed. Figure 1 shows the history of the Russian underlying market during the periods analyzed.

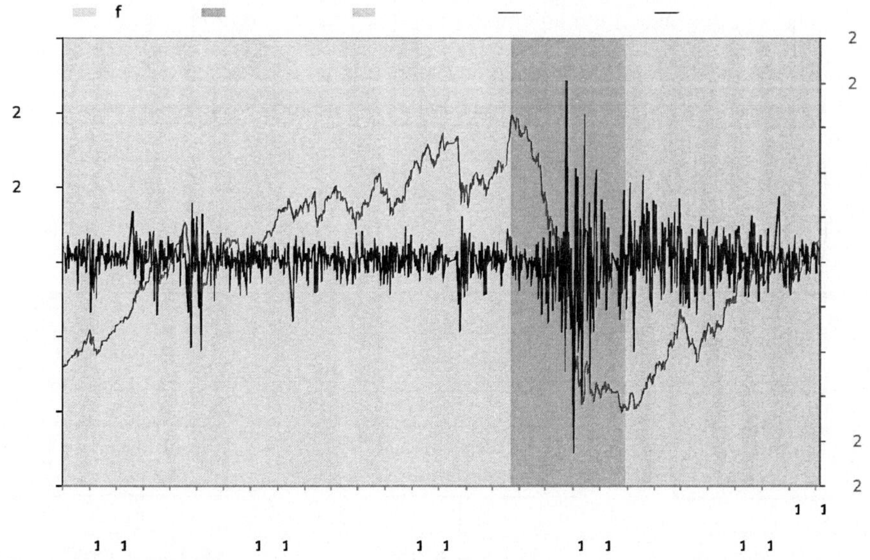

Fig. 1: Daily dynamics of RTS Index from 8th of April, 2005 to 4th of April, 2010

To show that option prices calculated on the basis of the Black-Sholes OPM cannot be considered effective, a traditional approach to Black-Sholes option pricing model is applied. For the Black-Sholes pricing model to derive fair (i.e. arbitrage-free) option prices it is essential for perfect hedges of the options and corresponding underlying assets to exist. It is well known that such riskless portfolios cannot be found in real markets, and the only market allowing perfect hedges is the complete market, which exists if and only if the underlying assets' log returns are i.i.d normal random values. To prove market incompleteness and consequent Black-Sholes OPM inapplicability it is necessary to show empiric distributions of log returns of the underlying assets differing from the normal distribution.

Considering the dynamics of market option prices in comparison with market prices, two hypotheses (*Hypothesis 1* and *Hypothesis 2*) alternative to *Hypothesis 0* about the option market were suggested (Figure 2):

Hypothesis 0: due to the small difference between market option prices and fair prices, short term super-profits are available to the market participants, thus, market price rapidly converges to the fair price — effective market equilibrium.

Hypothesis 1: market option prices and fair prices differ too much, so the expected benefits from hedging and arbitrage opportunities are not enough to motivate agents to trade on the option market — the market is illiquid.

Hypothesis 2: information is asymmetric and market participants cannot properly estimate arbitrage opportunities and hedging potentials, thereby form irrational expectations regarding the future market development dynamics, thus trades are concluded at prices different from fair prices — the market doesn`t perform its main function and appears to be ineffective.

The following part of the paper is devoted to the "testing" of these hypotheses according to the statistical analysis of the underlying assets' dynamics (stochastic processes) and the financial mathematics approach used in option pricing.

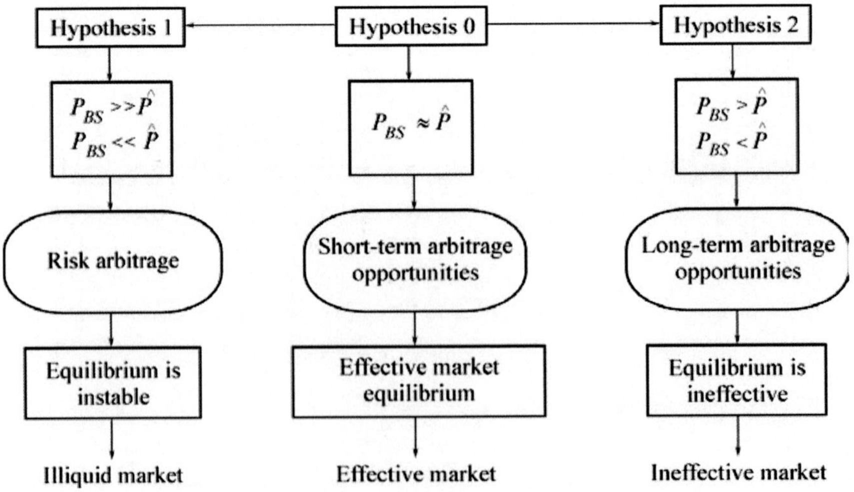

Fig. 2: Tested assumptions about option market work

Underlying Asset Prices Modelling in an Incomplete Market

The first step of the research is required to find the proper model of the return distribution of underlying assets. Figure 3 shows examples of the empirical distribution of some log returns (kernel densities) compared to the corresponding empirical estimates of normal densities. For these cases, the non-normality of log returns' distributions is obvious. To strengthen the visual results, the statistical Jarque – Berra test was applied: for more than 85% of the analyzed samples, the null hypothesis of normality is rejected with more than 99% confidence, and for 93% of the samples the corresponding confidence level is 95%, the minimal confidence level for rejecting normality is not less than 87%.

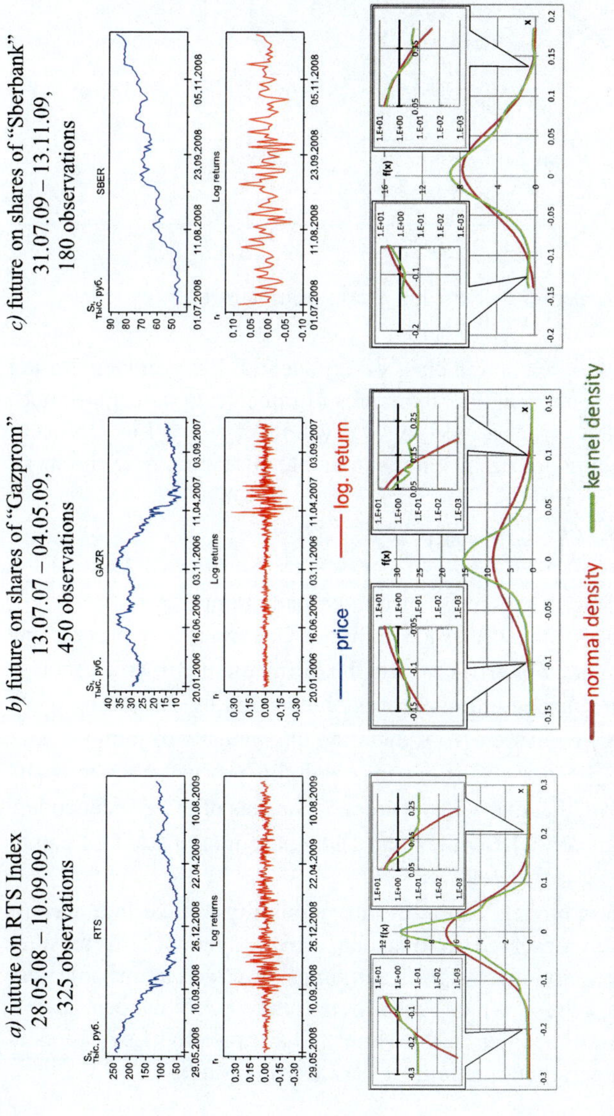

Fig. 3: Empirical distributions of futures' log returns for different periods of time compared to normal

The next step in the research is to suggest analytical models to account for the empirical facts seen in the log returns' distribution analysis. A literature review regarding financial time series and derivatives pricing shows three major ways to step away from normality to account for heavy tailed, asymmetric and leptokurtic distributions (Fig. 4).

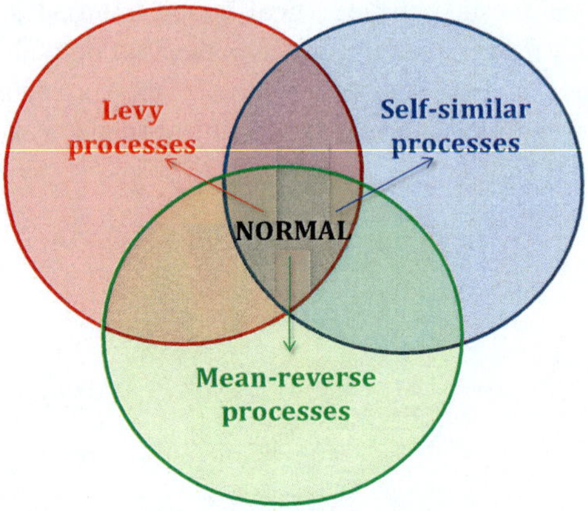

Fig. 4: Classes of models for underlying assets' log returns distributions

In this research, the approach based on the class of exponential Levy models for log returns of underlying assets is chosen. The dynamics of underlying assets are modeled as an exponential Levy process $S_t = S_0 e^{X_t}$, where X_t is a Levy process unambiguously corresponding to an infinitely divisible distribution (Schoutens, 2003):

$$X_t = \gamma t + \sigma W_t + Z_t,$$

where Z_t is a jump process with (possibly) infinitely many jumps.

The first part of the process $\gamma t + \sigma W_t$ is a continuous Gaussian Levy process and is described by two parameters: the drift (γ) and the diffusion of Brownian motion (σ). The other term Z_t is a discontinuous process incorporating the jumps of X_t and is described by the Levy measure $\nu(dx)$, dictating the intensity of jumps of size x. The number of jumps occurs according to a Poisson process with intensity parameter $\int \nu(dx)$. It follows that every Levy process consists of three independent parts: a linear deterministic part, a Brownian part and a pure jump part. This can be written as the Levy triplet $[\gamma, \sigma^2, \nu(dx)]$.

The choice of Levy class models caused by its possibility to take into account jumps of all magnitudes, as observed in financial actives dynamics: from small jumps, observed in diffusion motion, to significant jumps, observed in unstable periods of market life (shocks, crises), which, even though they rarely happen, lead to substantial losses. This possibility lies in the variety of exponential Levy models, corresponding to different parameterizations of the Levy measure.

All Levy models fall into two categories. The first category, called *jump-diffusion models*, includes a combination of diffusion part ($\sigma > 0$) and jump process with finite activity. Here the jumps represent rare events – crashes and large drawdowns. The second category consists of models where an infinite number of small jumps suppress the diffusion part in every interval ($\sigma = 0$): these are infinite activity models (Cont, Tankov, 2004). The parameter α in Fig. 5 determines the tail index of an α-stable distribution and parameter $\alpha_{\pm}$ describes positive and negative jumps of α-stable modifications (for more details see below).

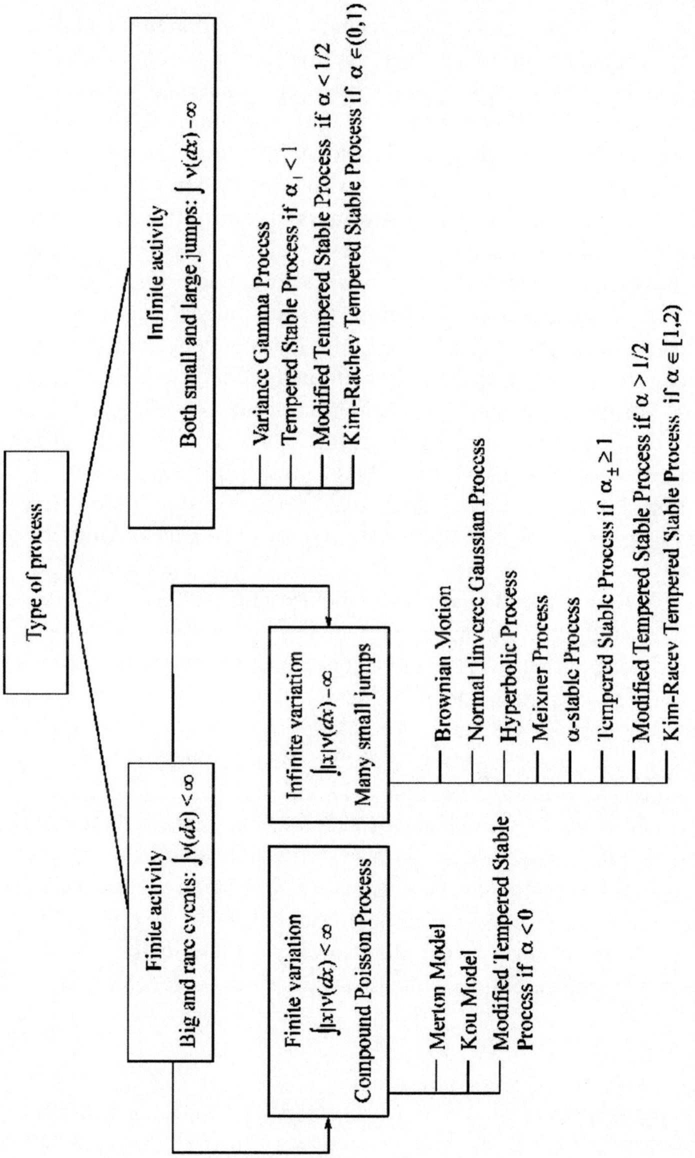

Fig. 5: Types of Levy processes

Thus the heavy tails, leptokurtosis and asymmetry of underlying assets' log returns of the empirical distributions in models based on Levy processes can consequently be explained as the result of jumps in the returns' dynamics. While the volatility of the diffusion part of the process represents the risks that can be effectively and perfectly hedged, the risk of unlikely, but rather significant, extreme changes in the returns' dynamics (i.e. the jumps) are the primary source of market incompleteness. From a risk management perspective, jumps allow one to quantify and take into account the risk of strong asset price movements over short time intervals, which appears non-existent in the diffusion framework.

Among the above, only stable distributions have attractive enough mathematical properties to be a viable alternative to normal distributions in trading, optimization, and risk management systems. A major drawback of all alternative models is their lack of stability, where stability means that the distribution family of the returns does not depend on the time interval over which the returns are considered. This gives a theoretical basis for the use of stable distributions when heavy tails are present and stable distributions are the only distributional family that has its own domain of attraction—that is, a large sum of appropriately standardized i.i.d random variables will have a distribution that converges to a stable one. This is a unique feature and its fundamental implications for financial modeling are the following: if changes in financial variable are driven by many independently occurring small shocks, then the only appropriate distributional model for these changes is a stable model, i.e., normal or non-normal stable (Samorodnitsky, Taqqu,1994).

The second property is also well-known from the Gaussian framework and it generalizes to the stable case. Specifically, by the Central Limit Theorem (CLT), appropriately normalized sums of independent and identically distributed (i.i.d) random variables with finite variance converge weakly to a normal random variable, and with infinite variance; by the Generalized Central Limit Theorem (GCLT) the sums converge weakly to a stable random variable (Rachev, 2003).

However, empirical studies show that tails of assets returns distributions are heavier relative to the normal distribution and thinner than the α-stable distribution. In response to those empirical inconsistencies, various alternatives to the α-stable distribution were proposed in the literature (Carr et al, 2004; Rachev et al., 2005; Kim et al., 2007; Rachev, Mitnik, 2000). The idea consists of tempering the tails to make them semi-heavy. Examples of some subclass of tempered stable processes are shown in Figure 5. The importance of tempered stable distributions comes from the fact that they combine both α-stable and Gaussian properties. Unlike α-stable distributions, tempered ones may have all moments finite, including exponential moments of certain order. Tempered stable tails decay much slower than the Gaussian and faster than α-stable tails. Nowadays these distributions are the prospective direction of infinitely-divisible distributions class development.

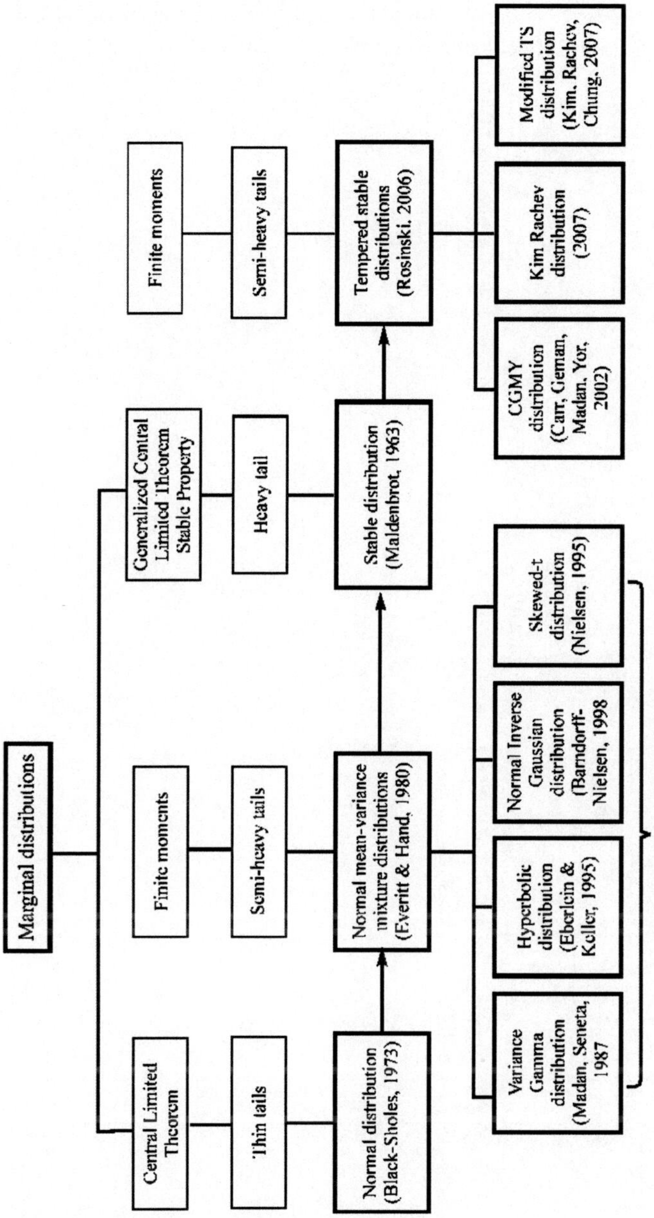

Fig. 6: Classification of infinitely-divisible distributions applied in finance

To be able to calculate arbitrage-free prices of options, a single model for each sample of log returns' dynamics (each corresponding to a single option) was estimated. In general 12 parameterizations of Levy processes were compared for each sample, including those shown in Figure 6, on the basis of maximum likelihood estimation (MLE) and Akaike information criteria (IC). For those classes of the distributions which cannot be calculated analytically in terms of a density function, a fast Fourier transform of the characteristic function was applied to calculate densities and apply MLE.

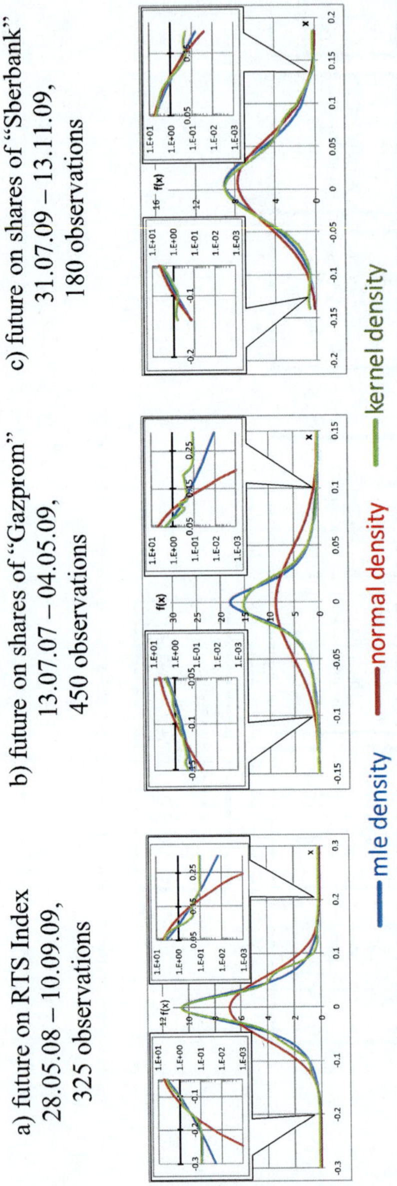

Fig. 7: Empirical distributions of log returns of RTS for different periods of time compared to normal densities and MLE densities of other jump-diffusion models

The investigation of the ability of alternative parametric families to represent the empirical facts of the financial market for the daily futures' return data produced the following results. MTS, NIG and Hyperbolic processes give reasonable fits for all subperiods: for more than 60% of the analyzed samples these distributions were chosen as statistically representative, based on the Akaike IC. However, the α-stable, Student's t and Miexner distributions fail to describe some features of the financial market in some/all sub-periods (Table 1).

Figure 7 extends figure 3 with the corresponding MLE densities for some samples. Density estimations show that in 35% of the analyzed samples the distributions with a diffusion component were statistically chosen and in 65% the pure jump diffusion models with infinite variation were chosen, in particular the Sberbank Stock future clearly demonstrates the fat "tailness" of empirical density with infinite variance. This phenomenon can be explained by the fact that in most cases realistic trajectories of the Russian market are characterized by frequent small jumps but the Sberbank Stock future dynamics contain discontinuities expressed in gaps in trade because most of all deals conclude at the over-the-counter securities market.

Table 1: Fitting results (frequency of process choosing)

	Distribution/Model	RTS Index Future (of total 100)	Gazprom Stock Future (of total 73)	Sberbank Stock Future (of total 73)
1	Normal	16	9	6
2	Merton JD	2	3	1
3	Kou JD	5	-	3
4	Gamma Variance, GV	4	6	2
5	Normal Inverse Gaussian, NIG	21	14	16
6	Hyperbolic	20	10	12
7	Meixner	-	-	-
8	α-stable	-	-	2
9	CGMY	6	9	7
10	Modified Tempered Stable, MTS	21	15	16
11	Kim-Rachev	5	7	8
12	t-Student	-	-	-

Risk-neutral Modelling of a Fair Option Price at Illiquid Market

The second step of the research is to calculate arbitrage-free prices of traded options corresponding to the estimates of the underlying market models. When a market is complete, the only way for it to exist is to be "normal" in log returns of the underlying assets, then at every moment the only price level for each derivative is arbitrage-free and one of the possible ways to calculate it is the Black-Sholes OPM. In case of FORTS, market incompleteness has been shown and another approach to arbitrage-free price calculation needs to be found.

In this paper, risk-neutral pricing is applied to calculate options prices corresponding to the empirical market facts. The essence of a risk-neutral OPM is in the fundamental theorems of pricing. When a market is incomplete and the underlying assets' prices follow some distribution law P called a market probability measure (expressed in a subjective investor`s estimation of the empirical distribution of market outcomes, e.g. in this research represented by some Levy process of log returns of underlying assets), there exists an equivalent martingale measure Q (possibly more than one for the case of incompleteness, and only one in case of a complete market), also called a risk-neutral probability law (or risk-neutral measure) such that Q-terms calculated expected values of any derivative payoff represent the arbitrage-free price of the derivative. Then this measure contains all information about risks connected with the underlying asset prices' changes.

The existence of the equivalent martingale measure allows one to reduce the pricing of options on the risky asset by calculating the expected values of the discounted payoffs not with respect to the physical (statistical) measure P, but with respect to the equivalent martingale measure Q (Harrison, Krepps, 1979; Harrison, Pliska, 1981).

Under the risk neutrality assumption, today's fair price of the option is equal to the expected value of its future payoff discounted by the risk free rate under appropriate probability measure (risk-neutral measure Q):

$$C(H) = \exp(r(t-T))E^{Q}[H|\Im_t],$$

where H is an option payoff; T is time to maturity of an option; $\Im_t$ is all available information at moment t.

The risk-neutral measure can be extracted in two ways: either by calibration of the risk-neutral option prices $C(H|Q)$ to the market ones $C^*(H)$, which is called the calibration problem, or by calibration of the theoretical distribution of underlying assets $F(S|Q)$ to the empirical one $F^*(S)$, which is called the pricing problem (Figure 8).

In developed countries with liquid option market, market prices are supposed to be arbitrage-free and so the calibration to the traded options is used for estimation of model parameters. But on the illiquid Russian option market the degree of market prices bias from arbitrage-free needs to be examined and therefore we cannot use the option prices as a criteria for calibration because there is no sense in calibrating to the unfair prices. The second reason for solving the pricing problem instead of the calibrating problem comes from lack of data about the dynamics of option prices for the risk-neutral market measure estimation.

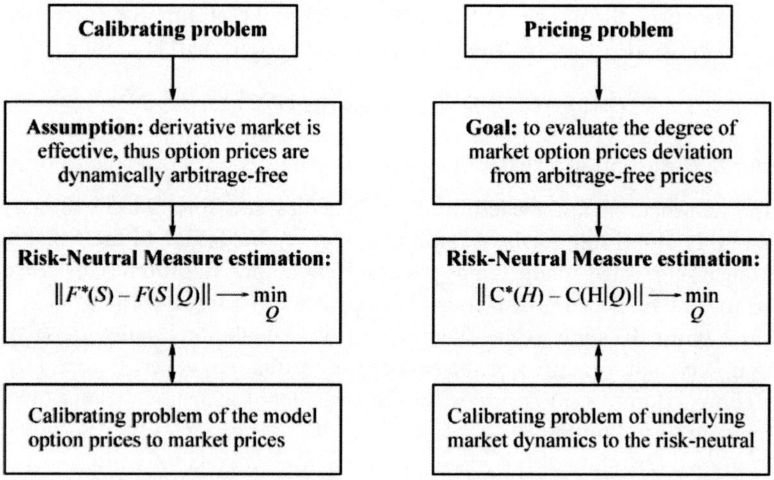

Fig. 8: Two approaches to risk-neutral measure estimation

Options traded on FORTS are American-type options on futures (also traded on FORTS) and therefore their payoffs can be calculated in the same way as vanilla options payoffs. To shorten the number of calculations needed to be performed, only call options are analyzed (corresponding arbitrage-free prices of puts are then derived from call-put parity).

Market incompleteness allows for multiple risk-neutral measures Q, and therefore we choose one possible way to shift from MLEs of jump-diffusion market models (representing market measures P) to the equivalent martingale processes — the mean-correcting shift; and Monte-Carlo simulations are used next to calculate the expected values of options payoffs corresponding to the modified measure. The whole process is known as 'Risk-neutral pricing by mean-correcting Monte-Carlo simulation'. The calculations are performed according to the following algorithm:

1. 10 000 samples of log returns are simulated from the minimum AIC MLE distribution, the number of points in each sample equals to the option maturity T (in days, as the observations are daily). These data are used to calculate the market measure coherent expected values of the underlying asset price for the moment of the option expiration $t=T$. The number of the points of the series is also T:

$$S_T^{e,t} = E^P\left(S_T \mid I_t\right),\ t=1,\dots,T.$$

2. For the same simulations of log returns the corresponding number of martingale measure coherent market trajectories are simulated, and the corresponding prices of the underlying asset for $t=T$ are calculated:

$$\widetilde{S}_{t,T}^{Q} = \widetilde{S}_{t,T}^{P} - S_T^{e,t} + S_{t-1}.$$

3. By construction, the prices $\tilde{S}^{Q}_{t,T}$ are martingales and therefore the corresponding prices of calls are arbitrage-free in terms of the current market model:

$$C^{Q}(K) = E^{Q}H_{C} = E\max\left(0; \tilde{S}^{Q}_{t,T} - K\right),$$

where K is the option's strike.

It is important that it is not needed for the risk-neutral measure Q to be directly calculated in this algorithm, as the martingale property holds due to the construction of the mean-corrected underlying prices. Hence the algorithm can be easily adjusted for any market model if it can be simulated by Monte-Carlo.

Figures 9 and 10 show some examples of the calculation results, these figures are also highly representative of the rest of the results. However, Figure 11 represents a comparison of option prices for the considered instruments, and these figures are examples of outliers.

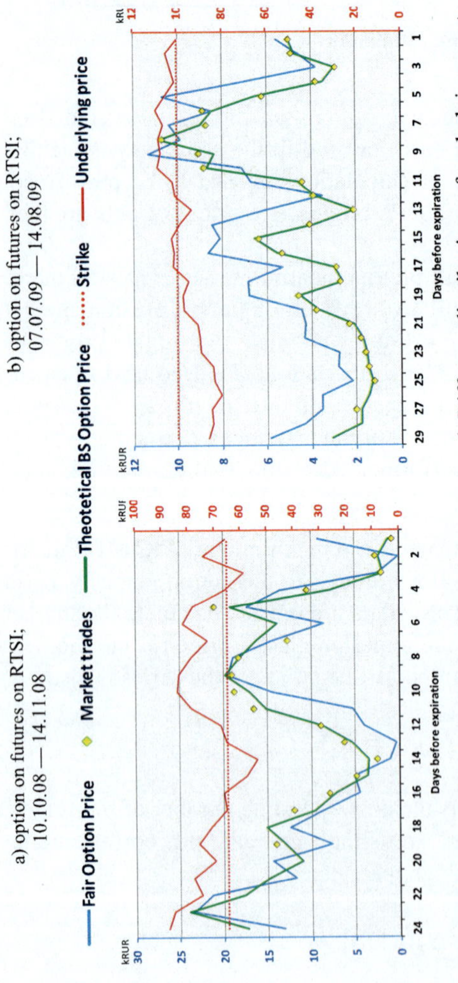

Fig. 9: Market and risk-neutral option prices compared. Different distributions of underlying assets log returns: a) Normal Inverse Gaussian; b) CGMY

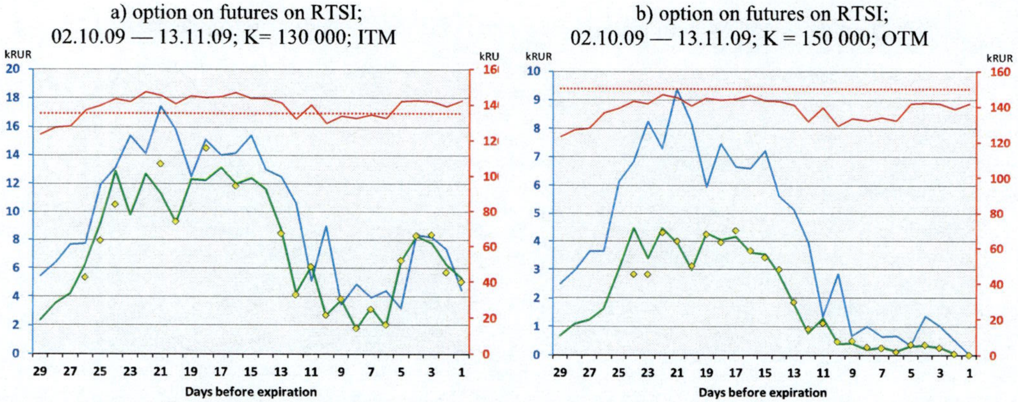

Fig. 10: Market and risk-neutral option prices compared. Different strikes of the same option and moneyness

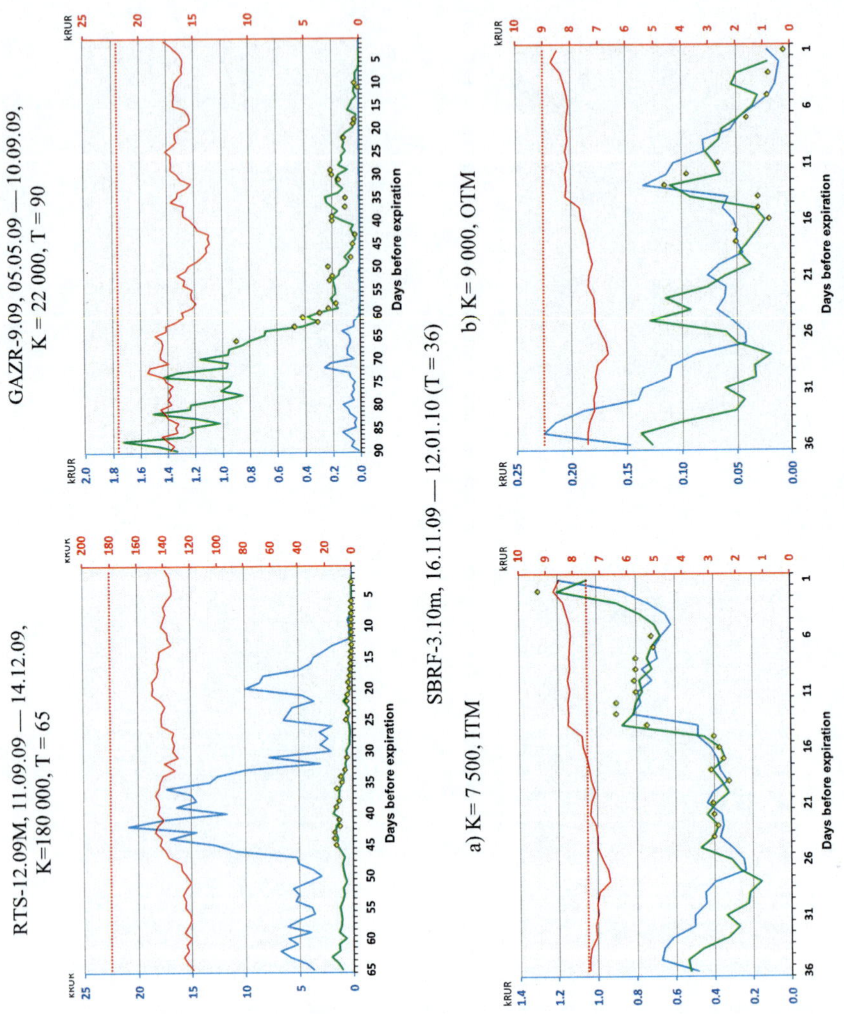

Fig. 11: Market and risk-neutral option prices compared. Different time to expiration of option

Based on the outcome of the calculations analysis and for the consequent conclusion on FORTS effectiveness it is necessary to mention that:

The first group of samples justifies the *Hypothesis 1* and includes out of the money options (when the underlying asset price does not exceed strike at the expiration date). As usual, the theoretical price of such contracts is underestimated from the emission and the option has positive risk-neutral value, i. e. promises positive future payoffs. Nevertheless, there are no trades until the option becomes out of the money and its risk-neutral value is equal to zero. In this way, trades made in the second part of the life of such options cannot be considered as effective market equilibrium, in spite of the convergence of risk-neutral and market prices, because the option promises "nothing" and sells by inestimable value.

The second group of samples demonstrates the *Hypothesis 2*. The trades on the market are active only when the BS price significantly underestimates the option value relative to a risk-neutral one. However, these low-priced trades do not cause to any price corrections leading to arbitrage-free market states, consequently the market rather fulfills mostly the speculative function than hedging.

The situation for the third group of samples cannot be completely assigned to only one of the hypotheses — trades all along the option life-time happen differently. At the beginning of the life the market is illiquid – the theoretical price is vastly overestimated, the number of trades are very poor (*Hypothesis 1*), and market price slowly converges to the risk-neutral, which leads to some short-term efficiency (*Hypothesis 0*). But the market liquidity doesn't rise significantly, hence the equilibrium is not stable. Trades recommence only when the theoretical price is underestimated relative to the risk-neutral, allowing for the arbitrage. That, however, doesn't lead to the price correcting during the significant period of time (*Hypothesis 2*). The effective equilibrium is established at the end of the option life, when it is much in the money.

The forth group of samples demonstrates the most effective work of the option market (*Hypothesis 0*). However the market liquidity is still low and the equilibrium never stays stable and therefore new arbitrage opportunities arise all along.

Testing of the considered hypotheses allows one to make the following inference about the option market (Table 2).

Table 2: The result of testing hypotheses

Hypothesis	Index RTS Futures, % (100 samples)	Gazprom Stock Futures, % (73 samples)	Sberbank Stock Futures, % (73 samples)	Total number of options, % (246 samples)
Hypothesis 0	9	7	21	12
Hypothesis 1	27	22	63	36
Hypothesis 2	64	71	16	52

The market mechanism offers significantly different from fair price option value estimations, thereby blocking the settling of long-term effective equilibrium. Once the equilibrium is settled in a price close to the fair price, it is unstable and does not contribute to the performance of market function, i.e. the market is not effective. Generally, the market mechanism systematically offers prices that underestimate the value of options, creating arbitrage opportunities. This shows the market ineffective again, as no price corrections leading to arbitrage-free market equilibrium appear.

Conclusion

Empirically, we find that there are advantages supporting a Levy class of processes in the fitting of the historical distribution and in the calibration of the risk-neutral distribution because of its tail property. The analysis of three options price cooperation (Black-Sholes price, market price and arbitrage-free price) with the consequent conclusion on FORTS effectiveness revealed the following items:

1) even when the fair (i.e. arbitrage-free or risk-neutral) prices of options are unknown, the ineffectiveness of FORTS seems quite obvious, as the market prices tend to stay close to those derived from Black–Sholes OPM prices of the options, which cannot be considered arbitrage free in an incomplete market;
2) hence, once the market model is chosen that is coherent with the empirical data, the corresponding fair prices prove the ineffectiveness of the market trades; the actual market prices differ more from the arbitrage-free ones when the distributions of log returns of underlying assets differ more from the normal; the jumps in the log returns of underlying assets dynamics are the reason for the market to underestimate the out-of-the-money options and overestimate the in-the-money ones. Nevertheless, the resulting arbitrage opportunities somehow do not force prices to change in the direction of fair ones, thus the market is systematically ineffective;
3) of course, according to the most simple rules of options pricing the prices all along tend to converge with an option's maturity expiring, which can be mistaken for effective market work; still this convergence doesn't seem to be due to arbitrage-driven demand and supply changing forces; this convergence is due to the role of the diffusion part of the log returns process, as the closer expiration is — the lower probability of extreme jumps that can significantly change the market trajectory (especially when options are far from being at-the-money).

To sum up the features exposed in this paper, one may say that staying close to Black-Sholes calculated market prices causes major long-running arbitrage between calls and puts, which does not tend to disappear towards the options' expiration, as it should for effective markets.

The obtained results show that if options are priced without allowing for adequate modeling of market features, options will create risks. On the other hand if the stylized facts of the financial time series are taken into consideration, they will reduce risks. This investigation contains the approach of more complete capturing of financial market characteristics.

References

Carr P., Geman H., Madan, D.B., & Yor, M. (2002). The Fine Structure of Asset Returns: An Empirical Investigation. The Journal of Business, 75(2), 305–332.

Cont, R., & Tankov, P. (2004). Financial Modelling with Jump Processes. Chapman & Hall/ CRC, Financial Mathematics Series.

Harrison, J. M., & Kreps, D. (1979). Martingales and arbitrage in multi periods security markets. J. Econom. Theory, 20(3), 381-408.

Harrison, J. M., & Pliska, S. (1981). Martingales and stochastic integrals in the theory of continuous trading. Stochastic Process. Appl., 11(3), 215-260.

Kim, Y. S., Rachev, S. T., Bianchi, M. L., & Fabozzi, F. J. (2007). A new tempered stable distribution and its application to finance. In Bol G., Rachev S. T., and Wuerth R., (Ed.), Risk Assessment: Decisions in Banking and Finance (pp.51–84). Physika Verlag, Springer.

Rachev, S.T. (2003). Handbook of Heavy Tailed Distributions in Finance. Elsevier.

Rachev, S.T., Menn, C., & Fabozzi, F.J. (2005). Fat-tailed and Skewed Asset Return Distributions: Implications for Risk Management, Portfolio Selection, and Option Pricing. John Wiley & Sons.

Rachev, S.T., & Mittnik, S. (2000). Stable Paretian Models in Finance. Wiley New York.

Rosinski, J. (2007). Tempering stable processes. Stochastic Processes and Their Applications, 117(6), 677–707.

Samorodnitsky, G., & Taqqu, M.S. (1994). Stable Non-Gaussian Random Processes: Stochastic Models with Infinite Variance. CRC Press.

Schoutens, W. (2003). Lévy Processes in Finance: Pricing Financial Derivatives. John Wiley and Sons.

Hierarchical and Ultrametric Models of Financial Crashes

Anna Pivovarova

Samara State Aerospace University, Samara, Russia. email: a-pivovarova@mail.ru

Abstract We explore the log-periodic behavior which is known to precede the critical events of some complex systems. Particularly, we consider the hierarchical model of financial crashes introduced by A. Johansen and D. Sornette, which reproduces the log-periodic power law behavior of the price before the critical point. Much attention is being paid to a problem of critical point invariance which is investigated by comparison of probability density functions of the crash times corresponding to systems with various total numbers of agents. In order to build the ultrametric modification of this model we introduce the dependence of an influence exponent on an ultrametric distance between agents. We found out that for this modification, invariance of the critical point remains true. We also introduce the new pure ultrametric model, which exhibits power law behavior modulated by decreasing-period oscillations.

Keywords: Mathematical modeling, log periodic power law, ultrametric distance, hierarchical structure, financial crashes

JEL classification: C02, D49, G01

Introduction

Empirical studies of the behavior of various complex systems exactly before big catastrophic events have shown that this behavior is characterized not only by growth of the relevant observables, but also by acceleration of the oscillations. Namely, oscillations with a decreasing period are often observed in financial market data and earthquake statistics (Sornette et al., 1996). Many recent studies have revealed that a good approximation for such behavior is a power law dependence modulated by log periodic structures (Sornette et al., 1996, Podlazov, 2009). On the other hand, it is known that power law and log periodicity occur in discrete scale-invariant systems (Sornette, 1998, Bikulov et al. 2006). Hence, the problem of exploring financial markets as discrete scale-invariant systems emerges. In this work, we will focus on the models that take into account the hierarchical structure of financial markets. We consider a model of market dynamics before crashes introduced by Johansen and Sornette (1998) as the most successful attempt in this framework.

The Johansen-Sornette hierarchical model (JS model) of financial crashes can be considered as an approach to describe hierarchically organized complex systems

D. Sornette et al. (Eds.), *Market Risk and Financial Markets Modeling*,
DOI 10.1007/978-3-642-27931-7_17, © Springer-Verlag Berlin Heidelberg 2012

with interacting elements. The aim of the present study is to examine, in the framework of simple models, how this approach can explain various phenomena in financial markets and be applied to solve actual market problems.

In the JS model, the hierarchical structure of the market refers to the hierarchical organization of the traders on the market. It is suggested that the proposed hierarchical structure may reflect the genuine hierarchical organization of stock markets, which can be either built-in structural organization or spontaneous structure resulting from the self-organization of the market (Huang et al., 1997). An example of the built-in hierarchy is the following: at the highest level of the hierarchy, we find currency blocks, at the next level below we find the countries, then major banks and institutions within a country and so forth down to individual traders. An important consequence of the hierarchical organization is that the action of a trader influences only a limited number of traders at the same level of the hierarchy and below. Due to a cascade effect, the decisions of the lower levels in turn influence the higher levels.

Over the whole study and while developing our own model we will follow the main simplifying assumptions made in the JS model. First of all, it is assumed that the sellers are necessarily a homogeneous group which remains fixed and neutral throughout the period in which the progressive cooperative activity between the buyers develops. It is expected that a moderate selling rate will not modify the results qualitatively, as long as the buyers remain a strong majority. The problem thus reduces to determining quantitatively the temporal behavior of the total number of buy positions. Secondly, irreversible evolution is being considered in which traders, when they put a buy order, then hold their position until the crash.

Johansen-Sornette Hierarchical Model of Financial Crashes

Individual traders are referred to as traders of order 0. According to the hierarchical organization, these traders are organized in groups of m traders and we consider each such group as a single "trader" of order 1. These groups of order 1 are also organized in groups of m so that each forms a group of order 2 and so forth. In this way, a hierarchical organization is obtained, where a group of order n is made of m^n individual traders. In order to obtain the analytical solution below we take $m=2$.

Considering the strategies of the agents, we may call them both fundamentalists and imitators. Each trader carries out his own fundamental analysis of the economy, of the expected dividends and of the strength of the stock company. This determines his time-to-buy. Hence, at time 0 each individual trader i of 0th level of the hierarchy has a preferred time t_i to by the stocks. All these times t_i are distributed according to the following cumulative distribution known as a Poisson distribution

$$P_0(t) = 1 - \exp\{-\lambda t\}.$$

Interaction between traders occurs as a result of their uncertainty. The trader is aware that his own analysis may be incomplete or even mistaken and he is thus eager to learn more from the action of his nearest neighbor. Then the information that the nearby trader has bought the stock is considered by the trader as a sufficient reason to reduce his own time-to-buy.

Quantitatively the effect of an acquisition by trader i at time t_i on the trader j can be expressed as the reduction of the time-to-buy t_j according to

$$t_{ij} = t_i + 2^{-\beta}\left(t_j - t_i\right),$$

where $\beta \geq 0$ is an influence exponent. The fact that $2^{-\beta} \leq 1$ ensures that $t_i \leq t_{ij} \leq t_j$. Thus, the distribution of the obtained time-to-buy for agent t_j becomes the following

$$P(t) = 1 - \exp\{-\lambda[t_i + 2^{\beta}(t - t_i)]\} \quad (1)$$

In the model the influence is assumed to be homogeneous, i.e. β is the same for all agents.

The described impact mechanism is essential to obtain threshold-like dynamics of the model. It is basically a positive feedback which together with the hierarchical structure gives rise to the power law growth and decreasing-period self-similar oscillations of the demand curve. Threshold-like self-similar oscillations occur as a consequence of information distribution limitations, namely the rule that other traders of the same group, and only them, have the privilege of incorporating the information about a trader's actions. Furthermore, the agent of order m is considered to be an active buyer when all its constituting traders of order $m-1$ have bought the stock. Then, due to a cascade process, the influence overlaps the whole hierarchy from the lowest level to the highest level.

In the special case of $m = 2$, which corresponds to a binary tree, the exact formula of probability for the trader of order N to buy the stock in the time interval $(t, t+dt)$ can be derived. Given that there are two traders of order $N-1$ constituting the trader of order N, this event corresponds to the situation when firstly one of two traders of order $N-1$ buys in the time interval $(t_1, t_1 + dt_1)$ and then the second would buy in the time interval $(t, t+dt)$. The probabilities of this two event are $p_{N-1}(t_1)$ and $\tilde{p}_{N-1}(t_1)$ respectively. Here $\tilde{p}_{N-1}(t_1)$ will refer to the probability density for the second trader of order $N-1$ to buy the stock provided that the first trader of order $N-1$ has already entered the market. Then from the Eq.(1) one has

$$\tilde{p}_{N-1}(t) = \frac{1}{2^{-\beta}}\, p_{N-1}\, \frac{t - \left(1 - 2^{-\beta}\right)t_1}{2^{-\beta}} \quad .$$

Taking into account all possible time values $t_1 \in (0,t)$ one finally obtains

$$p_N(t) = \frac{2}{2^{-\beta}} \int_0^t p_{N-1}(t_1) p_{N-1}\left(\frac{t-(1-2^{-\beta})t_1}{2^{-\beta}}\right) dt_1 \,. \tag{2}$$

The factor 2 occurs because either of the two traders of order *N*-1 can buy first.

In the framework of this model, there is a rigorous definition of a crash. Namely, the critical point t_c is defined as the time when all traders have finally placed their buy orders. In the limit of an infinite number of traders it means that at time $t < t_c$ the number of buyers accelerates progressively but remains small until at time t_c a finite fraction of traders have put buy orders, thus saturating the market. Thus, the crash is supposed to occur due to the impossibility of the market to sustain such speculation. In (Johansen and Sornette, 1998) it is shown that the distribution of times of crashes converges to a delta function as the number of traders goes to infinity, i.e. $p_N(t) \to p_\infty(t) \equiv \delta(t-t_c), \quad N \to \infty$. It should be noted that in the case of a finite number of traders, the distribution of times of crashes is obtained by N iterations of Eq.(1) starting with $p_0(t)$.

There is a special case $\beta = 1$ when we can obtain the exact expression for the distribution of crash times. Provided that the initial distribution of times-to-buy $p_0(t) = \lambda \exp\{-\lambda t\}$, iterations of Eq.(1) give the following expression for the probability for the agent of order N to buy in time interval $(t, t+dt)$ that is the same as the probability of a crash for the hierarchy consisting of N levels

$$p_N(t) = C_N t^{2^N-1} \lambda^{2^N} \exp\{-2^N \lambda t\}. \tag{3}$$

Clearly the distribution (3) converges to a δ- function as shown on fig. 1.

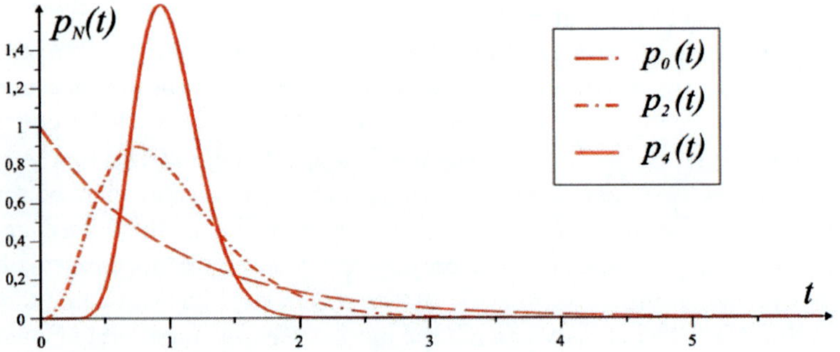

Fig. 1: Evolution of the probability distributions in Eq. (3)

The distributions (3) have their maximum points at

$$t_c = \frac{2^N - 1}{2^N \lambda} \xrightarrow[N\to\infty]{} \frac{1}{\lambda} \,.$$

This time, in the limit of infinite number of traders, is simply an average over all initial times-to-buy of individual traders.

In the general case $\beta \neq 1$ the exact expression for t_c cannot be derived analytically and we have to use numerical analysis. As a numerical solution, we plot the number of agents who have put buy orders versus time, which is basically a demand dynamics (fig. 2). It appears that there is a certain parameter space where the model exhibits almost power law growth, modulated by decreasing-period structures.

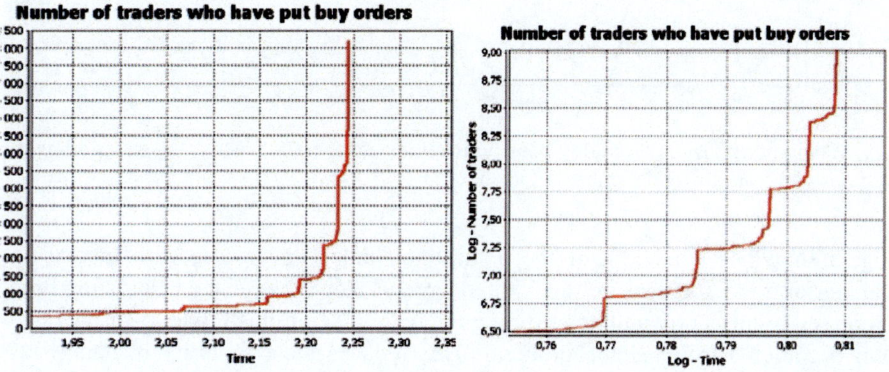

Fig. 2: The plots of number of agents who have put buy orders versus time with regular and log-log scales respectively. The values of the main parameters are $n = 13$ $(N = 8192)$, $\lambda = 0.01$, $\beta = 5$.

These results can be considered as a confirmation of the conjecture that the reason for the log-periodic structures on financial markets is its discreet scale invariance and a power law growth is a consequence of the presence of positive feedback.

In the limit of $N \to \infty$ the crash time t_c is the same for any initial realizations of times-to-buy. Nevertheless, when we want to obtain the numerical solution, we have to consider finite-hierarchical systems and the crash time will be different for every particular initial realization of times-to-buy. However, the spread of t_c should decrease with increasing number of traders (i.e. number of hierarchical levels). In order to confirm this statement we plot probability density functions of the crash times corresponding to systems with various total numbers of agents (see fig. 3). In order to plot one curve we use 200 simulations and the obtained range of times $t_c^{\,j}$ is divided into 20 spaces.

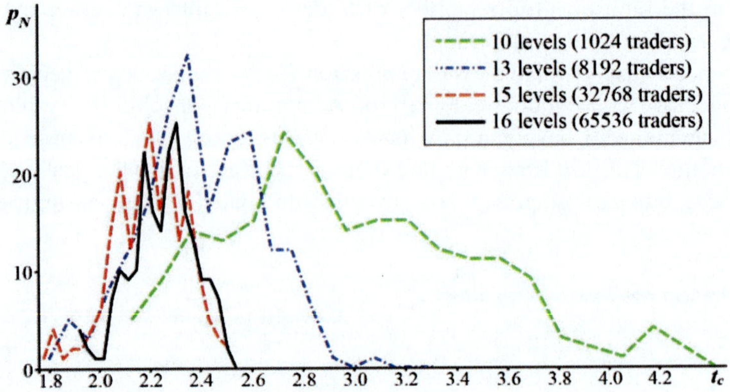

Fig. 3: Non-normalized probability density functions of the crash times $t_c^{\,j}$ corresponding to systems with various total numbers of agents.

Fig. 3 shows that a width of the distribution indeed decreases with increasing number of traders. However, the width decreases slowly while the calculating time increases significantly and determining the real value of crash time t_c for the system becomes a troublesome problem. This reduces the possibility of using this model for real trading and prediction.

Ultrametric Generalization

One of the simplifications in the model above, made in order to get an analytical solution, is homogeneity of the influence between the agents. A hierarchical organization allows us to introduce additional restrictions on information distribution. We suggest defining a certain distance between agents and introducing the dependence of an influence exponent on this distance.

The distance between two agents i and j is defined as $d_{ij} = m^{n_{ij}}$, where m is an arity of the tree of agents and n_{ij} is the number of levels from both agents i and j to their first mutual junction. This definition gives us an ultrametric distance, i.e. $d_{ik} \le \max(d_{ij}, d_{jk})$. Let us consider quantitatively the result of the impact of trader i on trader j. Let t_i and t_j be initial times-to-buy of agents i and j respectively, with $t_i < t_j$. Then at time t_i, the agent i enters the market and the agent j immediately receives this information and his own time-to-buy is modified to an earlier time t_{ij}, according to

$$t_{ij} = t_j - \frac{1}{(d_{ij})^{\beta}}(t_j - t_i).$$

Clearly, for this generalization we can also find a certain parameter range where demand dynamics exhibit power law growth modulated by log-periodic-like structures. Graphical results of the numeric calculation for this model are shown on fig. 4. This figure also represents the self-similarity of the obtained curve.

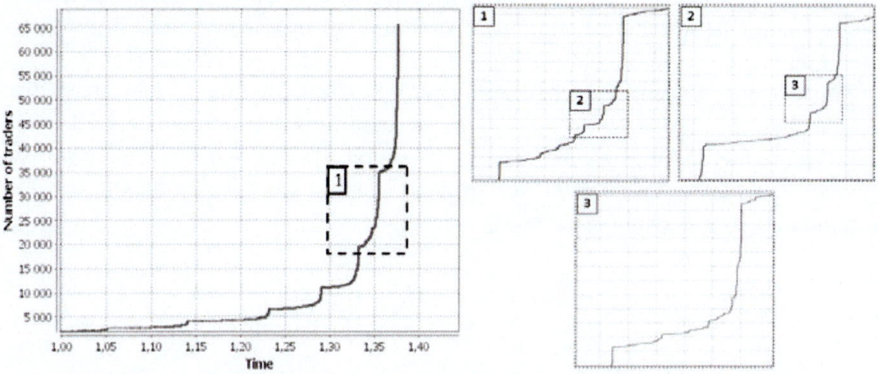

Fig. 4: Self-similarity of demand dynamics on different time scales

The important question that arises is whether an invariance of the critical point for this modification still remains true. Invariance of the crash point refers to the fact that in the limit of infinite number of traders the crash time becomes a nonzero constant, independent of initial realizations of times-to-buy. In order to answer this question, we plot probability density functions of the crash times for various total numbers of agents as described above. The results obtained show that the width decreases with increasing number of agents and the maximum point remains nonzero. In fig. 5 we compare non-normalized probability density functions for the JS model and for its ultrametric generalization. Thus, in the framework of the modified model, in order to calculate the actual crash point of a system with required degree of accuracy, we can use a hierarchical system with smaller number of agents.

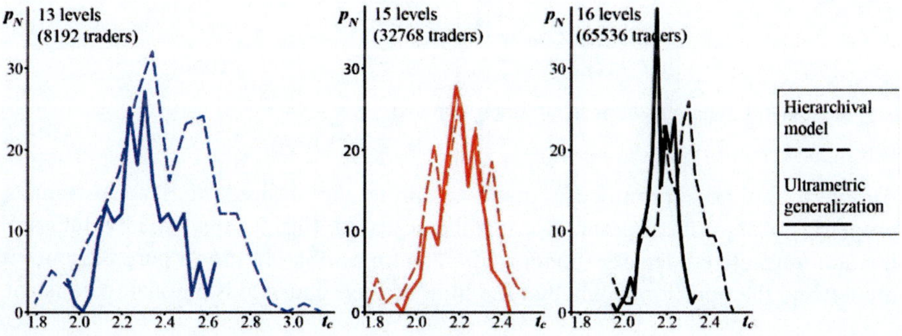

Fig. 5: Comparison of non-normalized probability density functions of crash times for two models (JS model and its ultrametric generalization)

Pure Ultrametric Model

It should be noted that the situation when an active agent influences only the nearest agent on the same level of hierarchy is rather a rough approximation of the real information distribution process. The actual imitation process seems to be highly heterogeneous. However, a hierarchical structure still needs to be taken into consideration.

Suppose that at time t_1, when an agent with the least time-to-buy enters the market, the information about his actions starts influencing immediately all other trader in the hierarchy. But this influence is smaller the further away (in terms of ultrametric distance) these agents are from each other. Then, new times-to-buy for all remaining agents change according to

$$t_i^* = t_i - \frac{1}{(d_{i1})^\beta}(t_i - t_1).$$

The main difference between this model and the models above is an absence of predefined threshold-like dynamics, which is a consequence of specific imitation rules, since every agent of hierarchy receives the information. We thus do not expect our model to exhibit log-periodic-like structures. The numerical solution of the model shows that in a fairly small neighborhood of the critical point, demand dynamics is also modulated by threshold-like structures with increasing amplitude and decreasing period (see fig. 6). Unfortunately, there are some difficulties with visual observation of these oscillations because of a "too quickly decreasing" period.

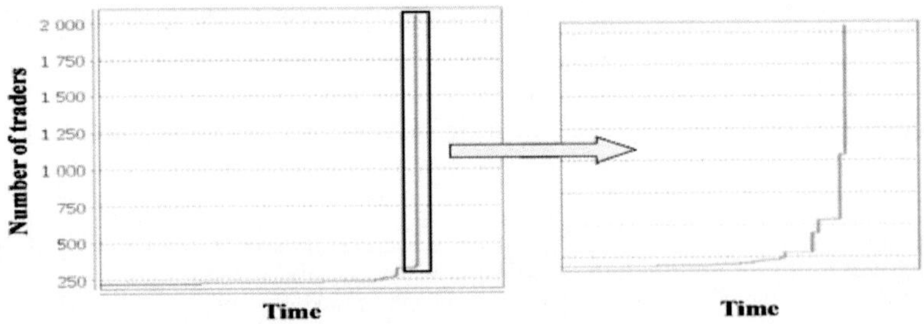

Fig. 6: Demand dynamics in pure ultrametric model

Although the new ultrametric model exhibits the desired demand dynamics, properties of its critical point appear to be arguable. Fig. 7 shows the evolution of the non-normalized density function of crash times obtained for a pure ultrametric model, and the question is whether the limit of this sequence is a nonzero constant.

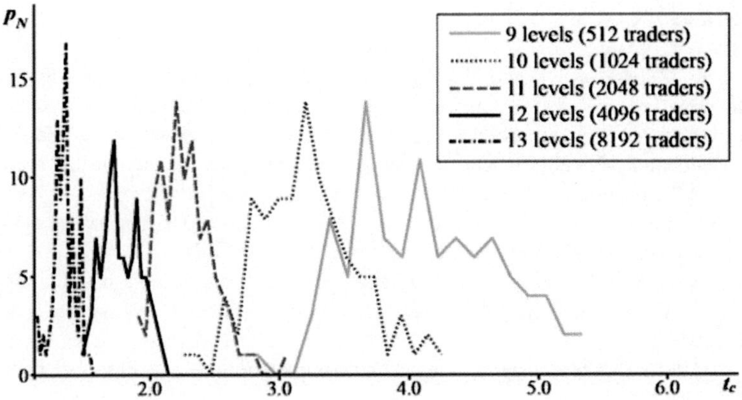

Fig. 7: Non-normalized density functions of crash times t_c^j for pure ultrametric model

Conclusion

The main purpose of hierarchical and ultrametric models is to explain the phenomenon observed for different complex systems before catastrophic events characterized by singular behavior. Ultrametricity, which describes hierarchical systems, is well known to give rise to log-periodic power law solutions and the question was where can we find hierarchy in stock markets. The proposed hierarchical organization of the traders seems to be consistent with the real situation on the market.

The model of Johansen and Sornette not only shows the possible origin of log-periodic power law behavior on the market, but also provides the tool for describing and analysis of the real hierarchical structures observed on the stock markets. We explore the properties of the critical point in this model in order to estimate the predictive potential of these models. Probability density functions of the crash times as a research tools show that the critical time is an intrinsic quality of hierarchical systems, i.e. in the limit of very large number of participants this time is independent of the randomness of the initial strategies of agents. We prove that for an ultrametric generalization of the JS model this invariance of the critical point remains true.

The last model proves that hierarchical and ultrametric structure on its own can give rise to log-periodic-like behavior while the imitation rule rather determines the type of feedback and consequently the general trend of observed dynamics.

All the models considered above can be useful in the nowadays very popular microscopic simulations of the stock market. It is obvious from many different researches that it can be a mistake to represent market participants as independent elements of the system, since some very important market phenomena (e.g. heavy tails in the distribution of returns) are the consequence of relations between agents (Cont and Bouchaud, 2001). Thus, one may represent agents organized hierarchically as described above and introduce certain imitation rules.

References

Bikulov A. K., Zubarev A. P., and Kaidalova L. V. (2006). Hierarchical dynamic model of financial market near a crash point and p-adic mathematical analysis. Vestn. Samar. Gos. Tekhn. Univ. Ser. Fiz.-Mat. Nauki. Samara State Technical University, 42, 135–140

Cont R., Bouchaud J.P. (2000). Herd behavior and aggregate fluctuations in speculative markets, Macroeconomic dynamics, Vol. 4, No.2, 170-96

Huang Y., Ouillon G., Saleur H., Sornette D. (1997). Spontaneous generation of discrete scale invariance in growth models, Phys. Rev. E, 55, 6433-6447.

Podlazov A.V. (2009). Blow-up with complex exponents. Log-periodic oscillations in the democratic fiber bundle model. Preprint, Inst. Appl. Math., the Russian Academy of Science, 35, 22.

Sornette D. (1998). Discrete scale invariance and complex dimensions, Physics Reports 297, Issue 5, 239-270.

Sornette D., and Johansen A. (1998) A hierarchical model of financial crashes. Physica A, 261, 581-598.

Sornette D., Johansen A., and Bouchaud J.P. (1996). Stock market crashes, Precursors and Replicas. Journal de Physique, France, 6, 167-175.

Catastrophe Theory in Forecasting Financial Crises

Anastassia Pleten

Institute of Economics and Industrial Engineering, Siberian Branch of RAS, Novosibirsk, Russia. email:anastasia.zaykova@gmail.com

Abstract Sometimes in an economy a system becomes susceptible to even a small exterior pulse, which can give a disproportionately strong response. Catastrophe theory allows us to define critical values of pressure upon the system at which a crisis becomes inevitable. Analysis of the quantitative characteristics gives us the chance to draw the qualitative outputs necessary for making management decisions, both on micro and on macro levels, depending on the scales of the analyzed system.

Keywords: Financial crises, Catastrophe theory

JEL classification: C02, D49, G01

Introduction

The constant development of the mechanisms of the market functioning of the Russian economy inevitably results in reinforcement of the phenomena connected with the cyclical development of national economy. Accordingly, it is impossible to neglect the fact that periods of fast growth are replaced by periods of deceleration of growth and even curtailment of production. That fact is conventional that in the conditions of a market economy, decisions are accepted by a lot of economic agents independently, as result of it constantly collecting disproportions which elimination is impossible without curtailment of production, growth of unemployment, inflation or other, crisis phenomena can serve. The globalization of the economy of both developed, and what are considered as the developing countries indicates that the presence of communications leading to the crisis phenomena in the economy of one country, launches a mechanism which can cause a chain reaction and make an essential impact on the economy of other countries.

The possibility of defining increases in so-called "pressure" in various sectors of economy and crises at various levels in time appears at the foreground in universal globalization. The scale of the free circulation of the financial flow considerably strengthens the danger of the emergence of instability in stock markets, credit organizations and banking as well as financial systems both on macro- and on meso-levels under the conditions of an almost total absence of a necessary system of regulation and forecasting of crisis situations.

D. Sornette et al. (Eds.), *Market Risk and Financial Markets Modeling*,
DOI 10.1007/978-3-642-27931-7_18,

As it is shown in observations of crisis situations in past years, it is possible to explain a variety of crises but there is no settled, unambiguously accepted point of view on the majority of the questions concerning reasons causing crises, and there are also no possibilities for their forecasting, and accordingly, their prevention. In spite of the fact that financial crises can not lead to recession in industrial sectors of the economy, the losses are becoming more and more significant in the last decades. Therefore the necessity to develop a technique that would identify financial crises in early stages is dictated not only by the world, but also by Russian experience. In addressing the scientific approach to the examination of financial crises, empirically tested methods are required that are viable both for the Russian Federation, and for the world economy as a whole.

At present there are three different econometric approaches that have already become the classics of crisis investigation. Through using one of these, it is possible to reveal the pacing factors influencing the development of crisis situations:

- the approach based on classical regression methods,
- the system of early indicators,
- the probabilistic approach with the usage of models of a binary choice.

The first one is based on the detection of the contribution of various factors in the formation of a currency crisis by means of the standard least-squares method; it is possible to define a necessary set of factors.

The second is the system of early indicators, which allows one to include in the analysis a larger number of considered factors, in comparison with the first method, that are prospective indicators of a crisis.

The third method of the analysis of mechanisms of crisis formation is the probabilistic approach. This method allows the estimation of the concrete contribution of each factor to crisis formation, and allows one to review the data of crisis presence in each country during various time frames; there are no restrictions in the number of factors under study (probit- and logit-models).

One of the most vital issues in forecasting economic crises is that from the point of view of economic theory, the balance in the market has been researched extensively, as well as the processes of the passage of economy from one equilibrium point to another, but the processes that have caused this passage have not been researched to the same extent.

Crises are divided both according to a regional indication as well as from the point of view of the time of their origin. The regional character of the financial crises is proved by empirical research. Glick and Rose (1998) have empirically proven the regional character of "the epidemic effect" for the case of currency crises, and have explained this by the high level of regionalization of trading contacts. From the point of view of the time of their origin, crises can differ considerably in the set of the factors that have caused them. In modern Russia, the following crises took place:

- the crisis in the interbanking market in 1995;
- the crisis in the stock market in 1997;

- the financial, currency crises and the crisis of a state debt (state credit obligations-federal loan bonds) in 1998;
- the currency and financial crisis in 2002;
- a credibility gap in the Russian banking system in 2004;
- the crisis of liquidity of the second half of 2008 – 2009.

In the scientific literature there is a set of various types of crises, but the crisis that has captured a world financial system in 2008 is probably one of the heaviest and longest. The present crisis is a structural crisis; thus, it is possible to consider all chains of world financial institutions inconsistent, and while world leaders and the outstanding financial analysts should search for ways to eliminate the impractical links of this circuit, each sector of domestic economy suffers to some extent. The banking sector of economy is the immediate participant the financial crisis.

The problems in the mortgage lending market in the USA became the trigger which has put the crisis mechanism in action. Though at the heart of the crisis there are other more fundamental reasons for the crisis. These can be divided into: macroeconomic, microeconomic and even institutional. It is not a secret to anybody that the inconsistency of financial institutions turned out to be the key contribution to the development of a crisis situation. The risk of the investors putting their means in mortgage securities had been artificially underestimated, and that became a cause of bankruptcy of the world leaders in the financial and insurance sectors of economy. The policy of low interest rates led by Federal Reserved System of the USA as an attempt to prevent cyclical recession of the economy of the USA allowed many large companies to receive cheap extra capital. Afterwards, the domestic companies have appeared involved in the international financial crisis as under the influence of superfluous liquidity process of formation of market bubbles was activated. As the Russian banks also used the possibility of engaging in cheap funds in the capital world market, the Russian market of credits has started to extend, that has led to growth of availability of monetary resources and the decrease of rates in domestic market.

The impairment of an investment position of the credit organizations has become the consequence of it.

Necessity of the development of techniques of early identification of financial crises is dictated not only by the world, but also the Russian experience. All the well-known scales and negative consequences of the crisis of 2008 are:

1. Rouble devaluation, though it is not such sharp as in 1998, but it essentially influences the incomes of the population. That is, the considerable decrease of income of the population against a rise in prices for the goods and services became the result of devaluation.
2. The influence of the financial crisis in Russia was felt by almost all enterprises, especially those oriented toward export. Companies with a million roubles turnover have frozen many investment programs under the conditions of the crisis and have begun to reduce the budget by all means possible. This in turn, involved mass lay-offs and a shortage of workplaces.

3. In the bank system, toughening of requirements of banks to potential borrowers, increase of rates under again given out credits, curtailing of many mortgage and consumer programs (for example, without-deposit and interest-free credits) are observed
4. The prices for the earth and real estate have essentially decreased because of a sharp fall of demand for these resources. But the financial crisis has played Russia a more positive role, having relieved the market of the artificial overestimate of real estate in terms of cost of objects and its continuous growth.

The negative consequences of the modern financial crisis are underlined by the necessity for learning and forecasting the tendencies of modern social and economic development and have also caused interest to non-linear theories. Such theories constructed on the basis of an analytical toolkit of systems of differential equations, give some new approaches to studying social and economic processes. One of the examples concerning non-linear theories is the catastrophe theory. The subject of catastrophe theory is study of the spasmodic changes arising in the form of a sudden answer of system to the smooth change of exterior conditions. The concept "catastrophe" with reference to studying the crisis processes carries dual semantic meaning: on the one hand, it characterizes crisis scales, on the other it contains an element of unpredictability in the development of economic processes.

For the analysis of economic events it is important that the catastrophe theory formulates an important regularity: after passing a threshold value, the system answers a proportional change of parameters with a quantum leap. The catastrophe theory ascertains infringements of linearity, proportionality and conformity between quantitative changes and qualitative transitions caused by them in system development. We will consider similar statements in an example:

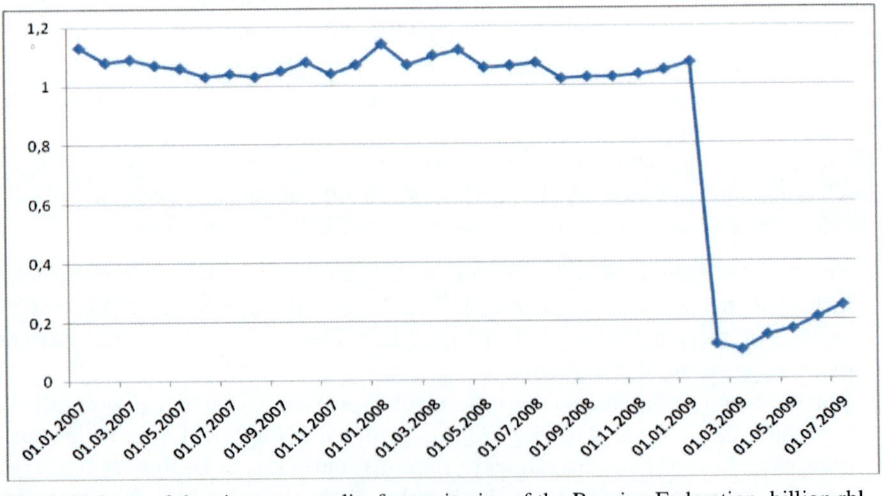

Fig. 1: Volume of the given out credits for territories of the Russian Federation, billion rbl.

In the figure the sharp decrease in volume of issued credits during the period from January, 1st 2009 to February, 1st 2009 is clearly visible. Such decreases are also catastrophes, or so-called tucks. The following figure can serve as an illustration to this statement:

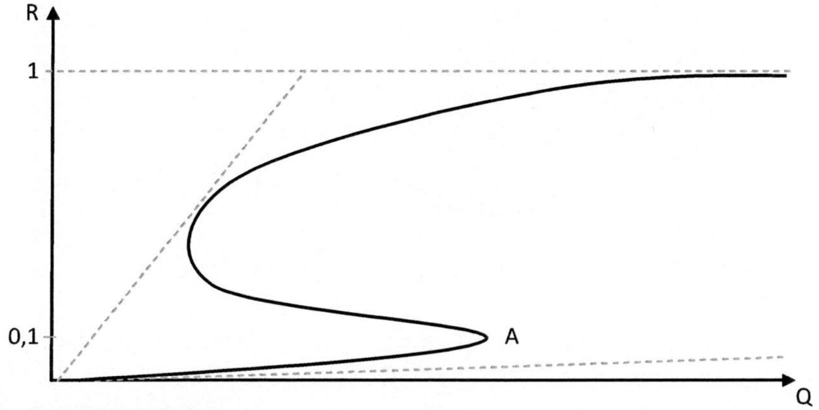

Fig. 2: A fold of Whitney

The so-called tuck of Whitney is represented in figure 2. (On figure 2 and 3 Q is volume of giving out credits and R is a measure of credit rick)..The point A is a stable equilibrium point, and upon passage to any other point on a curve or a tuck of Whitney, the balance is broken. A bank slowly moves on a curve upwards to the point A, an equilibrium point, by gradually increasing the volume of the credits produced and thereby maximizing the profit. If the balance in the financial sector of economy is broken, due to the influence of some external factors, the bank can get either to a point which is above equilibrium, or movelower from the point A. When hitting a point on the curve which is below the point A, the bank reduces the risk, but at the same time the volume of the credits given out also decreases. After the economic situation in the financial markets is stabilized, the bank will start with a view of increase have arrived over again to increase volume of given out credits.

The second variant of the succession of events after balance violation in the financial market occurs in the event that the bank hits the nail on a curve, above the equilibrium point A. In this case, the credit risk grows considerably together with the volume of the produced credits that essentially influences the financial stability of the bank. After a row of non-payments, the bank will be forced to declare itself bankrupt.

Accordingly, constant control of the position on the curve is necessary for the bank in order not to suddenly appear in a zone of high risk.

As it is known, the economy develops cyclically, hence, quite often the periods of economic growth are replaced the recession periods. Therefore, drawing a tuck of Whitney for the period of one cycle, we see a segment of the equilibrium positions of bank, as shown in a figure 3.

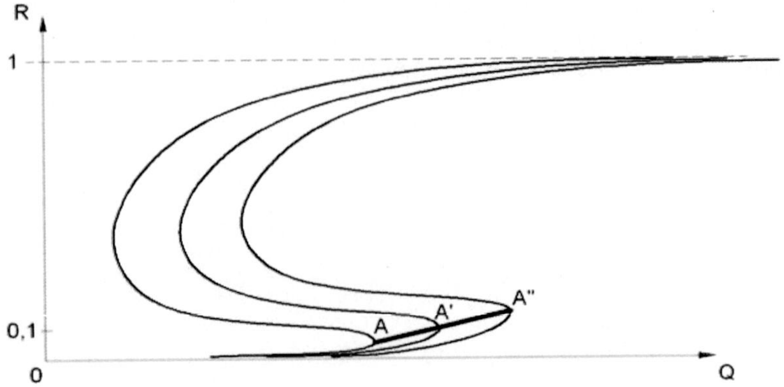

Fig. 3: A fold of Whitney taking into account cyclic development of economy

In a recession period, the curve is moved lower and more to the left from the curve corresponding to a normal state of the economy. During such moments, the equilibrium point is much lower. That is, a smaller risk corresponds to an optimal point A, while the points on the same curve to which there is a higher risk compared to the risk at point A, can lead the bank to bankruptcy. During a period of economic growth the situation is reversed; the curve is moved to the right and upwards. The equilibrium point on this curve will be the point A.

Thus, defining a set of parameters that influence the overheating of an economic system in this or that sector with the help of an econometric toolkit allows a possibility of forecasting a crisis, or, in terms of the considered theory – catastrophe. In other words, crisis situations in the economy are developed by a gradual increase of disproportions, defects of the market; accordingly, after the achievement of a certain threshold value of parameter, the system answers with a quantum leap, hence, there is a crisis.

On the whole, it is possible to draw the following conclusions based on the conducted research. At first, in the process of increasing instability the dynamics of parameters acquire a stochastic character. The system becomes susceptible to even a small exterior pulse in such a state, giving a disproportionately strong response. Catastrophe theory allows us to define critical values of pressure upon a system at which crises becomes inevitable.

Secondly, analysis of the quantitative characteristics gives the chance to make the qualitative outputs necessary for making management decisions, both on micro- and on macro-levels, depending on the scales of the analyzable system. Thus, it is useful for each separate bank to know at what point in a tuck of Whitney it is during each specific moment, for maintenance of financial stability. This calculation gives the bank the chance to influence a situation beforehand, by means of a change in the quantitative characteristics (in the example considered, the volume of the produced credits influences the change of an index of credit risk). Accordingly, such approach gives the chance both to foresee the approach of a financial crisis, and to influence the bank stability during any single moment of time.

References

Arnold V.I. (1990). The Catastrophe theory.

Demirguc-Kunt A., Detragiache A. (1998). The determinants of banking crisis in developing and developed countries. IMF Staff Papers, 56.

Glick, R., Rose, A. (1998). Contagion and trade: Why are currency crises regional? NBER Working Papers, 47.

Kaminsky G., Lizondo S. & Reinhart C.M. (1998). The leading indicators of currency crises. IMF Staff Papers, 48.

Sachs, J., Tornel, A. & Velasco, A. (1996). Financial crises in Emerging Markets. The lessons from 1995. Brookings Papers on Economic activity, 152, 147-215.

Zhuravleva U.A. (2010). Specification of system of indicators of financial stability of bank sector. Specification of system of indicators of financial stability of bank sector.

A Mathematical Model for Market Manipulations

Bismark Singh

Senior Undergraduate, Indian Institute of Technology, Delhi, India.
email: bismark.singh@gmail.com

Abstract A simple, hypothetical, probabilistic model is presented here to study how market manipulation done by an individual, towards his favor, also impact the success rates of others and vice versa. The mathematical modeling is intentionally developed into a form similar to that resulting from a game theory exercise, because the actions of one individual do not take place in isolation from the actions of others. The effect of not being content to stay at the level of one's peers is surveyed critically and the positive/negative bearings of this ideology are shown. Other results presented include how being selfish and following personal greed motives may possibly be the best choice available for an individual; how working in a team against a particular opponent could turn out to be not as individually advantageous as taking the risk of working alone.

Keywords: Game Theory, Market Manipulations, Economic Modeling, Strategy Planning in Market.

JEL classification: C60, C70.

Introduction

It is a well-established fact that every businessman tries to maximize his profits from a given customer base. In the competitive economic world we have today, this profit expansion, for one businessman, comes largely at the expense of another businessman. No person is satisfied to stay forever at a single, stagnating economic level and traders are constantly devising new, innovative strategies to earn more than others. Some of these strategies maybe negative while others may simply be aimed towards the quality improvement of their products (Slater, 2000). Whatever be the strategy, the central underlying fact is that every trader is trying to maximize his power to attract customers and thus trying to tilt the market balance in his favor.

However, a trader cannot manipulate the market independently. The outcome of his actions directly impacts the 'selling' potential of other traders and vice-versa (Aggarwal, 2003). This basis motivates us to look for a model in which actions of one trader are dependent on actions of another trader. In this study, one such mathematical model is presented, which uses a probability based approach towards market manipulations. It is attempted to look into the degree of manipulation possible by a single dealer at the expense of others. Questions with a moral connotation

D. Sornette et al. (Eds.), *Market Risk and Financial Markets Modeling*,
DOI 10.1007/978-3-642-27931-7_19,

(Macintosh, 1995) are deliberately ignored or overlooked as the aim of this study is to look at the impact of the manipulation and not its cause.

A game theoretic approach is preferred on the grounds that it provides a greater visual feel of the competition existing between the traders, the devisal of new strategies by a player to succeed and how these are handled by other players etc. (Macrae, 1982) Also, since profit at the expense of another dealer can be viewed as success or victory, the analogy appears to be apt.

Modeling

A group of N dealers is considered in this study. This group is divided into two teams (henceforth referred as players). The first team, which we address as Player 1, consists of the first dealer alone. The second team consists of the remaining N-1 dealers. A hypothetical game is played between these two players in which each tries to maximize his success over the other. In a physical scenario, these N dealers are competing in a market and trying to convince a group of N independent customers to purchase products from them. Thus the situation is not very different from a market of N dealers, selling products to a customer base of N customers.

The game is said to be partially won for a dealer if a single customer approaches him and thus purchases a product from him. Any approach to a dealer results in a purchase from him and thus it is sufficient for this event to be described just as a customer approaching the dealer. As all the dealers are symmetric, the probability for this event to take place for a single dealer is simply $1/N$. Success and failure are defined with respect to the dealer, who is our object of interest, and not the customer base, which is treated merely as an entity serving the dealer's purpose. Complete success is defined as the event when one or more customers approach a dealer i.e. the summation of one or more partial successes. Thus complete success for one player is not mutually exclusive of the complete success for the other player. Henceforth in this study, success is used to denote complete success unless otherwise explicitly stated. Also, success is defined with respect to Player 1, again unless otherwise explicitly stated.

We make the following assumptions to facilitate an easy to obtain solution and a simple to construct model:

1. The definition of success is not to be taken as implying failure for the other player. Success, as stated above, for one player can also mean success for another player. However, partial success is a mutually exclusive process for both the players.
2. There is no hierarchy in success – thus the power to attract a single customer is treated with equal respect and weightage as the power to attract more than one customer.
3. The customer base consists of N customers, identical in all respects which concern this study. No particular customer has a preference for a particular shopkeeper and if a shopkeeper manages to create or enhance a preference, then it is done in an unbiased manner with respect to all the customers.

4. No dealer is a customer and no customer is a dealer.
5. Player 2 consists of a group of similar N-1 dealers. None of these group members have individual preferences and individual behavior within this group does not exist at all.
6. All dealers sell exactly the same products, so there is no question of quality or preference for a customer to choose from. Any preference generated is similarly applied to the entire customer base and not to a specific set of customers.

Continuing from the objective of the game (viz. to achieve success), a player may decide to act from two different approaches. First, he may attempt to play the game fairly and thus his partial successes and failures follow a completely random process based on natural, un-tampered probabilistic distributions. We call a player who uses such an ideology a “Fair” player. The second possibility is that he may attempt to allure customers by either a positive or a negative mechanism, and thus increase his partial success probability. Physical scenarios of how this is possible are explained later. It should be noted that this is a more realistic scenario than the case of a fair player as every player desires to increase his stature in the market and thus finds ways to do that. Such a player is henceforth called a “Manipulative” player. The word ‘manipulative’ is used here without any positive or negative connotation and thus should not be taken with any moral value judgment.

Now we consider this game from three perspectives:

Fair Player, Fair Player

This is the case when both the players are fair and the game follows a completely natural unbiased probability distribution process. It is attempted to compute the success probability for player 1. Under the previously defined notation it follows that,

$$P(\textit{Single Partial Success}) = \frac{1}{N} \qquad (1)$$

The probability of single partial success for Player 2 is simply the complement of that of Player 1 as the events are mutually exclusively (as explained above). Thus it follows that,

$$'(\textit{Single Partial Success for Player } 2) = 1 - P(\textit{SinglePartial Success}) = 1 - \frac{1}{N} \qquad (2)$$

The probability of success for player 1 is the sum of the partial probabilities for a single success, double success, etc. up to N successes. This is equivalent to unity minus the probability for no success, or unity minus the probability that all customers go to player 2. Mathematically, the last statement can be expressed as,

$$P(\textit{Success}) = 1 - \left(1 - \frac{1}{N}\right)^{N} \qquad (3)$$

It must be noted that, from the government (or whatever party controls the market, if any), a greater number of dealers is desired because that is more beneficial for a customer. It leads to a greater variety (in terms of options of whom to buy from, although not in terms of quality because of the assumption) for the customer and a diminished chance of monopolization. But from the dealers' point of view this is not desirable because one expects that as the number of dealers increases, the probability of success for each dealer decreases. This is quantified in Fig.1, which is a graph of (3). Thus, every dealer wants there to be a lower overall number of dealers in the market, meaning that he would have a greater chance of attracting the customer. Further, every dealer would want to move towards establishing a monopoly in the market because that would result in the maximum success he could possibly have. Thus, he is not satisfied with a partial success probability, which is the same as everyone else, and tries to increase it from $1/N$. This is the basis of motivation for the second case.

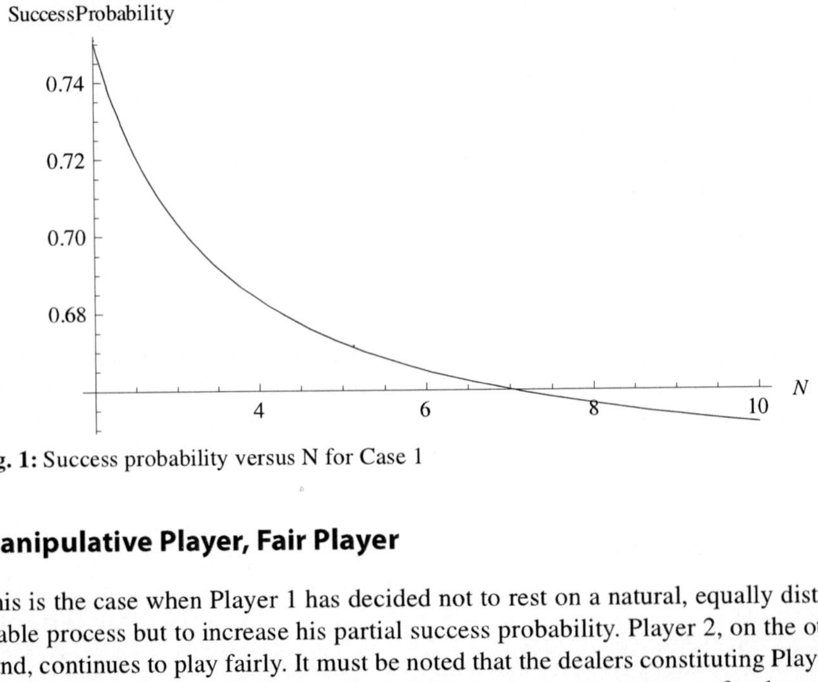

Fig. 1: Success probability versus N for Case 1

Manipulative Player, Fair Player

This is the case when Player 1 has decided not to rest on a natural, equally distributable process but to increase his partial success probability. Player 2, on the other hand, continues to play fairly. It must be noted that the dealers constituting Player 2 all play identically i.e. all play the game fairly. It does not concern us for the scope of this study how Player 1 manages to increase his partial success probability – we are more interested in looking at the impact it creates. However, for the sake of continuity, a few ways in which Player 1 could do so are described here,

1. He may manipulate with some controlling agency which forces other dealers to close their businesses on Sunday or at an earlier time than him.
2. He may get some regulations approved from the bureaucracy or some private companies which say that only products bearing his business stamp would be suitable for a particular office, e.g. bulk stationary orders for a particular office, medicines in a particular hospital etc.

This list could go on indefinitely but is curtailed here. Under this new scheme we use the following notation,

$$P(Partial\ Success) = \frac{a}{N} = \beta \tag{4}$$

where,

$$1 \le a \le N \tag{5}$$

It is easy to observe that a=1 corresponds to the case of a Fair Player and a=N corresponds to the case of Player 1 (a Manipulative Player) succeeding in establishing a perfect monopoly. Also for Player 2 as described before it follows that,

$$P(Partial\ \ Success\ \ for\ \ Player\ \ 2) = 1 - \beta \tag{6}$$

Summing up these probabilities as described in Case 1,

$$P(Success) = 1 - (1 - \beta)^N \tag{7}$$

The implications of this result are discussed later.

Manipulative Player, Manipulative Player

This case is the opposite of Case 2. Here all dealers combining to make Player 2 decide to increase their partial success probability while Player 1 chooses to be honest. Again, a few ways in which this is physically possible are described here,

1. Player 1 is new to a locality and thus not many customers trust/know him. Thus, even though he is selling the same product, he is unable to attract a similar customer base as Player 2.
2. All the dealers in Player 2 may decide to give a cheaper product free of cost with the main product. This may also be a custom/tradition prevalent in the area, which Player 1 does not know about. Thus the customers may prefer Player 2 as he (they) offers (offer) them a greater value for money.

Again this list is not exhaustive by any means. Now if all the dealers in Player 2 increase their probability (by the same amount) then,

$$P(\ Partial\ Success\ for\ Player\ 2) = \frac{a}{N}.\frac{a}{N}.\frac{a}{N}.....(N-1\ times).\frac{a}{N} = \frac{a}{N}(N-1) = \alpha \tag{8}$$

$$P(Partial\ Success) = 1 - \alpha \tag{9}$$

Thus it follows that

$$P(Success\ \ ) = 1 - \alpha^N \tag{10}$$

Further, using the fact that probability can only lie between zero and unity we get an upper bound on a,

$$1 \leq a \leq \frac{N}{N-1} \tag{11}$$

Again, a=1 implies the case of an honest player and $a = \frac{N}{N-1}$ implies the case when Player 1 has no chance of a partial success. However, the crucial difference between this case and Case 2 is the presence of a severe upper bound on a. This bound has several implications. It should be noted that in Case 2, a can take all possible values. However, in Case 3, the maximum manipulation for dealers of Player 2, working as a team against Player 1, is $1/(N\text{-}1)$ for each dealer. This quantity is a number lesser than 1, i.e. no dealer working in a team (against a single opponent) can achieve a perfect monopoly for himself. However, as noticed in Case 2, when a dealer is working independently towards manipulation, he can theoretically monopolize the market entirely towards his favor. Thus an interesting 'selfish' paradox is set up. Working on egocentric principles and attempting to maximize one's partial success probability without any team help can be more advantageous, rather than working in a team against a single player.

Results and Discussions

A market of 5 customers and 5 dealers is analyzed under the above model. The graphs in Fig. 2 show the probability variations with a. The value of a is restricted between the bounds described in (11) so as to compare Cases 2 and 3.

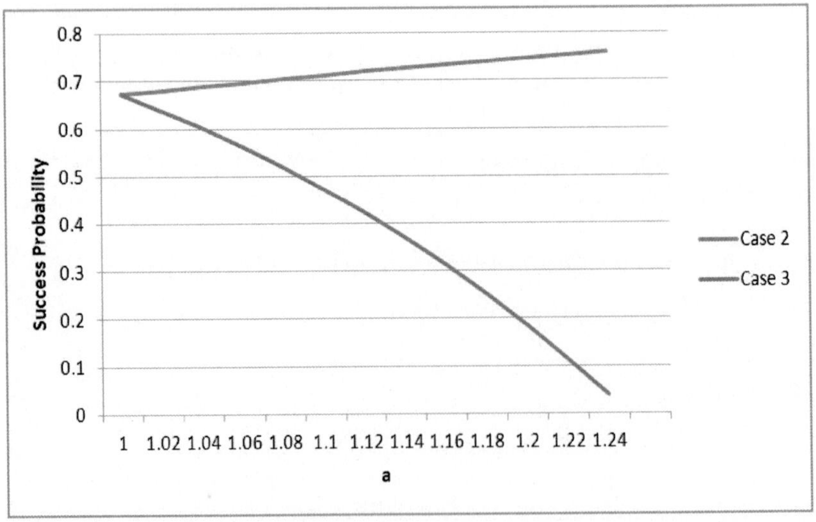

Fig. 2: Success probability for Case 2 and Case 3 versus a

It is observed from Fig. 2 that there exists a very steep downward slope for Case 3 as *a* increases. This is expected, because as Player 2 increases his partial success probability (by an increase in *a*) the success probability of Player 1 must fall. However, in the same domain interval for *a*, when we analyze Case 2, the increase in success probability for Player 1 is not so substantial. At an outward level, one may be tempted to conclude from Fig. 2 that Player 1 has a greater risk of losing out (shown in Case 3) rather than winning (shown in Case 2), but attention is brought to the horizontal axis of the graph. The range of values of *a* are complete for Case 3 but not so for Case 2, which allows a much larger value range for *a*. Results for this range are provided in Fig. 3.

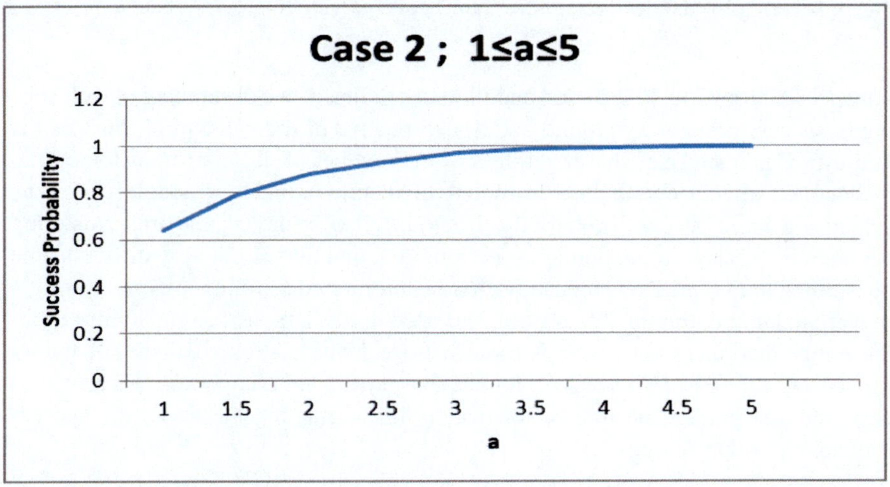

Fig. 3: Success probability versus a for complete range of *a* values

It follows from Fig. 3 that a slight manipulation by Player 1 to change *a* from 1(Fair Player) to say, a=2 results in a phenomenal increase in success probability. A value of a=2 can be theoretically thought of as Player 1 managing to oust one dealer from the market, thereby increasing his probability to 0.87 (which is a very large success rate). The argument stressed here is that a substantial probability increase can result from even a slight manipulation.

More general graphs are now discussed, which show probability variations with *a* for different values of N.

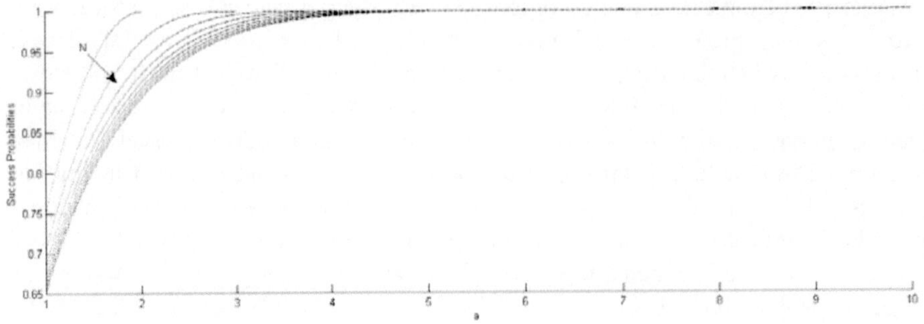

Fig. 4: Success probabilities versus *a* for Case 2, with varying N

Values of N from 2 to 10 are used and plotted. In Fig. 4, we observe a large clustering in success probability around a=2.5, irrespective of the value of N. This fact is interesting as it suggests that regardless of the number of dealers (or customers) in the market, after a certain fixed amount of manipulation by a single player he achieves a large success probability. It should also be noted that this clustering occurs fairly 'early' in the domain spectrum of a, and thus is not very difficult/time consuming to obtain. This fact can further be interpreted as follows: even if a single player is manipulating in a market of N (variable) dealers, he has the ability to tilt the entire market in his favor, without a huge manipulation. It does not matter immensely to the overall scenario how many players are competing. However, as expected, the greater the number of dealers in the market, the lesser the success probability within this clustering.

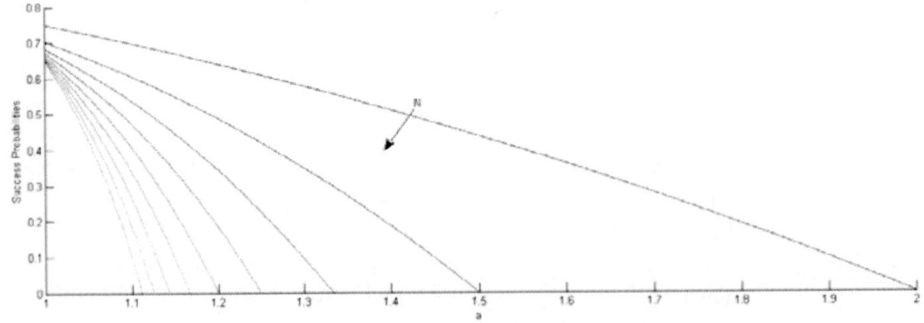

Fig. 5: Success probabilities versus *a* for Case 3, with varying N

In Fig.5, Case 3 is presented for different values of N. No analogous clustering at a particular value is obtained as in Case 2, but the change in magnitude of the slopes should be noticed. The downward slopes increase in magnitude as the value of N increases, implying sharper decreases in success probabilities for Player 1 as the number of players increase. Thus, from the perspective of Player 1, a lower number of overall dealers is desired. Further, as the number of dealers increases, the maximum value of a actually decreases – a fact which is detrimental not only to Player 1 but also to the individual team members of Player 2. Again the selfish paradox comes into play, where a member of Player 2 must decide and choose whether to stay in the team (and have a bound on his success maximization) or compete individually (and risk going against a group).

Conclusion

From this brief analysis of the hypothetical system considered, it can be concluded that a fair play approach need not always be the best possible choice/ option for a dealer competing in a symmetric market. This fact being intuitively obvious to every participating dealer, he attempts to use a manipulative strategy for greater success. This is possible in either a team effort or an individual effort. It is shown that for an individual working in a team, the team receives a greater success probability (than an individual working alone); however, the success is distributed amongst its members. Contrary to the intuitive effect expected of a team effort being more rewarding than an individualistic approach, this divided success is shown to have a maximum limit, which is lower than if the dealer was competing alone. Hence, the famous axiom – *the greater the risk, the greater are the possible rewards* is validated again.

Acknowledgements

The author would like to thank the organizers of Perm Winter School, in particular to Prof. Sergey Ivliev (Perm State University), for inviting him and for the partial travel grant provided.

References

Aggarwal, Rajesh K. and Wu (2003), Guojun, Stock Market Manipulation – Theory and Evidence AFA 2004 San Diego Meetings.

Macintosh, Norman B.(1995) The Ethics of profit manipulation: A Dialectic of Control Analysis, Critical Perspectives on Accounting, Vol. 6, Issue 4, pp. 289-315.

Macrae, John (1982) Underdevelopment and the economics of corruption: A game theory approach, World Development, Vol. 10, No. 8, pp. 677-687.

Slater, Stanley F. and Narver, John C. (2000), The Positive Effect of a Market Orientation on Business Profitability: A Balanced Replication, Journal of Business Research, Vol. 48, Issue 1, pp. 69-73.

Adaption of World Experience in Insider Dealing Regulation to the Specifity of the Russian Market

Alexander Starikov

South-Ural State University, Chelyabinsk, Russia. email: star_tur@mail.ru

Abstract This article considers the Federal Law of the Russian Federation «On Insider Dealing and Market Manipulation». It includes a comparative analysis of articles of the recently passed Law of Russia and legal regulations of insider dealing in the US and the countries of EU. The article covers the common features, assumed as a basis for the Russian Law development, and the key differences between them. Moreover, in the article the problems of regulation of insider dealing in Russia are shown, and the complementary measures to increase its efficiency are laid down.

Keywords: insider information, insider, market manipulation, state regulation of insider dealing

JEL classification: K 22, G 28, K 29

Introduction

Development of the stock exchange is one of the most important fields for economic reforms of Russia. Thus, B. Alekhin emphasizes that «it gives as much money, as it is needed; the Tax Service gives as much money, as it can raise. The market, but not the taxes, is the true economic basis for the authorities chain. If Russia has ever a chance of economic prosperity, it is surely connected with securities market» (Alekhin, 2001, p. 27). At the same time, one of the key laws regulating the dealing on the financial and commodity markets, has become the Federal Law «On Insider Dealing and Market Manipulation» as of July 27, 2010 (further – the Law), which comes into effect from January 27, 2011. First of all, among the countries that aspire to play the role of the world financial center, Russia is the only one which does not have any practice in counteraction to illegal insider dealing and market manipulation of prices on the exchange. Secondly, as the Crisis has shown, under the condition of market breakdown the problem of insider dealing becomes the most burning. This is so because during such periods trading volumes sharply drop and deviations in the dealings of certain traders become especially appreciable and, therefore, especially dangerous for the whole market .

An explanatory note to the Law states that during the Law elaboration, the main foreign models of insider transactions and manipulation were being analyzed, including those used in the US and Great Britain and also the European model

D. Sornette et al. (Eds.), *Market Risk and Financial Markets Modeling*,
DOI 10.1007/978-3-642-27931-7_20,

established by the EU Directives and developed in the legislation of Germany (Explanatory note, 2009).

The US legislation interprets insider information as relevant, unpublished (not made public) information on the securities which are the objects of the transactions (Act, 1934). The relevance of the information is defined by three factors. Firstly, it is the importance of the person who owns the information and takes advantage of it. Thus, the American courts as a whole, considering the insider trade cases, decided that «...the transactions closed by insiders (and the revenue earned) can serve as a sign of the information relevance» (Kiseleva, 2004, p. 4). The second factor is the market reaction to this information (for example, significant price variance of the financial instrument), when it is made public. Lastly, if a person carries out insider trade on the basis of the information received from corporate insiders, who are named “prompters”, the significance of this information is measured by the importance of the “prompter”.

As for Russia, until the Law was passed, the legal definition of insider information in court practice and acts of Federal Financial Markets Service (further – the FFMS) was equal to the definition of official information, given in the Federal Law “On Securities Market” (Federal Law, 1996). Without mentioning all the discrepancies in the definition of the legal concept, we shall mark out the key difference: the previous definition did not contain the most important attribute of insider information – the ability to lead to a significant price variance of the financial instruments, the foreign currency or the goods when published.

Now the Law, at last, gives the legal definition of insider information, according to which it shall have the following attributes: it must be precise, concrete, not made public; be capable of significantly influencing the prices of the financial instrument, the foreign currency or the goods; be included in the list of insider information, approved by the FFMS (Federal Law, 2010). The Law definition is given in the wide sense. This is probably the reason why the FFMS is charged with approving the list of information that can be recognized as insider information. Actually, without this list the Law will not fully go into effect, and it will be impossible to put it into practice, as development of such a list will need some time.

It should be noted that the insider information definition in the Russian Law, as well as some of its other definitions, are based on the EU Directives, particularly on the Directive 2003/6/ “On Insider Dealing and Market Manipulation (Market Abuse)”.

Let us consider the main approaches to identifying an insiders’ circle. The concept underlying the US legislation makes it possible to divide insiders into primary and secondary ones. Primary insiders are corporate ones (executive managers of the issuer, its workers, including external advisers), who own the relevant unpublished information ex officio in the company and perform towards the issuer the fiduciary duty not to use this information for personal gain. The Classical theory of insider trade (“Abstain-or-disclose” theory) is applied to this group. In other words, employees and external advisers of the company shall disclose the relevant information and make it accessible to the interested investors or to abstain from trading with the financial assets until this information is made public.

As for secondary insiders, the theory of information misappropriation is applied to determine the liability of the persons not obliged to keep loyal to the issuer, but involved in the transactions using the insider information. According to this theory, the law is violated if the person, strange to the company, conducts the transaction using confidential information and, thereby, breaches the loyalty of the person being a source of this information even if the source of the information is not a participant in the transaction. The misappropriation theory does not focus on the insider's duty to the company, but on the basis that if the trader obtains the information as a result of a breach of any fiduciary duty to the company, there is liability. It should be noted that this theory is applied not only to established business relations, but also to personal (usually family) relations (Shirinyan, 2004).

The further development of judiciary practice in the US and the appearance of the theory of misappropriation has brought together the approaches applied in the European and American legislations in the case of prosecuting persons who are not insiders in a classical interpretation.

Let us return to the Russian practice. In the official Law, the complete list of the persons who can be recognized as insiders is given. Formally, they can be divided into 2 basic groups:

1. State authorities and institutions of local government, and also their heads.
2. Legal persons, who are issuers; managing companies; business entities, having dominance on the market; clearing houses; and also other companies directly connected to the securities market, including natural persons being part of their boards or having access to insider information under civil contracts (for example, appraisers and auditors).

The Law on insider information does not specify whether the official or contractual duties of the above-mentioned natural persons should be connected with the dealing on the financial market. Thus, an natural person that conducts labour or has a civil contract can be recognized as an insider. At the same time, this definition does not include the persons to whom such information can be passed by those having a direct access to it (for example, affiliated persons, relatives of insiders).

In spite of the American experience, the Russian legislators have purposefully rejected the idea of fixing the definition of a secondary insider. This is explained by that without practice of the Law application even operating personnel can be recognized as insiders. This could have complicated the practice of impleading insiders, owing to the inflexibility of the Russian legislation. Meanwhile, the Law fixes the general rule, according to which any person illegally using insider information or performing market manipulation takes on liability in accordance with the legislation of Russia.

Definitions of illegal dealing with insider information are quite similar in the legislations of different countries. It is generally adopted that a person has no right to make a transaction with securities using insider information. However, we shall pay attention to the difference between the key concepts underlying the development and improvement of legislations in the American and European models.

The analysis of the US legislation shows that the main concept of illegal insider information use is that the person who conducts the trade or passes information breaches the fiduciary duty.

The European Directive 2003/6/EC seeks to deal with the problem by moving away from the concept of fiduciary duty, a relationship between an insider and the company, to the idea of the fraud on the market, when the market as a whole is deemed to be harmed. This concept has been assumed as a basis for the Law development for the Russian market.

It should be also noted that the real challenge is to prove that the deal has been concluded by using insider information. This burning problem is somewhat complicated, because Russia, the same as the EU countries, took the path of adopting the special legislation directed at the regulation of insider dealing. At the same time, in the US, the legislation regulating insider dealing results from the administrative and judicial interpretation of the laws regulating fraud and deceit. This difference makes the American legislation more flexible and dynamic to all unprecedented situations of insider information use on the financial market.

Moreover, the regulating authorities of Russia are at the very beginning of forming their practice for proving the facts of illegal insider information use and market manipulation. The FFMS has constantly reported about the frequent cases of price manipulation on the Russian market, but only two cases have been proven. In November, 2007, a client of the "Nord Capital" company, the Cypriot firm "Palmaris Holding Ltd" was convicted of price manipulation of "RITEK" shares. The company acted as a buyer and a seller of the shares at the same time, and, as a result, the rates of "RITEK" shares took off more than 30 %. After checking this, the FFMS sent a direction to the broker of the "Palmaris" company to prevent the execution of its orders to conduct transactions. There were no other sanctions applied to the "Palmaris" company. The second case is connected to the "RichBrokerCredit" company, whose shares rose in price by 80 % in a month due to the price manipulation by its executives. Again, the manipulators were not brought to account, and the only negative consequence was that the shares were delisted from the RTS and the "Saint Petersburg" stock exchange.

In the US, the Securities and Exchange Commission (further – SEC) annually investigates more than 50 cases connected with insider information, and institutes criminal proceedings against unfair market participants. So, for example, in January, 2008 a sentence was passed upon an analyst of the investment bank Goldman Sachs. The analyst was a Russian by origin, Evgeny Plotkin, who was found guilty of 8 cases of illegal insider trading, in particular the purchase of "Reebok" shares before its merger with "Adidas Salomon AG" and also of the illegal use of confidential information from the printing house "Business Week". Plotkin was sentenced to imprisonment for 4 years and 9 months on condition of paying the penalty of 6.7 million dollars for benefit of the state. If Plotkin had not admitted guilt, the American court could have sentenced him to a deprivation of freedom for 165 years.

In October, 2009 the SEC initiated a criminal case against a 52-year-old American billionaire and the founder and principal shareholder of the large hedge fund,

"Galleon Group LLC", Raj Rajaratnam, and a former director of "McKinsey and Co", Anil Kumar, who used in their securities trade insider information from such companies as Intel, IBM, Google, and AMD. The number of the accused in this case has risen to 19 people. Among Rajaratnam's accomplices are the top managers of Intel, IBM, AMD and eBay, along with lawyers, analytics and traders. According to the SEC, the profit of "Galleon Group" from the insider information transactions makes up approximately 33 million dollars. The FFMS and the Russian authorities of internal affairs should follow the SEC and the FBI's example, which could not only plant their agent trader in the hedge fund, but also obtain a guilt confession from five of the suspects, including the former director of the consulting company "McKinsey and Co", as well as their cooperation with the authorities. If Rajaratnam is found guilty, he could be imprisoned for up to 145 years, and his accomplice, the head of "New Castle Funds LLC", D. Chiesi – up to 155 years. However, even in such a financially developed country, as the US, the proving of participation in insider information dealing is quite a difficult process, demanding the high qualification of the state regulator's officials.

One of the particular features of the Russian Law adoption was that it raised heated discussions concerning the liability of the media. Thus, close attention was drawn to this problem, even in the higher echelons of authority. The original Law fixed liability of the media and persons connected to it for insider information dissemination. However, as a result of long-run discussions and the cooperation with the journalistic community, the legislators met their wishes and established the possibility of identifying a source of the information, on condition of its word-by-word reproduction, as a reason for exemption from liability. However, the Law does not exempt the media from liability in cases of earning an income from the information spread, receiving a counter concession or rejecting to disclose a source of the information.

In the EU Directive, dissemination of information through the media, including rumours and false or misleading news, when the person spreading the news knew, or ought to have known, that the published information is false or misleading shall also mean market manipulation. However, in practice, the European community did not pay as much attention to this question as in Russia, probably due to the more advanced legislation regulating the fields of protection of the freedom of speech and information dissemination rights, and also the rights of the media.

The Law brings a number of amendments to the Administrative and Criminal Code of Russia which, regarding illegal insider information use, will go into force in one year and in three years after the Law enactment, respectively. The legislation fixes the minimum administrative sanction for legal persons, which is a penalty of no less than 700 000 roubles. The maximum punishments, specified in the Criminal code, are a deprivation of the right of a person to occupy their certain position or to be engaged in their certain field for a period up to 5 years, a penalty of up to 1 000 000 roubles or imprisonment for up to 7 years. We hope that, before the amendments come into force, the practice of the application of this Law will have already been formed, and it will not become an additional instrument making pressure on business.

In the US there is also criminal liability for the violation of insider information use. In particular, a penalty from 100 000 up to 1 million dollars for physical persons and up to 2500 million dollars for legal persons is determined. The maximum imprisonment was increased from 5 to 10 years. In addition, a penalty of up to 1 million dollars or triple size of the profit received by the insider, can also be imposed on the so-called supervising person found guilty of allowing, deliberately or as a result of his negligence, the opportunity of insider information use by the person under his management.

Taking into account the above, it is obvious that in the US various kinds of liability are created for a given violation. This expands the possibilities for the state authorities to carry out more efficient counteraction to illegal trading dealing and allows them to be more flexible in prevention and suppression of the law violations (SEC, 1998). It is much easier to suppress illegal dealing, impose the penalty or receive compensation for the damage in a civil process than to prove guilt in criminal cases. At the same time, in the most dangerous cases, important for the market community, criminal cases are also brought. Thus, from this point of view, establishing in the Russian legislation various kinds of liability for illegal insider trade, depending on the gravity of the committed violation, seems to be quite a reasonable measure.

In the European Directive the persons guilty of the given violations shall incur, at least, administrative liability. The governments shall ensure appropriate administrative measures that are "effective, proportional and dissuasive" (Directive, 2003, p. 23). Criminal sanctions can also be imposed on the guilty persons. However, differences in punishment for the same crime in different countries of the EU can actually be significant. Perhaps the most harsh punishments for financial crimes are provided in Great Britain, where it is possible not only to pay the penalty of many millions, but also to go to prison for a period of up to 7 years for illegal insider dealing. Meanwhile, the applicable legislations of many countries of the EU do not provide criminal liability for illegal insider information use. Moreover, in 15 out of 27 participant countries of the EU, the sum of the penalty for illegal enrichment can turn out to be less than the profit received in the criminal way (Shapovalov, 2005).

Analyzing the Law of Russia in order to assess the severity of punishments, it is very important not to forget the key point. The purpose of the Law is not to punish as many people as possible most strictly, but is to exclude any possibility of illegal influence on the market. It is necessary to create a system, in which only the most loose traders would dare to attempt price manipulation. And by definition there are few of such marginal persons on the market, therefore cases of criminal sanctions imposed against the unfair traders will be scarce.

However, the current statistics of application of the current Criminal Code articles, which and specify liability for an abuse of securities emission or for malignant evasion from providing the investor or the supervising body with the information, have shown the extremely inefficient work of the law enforcement agencies with these kinds of crime. Thereby, we consider it reasonable to take some complementary measures, directed to the control and supervision in the financial sphere.

1. An active involvement of the self-regulatory organizations (further – SRO) in this process.

The SROs are noncommercial organizations based on a membership, exercising some degree of regulatory authority over an industry, market or profession (Federal Law, 2007). In spite of the fact that in the Law «On Securities Market» a narrower concept of a self-regulatory organization of securities market participants is given (most known examples are the National Association of Securities Market Participants, NAUFOR, and National Securities Market Association, NSMA), we consciously use the wider concept of the SRO, as the cooperation of the state regulator, in our opinion, should take place not only with securities market participants, but also with commodity market participants, because, in fact, at all levels market participants are interested in the development of the economy as a whole, and the Law, indeed, is applied to both financial and commodity markets.

According to the legislation, the SRO develops and approves the standards and rules of entrepreneurial or professional activity which are obligatory for all members of the SRO. These standards and rules shall not contravene the federal laws and other legal acts, but can establish additional requirements to entrepreneurial or professional activity. Therefore, SROs could work out the codes of fair dealing for the market participants and monitor that these codes are strictly followed. In case of their breach the SRO would direct the information to the state regulator, and it, in turn, would draw the attention of the law enforcement bodies to these facts. It is difficult to imagine that the SROs would not support the following suggestions of the state regulator, because illegal insider dealing harms not only the FFMS, but the interests of the market participants and investors, and finally the economy as a whole.

It should be also observed that the Law adds to the SRO's powers the right to conduct checks of the non-standard transactions concluded by its members on the instructions of the trade organizer.

2. A collaboration with the Ministry of communications for creating a joint working group including journalists for signing a Memorandum of cooperation.

It is really necessary to share the information and to investigate it together for the most complicated cases, which are connected with insider information disclosure or market manipulation, and affect the media. Such cooperation shall favour development of the legislation concerning relations between the FFMS and the media, and increase its transparency as a whole.

3. A monitoring of the information spread via Internet communities and other informal means of communication, and also a penetration of the state regulator executives in them.

As foreign experience shows, insider information misuse and market manipulation attempts have especially shifted to various Internet forums, blogs, etc. The false or misleading information can be spread not only via authoritative publications, but also via the blog of a person hiding himself under a nickname.

In connection with the acceleration of the rate of development of information dissemination via informal Internet communities and involvement of a massively increasing number of market participants in them, the control and supervision over the respective field seem to be effective measures for disclosing the Law violations.

4. A development of the present monitoring system of the securities market and an elaboration of the internal regulations of working with it.

The monitoring system of non-standard transactions on the Russian securities market, recently put into operation, has been developed on the basis of the software of the "NICE Actimize" company, which is used by financial regulators of the Netherlands and Great Britain and also by many international banks, for example HSBC and Barclays.

It is planned that a special department of the FFMS will deal with the monitoring system, and its executives will reveal in a real-time mode the queer transactions which can be united into five groups: price manipulation; price fixing; transactions without economic sense; transactions conducted with the use of insider information; and the placing of fictitious orders. The monitoring system of the FFMS is capable of processing up to 10 million of the market participants' orders and more than 1.2 million of real transactions daily.

Nevertheless, when determining the necessity of adopting the monitoring system for the Russian securities market, we should also note that the preliminary results should be treated cautiously. The efficient performance of the program directly depends on the adjustment parameters and the accepted criteria for identifying the facts of market manipulation. Thus, a chief executive of the "Russian Exchange Union", A. Gavrilenko, states that the monitoring system has been put into operation «just in three months, and its adoption has not included any discussions with the market participants, though it has been developed by a foreign company» (Mazunin, 2010).

Thereby, the monitoring system needs to be developed and adapted to the specificity of the Russian market. In addition, it is important to elaborate the internal regulations of working with the monitoring system, which will partly solve a problem of insufficient awareness of the market participants, especially of the regional companies.

There is also a complicated problem of legal regulation of the monitoring system. According to a director general of the "Group of Information Security" ("Group-IB"), Ilya Sachkov, the given technical system will not have a legal effect without a security policy corresponding with the Russian legislation, and without a notification of the users that their dealings are recorded (Sachkov, 2008, p. 6).

5. A development of the legal acts by the state regulator, establishing the exact and clearly defined criteria for the significant price variance and other facts identifying market manipulation.

According to a head of the FFMS, Mr. Milovidov, after two months of the monitoring system's work in a test mode, most signals have fallen on the market manipulation in the form of significant security price variance (Mazunin, 2010). This could be due to the fact that the conservative parameters of price variance are adjusted in the system. Therefore, it is necessary for the FFMS to develop a certain instruction, establishing what is considered to be a significant price variance.

At the same time, it is essential to work out the criteria for a significant change in demand, supply and trading volume on the market. The respective criteria should be established on the basis of analysis of the monitoring system signals from the very beginning of its implementation on the financial market and of the transactions underlying them.

Furthermore, the Law also does not give a definition of a non-standard transaction. The enactment of the Federal Securities Commission (FSC) 03-8 contains a concept of the queer transaction, which is defined as a securities transaction or order, the conclusion or significant conditions of which give grounds for assuming the presence of price manipulation in the traders dealing (Enactment, 2003). In this connection, it is not actually obvious whether it is possible to consider these two concepts as synonyms.

In our opinion, the presented measures would speed up and ease an adaptation of the recently adopted legislation to the specificity of the Russian market.

In conclusion, besides the developing of the supervision regulations and adopting of the violations liability, the Law removes the last barrier which has blocked the signing of the multilateral memorandum with the International Organization of Securities Commissions (IOSCO) and the further development of the cooperation of Russia with the group of international regulators. Moreover, a direct participation in this international organization would also allow Russia to influence the future development of the international regulations for financial markets for the benefit of national interests.

References

Alekhin, B. (2001) Is there a stock market in Russia? Stock Market, 23, 27-31.

Directive (2003) "On insider dealing and market manipulation (market abuse)". 2003/6/EC, OJ L 096, pp. 0016-0025.

Enactment of FSC (2003) "On adoption of the statute on monitoring of the persons dealings containing signs of market manipulation" 03-8. Russian Newspaper, p. 3.

Explanatory note (2009) to the Federal Law "On counteraction to insider dealing and market manipulation". http://www.nccg.ru/site.xp/049049049124049055048056.html.

Federal Law (1996) "On securities market" 39.

Federal Law (2007) "On self-regulatory organizations" 315.

Federal Law (2010) "On counteraction to insider dealing and market manipulation and amendments to certain legislative acts of Russian Federation" 224.

Kiseleva, I. (2004) Insider dealing regulation on the securities market of the US. Stock Market, 19, 3-7.

Mazunin A. (2010) FFMS discloses the stock market. Kommersant, p. 10.

Sachkov, I. (2008) The process of control needs to be adapted. Economy and life, p. 6.

Shapovalov, A. (2005) Legal insider dealing regulation in the EU. Stock Market., 5, 38-43.

Shirinyan, I. (2004) World experience in insider information use on securities market. Stock Market, 13, 38-42.

Securities Exchange Act of the US (1934). http://taft.law.uc.edu/CCL/34Act/index.html.

Speech by SEC Staff: Insider Trading – A U.S. Perspective (1998). Cambridge. http://www.sec.gov/news/speech/ /speecharchive/1998/spch221.htm.

Agent-Based Model of the Stock Market

Alexander Steryakov

Samara State Aerospace University, Samara, Russia. email: lubopitnij@mail.ru

Abstract In the framework of microscopic simulation, a mathematical model of the stock exchange is developed for the case of one type of shares. The model exhibits self-maintained trading, which results in a price formation that is sensitive only to the values of internal market parameters. The system responds to external influence and the response is consistent with real market dynamics. Some of the statistical properties of the resulting price time series, which are similar to real stock market time series, are consistent with the so-called stylized facts of real market data. We provide a mathematical formalization of the model for the agents and all the steps of the agents' interactions. The program "Exchange simulator", which is a computer representation of our model is developed and implemented. The program contains useful tools for deep exploration of the system. There is an opportunity to affect the system by means of external user trading. The program may be used as a simple stock market trainer.

Keywords: Stock market, agent-based model, computer modeling, microscopic simulation, stylized facts, statistical properties, assets

JEL classification: C02, D40, G17

Introduction

The standard classical models of financial markets, based on the assumption of the existence of a representative agent with full information and rational expectations, made in order to obtain analytical tractability, are regarded with increasing skepticism by a growing number of scientists working in the field of finance and economic theory. In the last two decades, contrary to classical models, a new class of contributions has arrived, which can be joined under the label "agent-based models". One could roughly divide these contributions into two partially overlapping classes. The first class contains models where the results come from a rigorous analytical investigation. Among many examples, let us mention Chiarella (1992), Chiarella and He (2001), Lux (1998), Brock and Hommes (1998). The second class consists of models based on the presentation and discussion of extensive computer simulations. Such an approach was used, among many others, in Levy et al. (1994, 1995, 2000), Arthur et al. (1997) and Bottazzi et al. (2005).

Traders operating in the stock market behave in various manners depending on their individual preferences, expectations, wealth, memory and data processing

D. Sornette et al. (Eds.), *Market Risk and Financial Markets Modeling*,
DOI 10.1007/978-3-642-27931-7_21,

capabilities. As we have mentioned above, in order to obtain analytical results, classical macroeconomic models were forced to assume a "representative" agent. While for very long time spans and very coarse averages such an approach might have some relevance, it becomes impractical for the detailed study of short-term market fluctuations.

Microscopic simulation, as an alternative to the representative individual framework, is suggested in the physical sciences as a tool for the study of complex systems with many interacting "microscopic" elements. Such complex systems generally do not yield to analytical treatment. The main idea of the microscopic simulation methodology is to study complex systems by representing each of the microscopic elements individually on a computer and simulating the behavior of the entire system, keeping track of all of the elements and their interactions in each time period. Throughout the simulation, global, or "macroscopic", variables that are of interest can be recorded, and their dynamics can be investigated.

We suppose that microscopic simulation is the most adequate tool to investigate financial systems, since the stock market is a complex system with many interacting autonomous traders. Moreover, in the context of economics and finance, employing this methodology allows the relaxation of assumptions that are made for the sake of analytic tractability. It also gives us a chance to accurately describe the real-world investors' behavior.

The first "modern" multi-agent model is the one proposed by Kim and Markowitz (1989). The major motivation for their microsimulation study was the stock market crash in 1987, and the authors tried to explore the relationship between the share of agents pursuing portfolio insurance strategies and the volatility of the market. Their model, of course, was not designed to address other puzzles in empirical finance, like the "stylized facts".

Later, the group M. Levy et al. (1994) developed a more realistic model in the framework of Econophysics. A traditional utility maximization paradigm was applied to model agents' behavior. The characteristics of the time series generated by their model seem to exhibit a few (but by no means all) of the empirical stylized facts. The model was generally aimed at explaining the origin of global bubbles and crashes. This fact and the rather homogeneous agents in the model lead to the lack of diversity of the obtained price dynamics and the poor consistency of the obtained dynamics with those observed in a real market.

The aim of this work is a simulation of the trading process on an artificial market made in the framework of agent-based models. The result is supposed to be an artificial market in which the trading process among the traders occurs as described by a mathematical model. The resulting data such as price and volumes timelines should be consistent with those observed in a real market. In addition, the market should be able to respond in some predictable way to the exogenous influence made by an external trader who is supposed to be the user of our software. Thus, in order to describe the whole market we need to develop the agent model and the way these agents interact with each other, e.g. a particular market tool.

Agent Model

Suppose that each agent on the market possesses a portfolio consisting of a riskless asset (bond with fixed rate of return) and a risky asset (stocks paying constant dividend). In addition, agents are expected to be utility maximizers, thus each agent possesses his own utility, which is a function of his total wealth. Hence, the time behavior of each agent can be described as a periodic changing of the portfolio composition in such a way that expected future value of the portfolio based on the forecasted price and its variance maximizes the utility function of the agent.

We use the following notations: $B_i(t)$ is an amount of riskless asset (or cash) held by investor i at time t; $A_i(t)$ is the number of shares held by investor i at time t; $P(t)$ is the stock price fixed by the market at time t; r is a riskless interest rate at time t; δ is a dividend paid each time step; the timeline is supposed to be discrete as $t = 1,2,3,...$

According to the assumptions above, the total wealth of the agent i at time t is

$$W_i(t) = B_i(t) + A_i(t)P(t).$$

Let

$$\pi_i(t) = \frac{A_i(t)P(t)}{W_i(t)}$$

be the fraction of an agent's wealth invested in the risky asset. Then we can rewrite the total wealth as

$$W_i(t) = (1 - \pi_i(t))W_i(t) + \pi_i(t)W_i(t),$$

where the first and the second terms correspond respectively to values of riskless and risky assets.

The trading activity of the agents can be described as follows. Let $\pi_i(t-2)$ be the fraction of wealth that agent i invests in the risky asset at time $t-1$, and $P(t-1)$ be the actual stock price. The fact that every agent wishes to change the fraction of risky asset to a new value $\pi_i(t-1)$ leads to changes in demand and supply. As a result, a new equilibrium price $P(t)$ is set. After that, each agent is eager to change the fraction of stocks to a new value $\pi_i(t)$ in such a way that the value of wealth $W_i(t+1)$ is the most desirable for him. At that time t, the agent is aware of the price $P(t)$, but he is unaware of the price $P(t+1)$. However, on the basis of the information he possesses by the time t, the investor can predict the future stock price and using this forecasted quantity choose the value of $\pi_i(t)$.

Let $P(t)$ and $\pi_i(t)$ be the stock price and the fraction of risky asset respectively at time t. Then the future value of such portfolio at time $t+1$ is given by

$$W_i(t+1) = (1-\pi_i(t))W_i(t)(1+r) +$$
$$+\pi_i(t)W_i(t)\ 1+\frac{P(t+1)-P(t)}{P(t)}+\frac{\delta}{P(t)}\ . \tag{1}$$

From Eq.(1) one obtains

$$W_i(t+1) = W_i(t)\times$$
$$\times\ 1+r+\pi_i(t)\ \frac{P(t+1)-P(t)}{P(t)}+\frac{\delta}{P(t)}-r\ =, \tag{2}$$
$$= W_i(t)\ 1+r+\pi_i(t)\ \rho(t+1)+\frac{\delta}{P(t)}-r$$

where $\rho(t+1) = \dfrac{P(t+1)-P(t)}{P(t)}$ is the stock rate of returns.

We assume that each agent has his own utility function $U_i(W_i)$, which depends on the total wealth. There are several common types of utility function, e.g. a power utility function

$$U_i(W_i) = \frac{W_i^{\beta-1}-1}{\beta-1}\ ,$$

and an exponential utility function

$$U_i(W_i) = 1-\exp(-\beta W_i)\ . \tag{3}$$

We suppose that agent i uses the following expression to predict the value of $\rho(t+1)$

$$\rho_i(t+1) = \mu_i(t+1)+\sigma_i(t+1)\xi(t+1)\ , \tag{4}$$

where $\xi(t+1)$ is a normally distributed random variable with zero mean and unit variance. $\mu_i(t+1)$ and $\sigma_i^2(t+1)$ are forecasted values of mean and variance of stock returns $\rho(t+1)$, respectively. Due to the randomness of $\rho_i(t+1)$, $W_i(t+1)$ also becomes random variable. From Eqs. (2) and (4) one obtains

$$W_i(t+1) = W_i(t)\ 1+\pi_i(t)\ \frac{\delta}{P(t)}-r+\mu_i(t+1)\ +r\ +\ .$$
$$+W_i(t)\pi_i(t)\sigma_i(t+1)\xi(t+1)$$

Then the utility function $U_i(W_i(t+1))$ is also random

$$U_i(W_i(t+1)) = = U_i \left(\begin{array}{l} W_i(t) + W_i(t) \; \pi_i(t) \left(\dfrac{\delta}{P(t)} - r + \mu_i(t+1) \right) + r \; + \\ + W_i(t)\pi_i(t)\sigma_i(t+1)\xi(t+1) \end{array} \right).$$

The agent acts so that the value of his expected utility

$$\mathrm{E}\big(U_i(W_i(t+1))\big) = = \mathrm{E}\left[U_i \left(\begin{array}{l} W_i(t) + W_i(t) \; \pi_i(t) \left(\dfrac{\delta}{P(t)} - r + \mu_i(t+1) \right) + r \; + \\ + W_i(t)\pi_i(t)\sigma_i(t+1)\xi(t+1) \end{array} \right) \right]$$

is maximized. Choosing the utility function as in Eq. (3) and using the fact that for a normally distributed random variable ξ with zero mean and unit variance the following expression

$$\mathrm{E}\big(\exp(a + b\xi)\big) = \exp\left(a + \frac{b^2}{2}\right)$$

is valid, we obtain

$$\mathrm{E}\big(U_i(W_i(t+1))\big) = = \mathrm{E}\left[1 - \exp\left(\begin{array}{l} -\beta W_i(t) \left(1 + \pi_i(t) \left(\dfrac{\delta}{P(t)} - r + \mu_i(t+1) \right) + r \right) - \\ -\beta W_i(t)\pi_i(t)\sigma_i(t+1)\xi(t+1) \end{array} \right) \right] = = 1 - \exp\left(\begin{array}{l} -\beta W_i(t) \left(1 + \pi_i(t) \left(\dfrac{\delta}{P(t)} - r + \mu_i(t+1) \right) + r \right) + \\ + \dfrac{1}{2}\beta^2 W_i(t)^2 \pi_i(t)^2 \sigma_i(t+1)^2 \end{array} \right).$$

Solving the equation $\dfrac{d\,\mathrm{E}\big(U_i(W_i(t+1))\big)}{d\pi_i(t+1)} = 0$ for $\pi_i(t)$ finally gives

$$\pi_i(t) = \frac{\mu_i(t+1) + \delta / P(t) - r}{\beta W_i(t) \sigma_i^2(t+1)} . \tag{5}$$

According to our assumptions, in order to make his decision, the trader needs to have forecasted values of mean $\mu_i(t+1)$ and variance $\sigma_i^2(t+1)$ of returns. We will consider two classes of agents distinguished by prediction strategies: trend followers and fundamentalists.

Trend followers obtain forecasted variables using exponentially weighted moving averages of past data

$$\mu_i(t+1) = (1-\lambda_i) \sum_{n=0}^{\infty} \lambda_i^n \rho(t-n) ,$$

$$\sigma_i(t+1)^2 = (1-\lambda_i) \sum_{n=0}^{\infty} \lambda_i^n \left(\rho(t-n) - \mu_i(t-n)\right)^2 .$$

In the case of using only one last value we have

$$\mu_i(t+1) = \lambda_i \mu_i(t) + (1-\lambda_i)\rho(t) , \tag{6}$$

$$\sigma_i(t+1)^2 = \lambda_i \sigma_i(t)^2 + (1-\lambda_i)\left(\rho(t) - \mu_i(t)\right)^2 . \tag{7}$$

Fundamentalists believe that that the objective "correct" price $\overline{P} = \frac{d}{r}$, which is called the fundamental price, exists on the market. This idea changes their beliefs regarding the mean of returns but does not change the forecast of variance. Hence, the final expression for their forecast is

$$\mu_i(t+1) = \theta_i \left(\frac{\overline{P}}{P(t)} - 1\right) , \tag{8}$$

$$\sigma_i(t+1)^2 = \lambda_i \sigma_i(t)^2 + (1-\lambda_i)\left(\rho(t) - \mu_i(t)\right)^2 . \tag{9}$$

Once the agent obtains the forecasted values (using either Eqs. (6) and (7) or Eqs. (8) and (9)), he calculates the desirable value of the fraction of risky asset in his portfolio using Eq. (5). Then the trader evaluates the number of shares $A_i(t)$ corresponding to this value of $\pi_i(t)$

$$A_i(t+1) = \frac{\pi_i(t) W_i(t)}{P(t)} .$$

Thus, the number of shares which an investor needs to sell or buy in order to have the required structure of his portfolio is $|\Delta_i|$, where $\Delta_i = A_i(t+1) - A_i(t)$. Here $\Delta < 0$ corresponds to a seller and $\Delta > 0$ corresponds to a buyer.

Interaction Between Agents

As we have mentioned above, an interaction between traders is performed by means of a particular market tool, namely, the order book. An interaction basically represents the deal-making process between active agents. This process can be divided into four successive steps.

Step 1. Each agent forms the order. Once the trader makes his decision, i.e. makes all the calculations above, the order consisting of three elements is formed. These elements are order size, i.e. the number of shares, order price, i.e. the price that a trader is willing to pay to buy or willing to accept to sell, and order sign. The order sign represents whether the agent wants to buy or sell his stocks. As follows form the model above, the size of the order of agent i is $|\Delta_i|$ and the order sign is determined by the sign of Δ_i: if $\Delta_i < 0$ the trader wants to buy, otherwise ($\Delta_i > 0$) to sell.

The second element of the order is an order price. Here we take in to account the fact that each buyer wants to buy at a lower price, conversely sellers try to make the price as high as possible. Thus, depending on the order sign the order price is given by

$$P_{bid} = P(t)(1 - \nu * \zeta) \tag{10}$$

in case of a buy order and

$$P_{ask} = P(t)(1 + \nu * \zeta) \tag{11}$$

for sell orders. Here ζ is a uniformly distributed random variable on $[0,1)$, and ν is a deviation factor which represents the spread on the market.

Step 2. All orders are placed in the order book. A stock market database always contains a queue of unfulfilled orders: offers, i.e. sell orders, and bids, i.e. buy orders. Generally, there is a certain spread, which is the difference between the highest bid price and the lowest ask price. Orders placed in the order book are sorted by their price. Our model implements all the basic functions of this real financial tool. The last two steps describe the trading process itself.

Step 3. Rearrangement of the order book. On the real market, sellers and buyers have to make mutual price concessions in order to satisfy the interests of both sides of the deal. According to our model, after step 2 we obtain an order book with a nonzero spread, hence no deals are possible. Consequently, we have to introduce the process that leads to the required rearrangements in the order book and is consistent with the process of mutual price concessions observed on the real market.

Let P_a be the price the seller is willing to sell his stock and P_b be the price the buyer is willing to pay for this stock, besides $P_a > P_b$. In order to satisfy interests of both sides of the deal both seller and buyer have to change their prices so that $P_b \geq P_a$.

Let us consider in detail the behavior of each side of the deal. Let x be a random variable equal to the new price the buyer is willing to pay. It seems reasonable to propose that this variable has the following triangle density function

$$f(x)=\begin{cases}0, & x<P_b\\ \dfrac{2x-2P_b}{(P_a-P_b)^2}, & P_b<x<P_a.\\ 0, & x>P_a\end{cases}$$

The corresponding cumulative distribution function is given by

$$F(x)=\begin{cases}0, & x<P_b\\ \dfrac{(x-P_b)^2}{(P_a-P_b)^2}, & P_b<x<P_a.\\ 1, & x>P_a\end{cases}$$

In order to generate this random number on a computer we use the well-known inverse function method, allowing generation of desired random numbers using only a uniform random-number generator. Firstly, we find the inverse of a function $F(x)$, i.e. the positive definite function $x=G(y)$ defined on $[0,1]$

$$x=P_b+(P_a-P_b)\sqrt{y}\,.$$

Then, if y is a uniformly distributed random variable between zero and one, x becomes a random variable with the desired triangle distribution.

Now, let x be a random variable equal to the new price offered by seller. Similar to the case above, we can assume that its density function is triangle. Then for the density and cumulative distribution functions we have

$$f(x)=\begin{cases}0, & x<P_b\\ -\dfrac{2x+2P_a}{(P_a-P_b)^2}, & P_b<x<P_a,\\ 0, & x>P_a\end{cases}$$

$$F(x)=\begin{cases}0, x<P_b\\ \dfrac{x^2+2P_ax+P_b^{\,2}-2P_aP_b}{(P_a-P_b)^2}, P_b<x<P_a.\\ 1, x>P_a\end{cases}$$

The corresponding inverse of the function $F(x)$ is given by

$$x=P_a-(P_a-P_b)\sqrt{1-y}\,.$$

A new order book is obtained by applying this algorithm to each active trader. As a result, agents change their places in order book and it become possible to find the orders that can be fulfilled.

Step 4. Deal-making process. After step 3 we have the order book with a negative spread. Negative spread is never observed on the real markets since the corresponding orders are immediately fulfilled and spread again becomes positive. We tried to model the deal-making process in such a way that it would reflect the real market situation as best as possible. For that reason, the deal is made between a buy order with the highest price and a sell order with the lowest price. We continue to make such deals until the spread becomes positive. After each transaction, the portfolio structure and the total wealth of the involved agents are properly changed.

The price of the last transaction is considered to be the current price of the stock and is added to the price time series of the modeled market. The remaining unfulfilled orders are removed from the book and the whole process starts all over again with the new time iteration.

Computer Representation

The aim of present work was not only to develop a mathematical model, but also to create a powerful tool for its observation and analysis. For this reason, we have designed and elaborated the computer program "Exchange simulator" by means of the object-oriented programming language Java SE v1.6 and NetBeans IDE.

The "Exchange simulator" application consists of three windows (see Fig. 1): the main window containing control elements and a visualizing panel; an "Exchange properties" window, that provides input of the market parameters; and a user-trading window, which allows a user to enter the market and take part in the trading process.

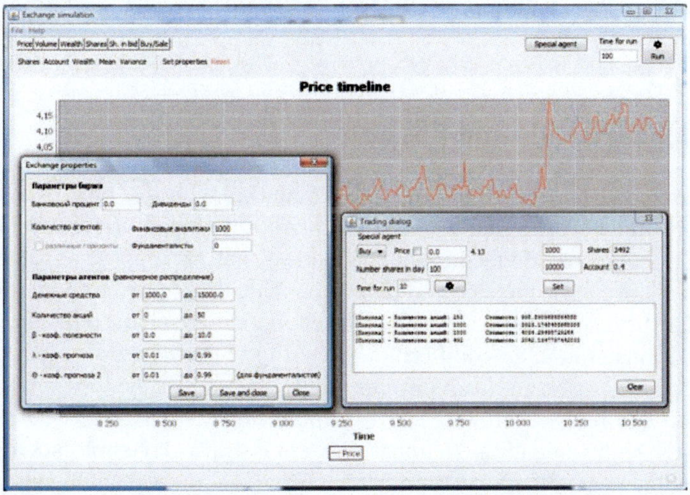

Fig. 1: General view of the developed application "Exchange simulator"

The program is operated in a step-by-step mode, i.e. a researcher enters the necessary market parameters and the number of steps he wants to calculate and then pushes the run button. The main parameters of the modeled stock market are the number of agents (for both types), riskless interest rate, dividends, initial values of cash and stock number for the agents, the parameter of the utility function and the parameters of the agent forecasts. For each agent property, the user may enter either one value or two boundary values. In the second case, the parameter will be uniformly distributed on a given interval among the agents. All the resulting data can be written to text files for further processing.

For convenience, we visualize dynamics of the most significant market variables. We use two types of plots: a value-time chart and an instantaneous distribution diagram that shows an instantaneous statistical distribution of the required variable among the agents. The first type is used to visualize stock price, trading volumes, the mean amount of buy and sell orders, the number of active buyers and sellers. The second type is a good way to observe the agents state (e.g. distributions of forecasted mean and variance of returns, total wealth and stock number among agents).

When we think about artificial markets, the following reasonable questions immediately arise. How will our stock market response to the exogenous influence made by external buyer or seller? Is this response consistent with the real stock market performance? In order to answer these questions, we introduce special feature in our program, which allows a user to enter the market with arbitrary wealth and stock number and take part in trading by putting his orders. While trading on the market, the user may observe changes in his own wealth and portfolio structure and keep track of his deals. Hence, besides the general usage of our program as a tool for model investigation, it can be used as a simple trading trainer.

It should be mentioned that we developed our program by means of an object-oriented programming language in order to be able to easily update the model (e.g. we can easily change the agent model or introduce a new step of interaction between agents).

Numerical Analysis and Results

For our computer experiments we create the market with one type of agent (trend followers); initial wealth and stock number are distributed uniformly on a given interval among agents, dividends and the riskless rate are suppose to be zero. Thus, we obtain a closed system, since no money or shares are transferred in or out of the market. The price dynamics for such a closed market are characterized by the chaotic oscillations around an equilibrium price. Fig. 2 shows how system converges to these dynamics starting from different initial states (for the top panel the initial price is 3.5 and for the bottom panel the initial price is 9.0). Other conditions are the same for both simulations (number of agent is 1000, deviation factor V is 0.15, other parameters are distributed uniformly on a given interval among agents: initial wealth is from 1000 to 5000, initial stock is from 0 to 50, parameter of agents' prediction λ is from 0.01 to 0.99 and parameter of utility function β is from 0 to 10).

We found out that the value of an equilibrium price is determined by the proportion of total money to total stock number in the market. We investigated this correlation and obtained the result that the equilibrium price is linearly dependent on this ratio.

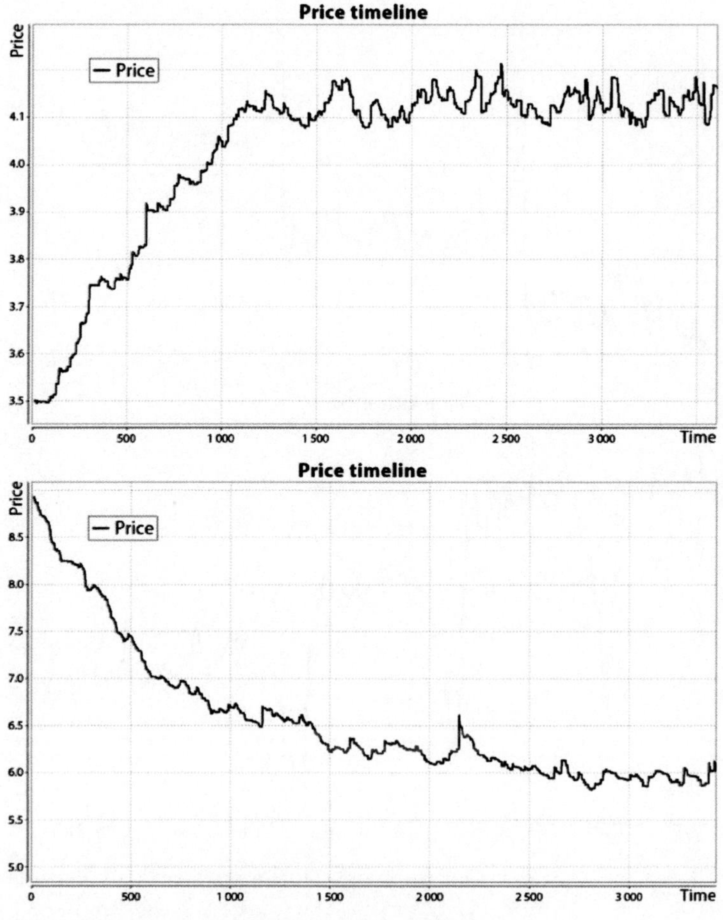

Fig. 2: Price dynamics observed on the closed market

It is clear from the result above that in the case of an open market we should observe an upward or downward trend, depending on how the ratio of total money and total stock number is changed. A similar situation occurs when an external agent enters the market. We use the user-trading mode in order to examine the consequences of such exogenous influence. The top panel of Fig. 3 shows the dynamics of a closed market with an external buyer entering the market twice. The bottom panel of the same figure shows the dynamics of closed market with an external seller entering the market three times. In both cases, the external agent buys or sells around 8-10% of all shares in the market. We see that after a sudden change the price dynamics converges to oscillations around the new equilibrium price.

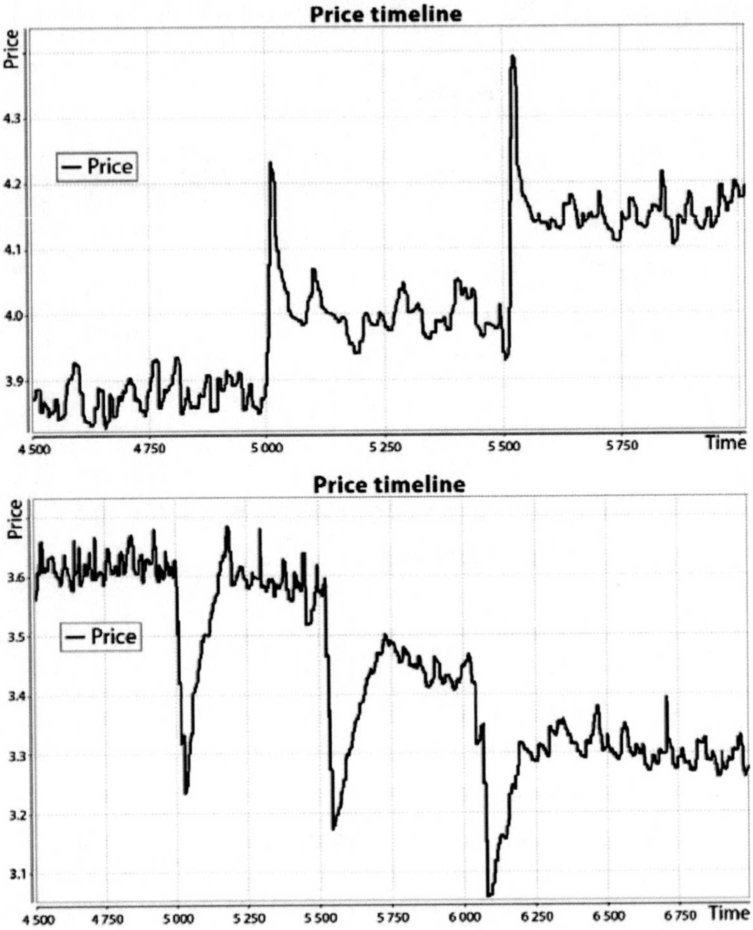

Fig. 3: Price dynamics observed on the closed market with external buyer (top) and seller (bottom)

The next step is to explore the statistical properties of the time series generated by our model. In particular, we are interested in the autocorrelation function of the stock returns. It turns out that the form of this function strongly depends on the deviation factor ν, which characterized the size of random component in the order prices (see Eqs. (10) and (11)). When ν is small (from around 0.01 up to 0.2), the correlation between price changes remains significant up to times equal to 100 trading steps. Increasing ν (around 0.3-0.4) leads not only to a weakening of the correlation but also to anticorrelation on short time scales. Further increasing ν (from 0.7-0.8) gives an absence of correlation except for presence of anticorrelation on very short time scales. The corresponding autocorrelation functions are shown in Fig. 4.

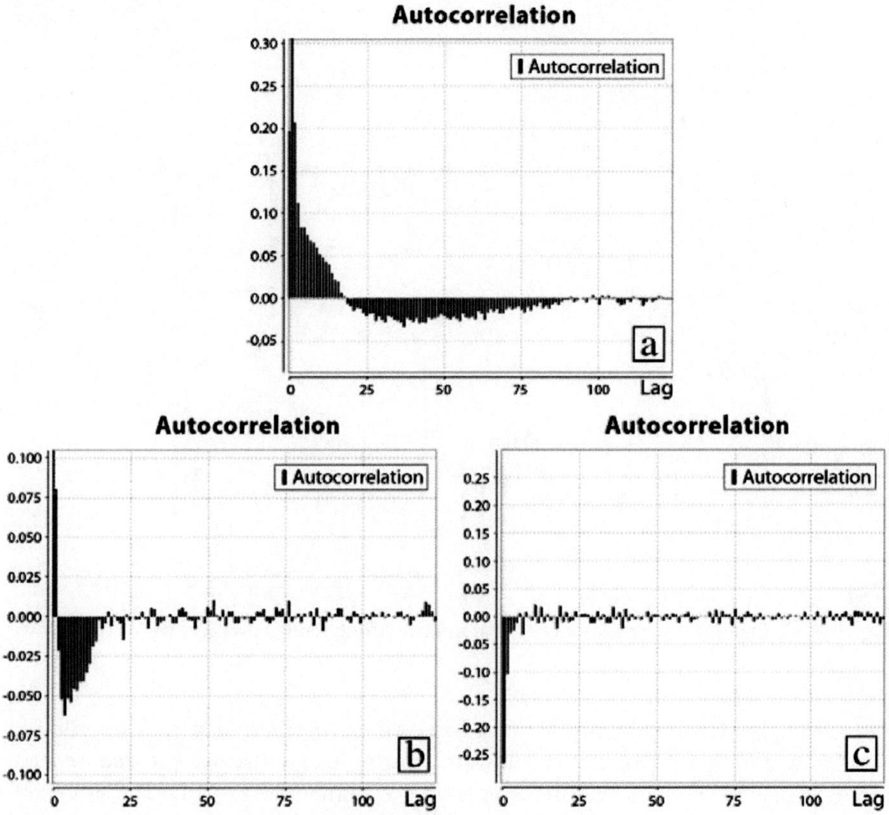

Fig. 4: Autocorrelation functions depending on deviation factor ν () ν=0.025, (b) ν=0.35, (c) ν=1

It has been widely documented that price returns in liquid markets do not exhibit any significant correlation except for anticorrelation on very small time scales. Thus, we can choose the parameters of our market such that the price time series generated by our model are consistent with real market data, at least according to their autocorrelation properties. Investigation of other stylized statistical properties is the matter of further research.

We also discover a strong dependence of obtained price dynamics on the factor β of the utility function (see Eq. (3)). Fig. 5 depicts examples of typical price behavior with various β.

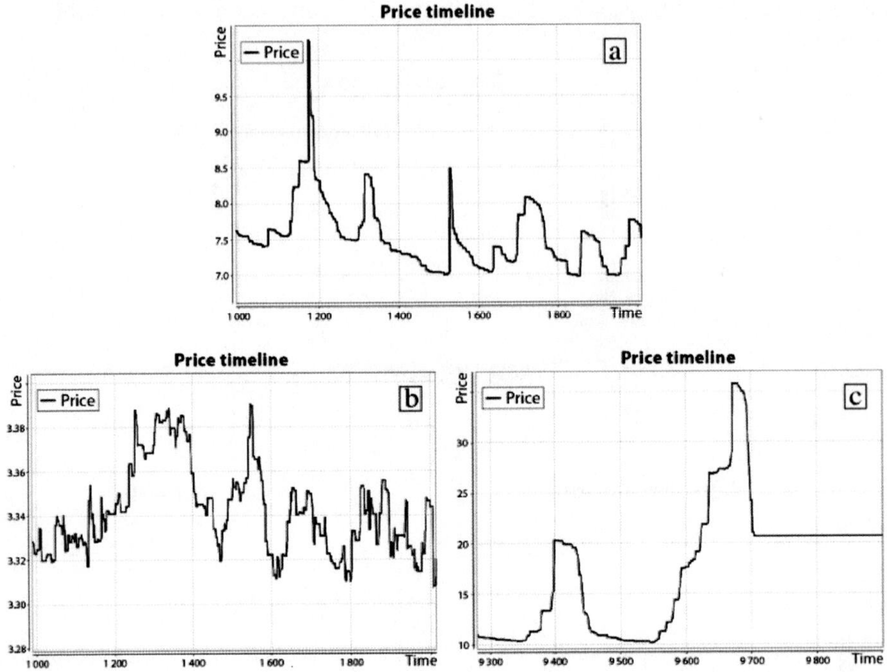

Fig. 5: Price dynamics for different factor β in utility function (a) β=1, (b) β=10, (c) β=0.01

Decreasing β leads not only to increasing of the oscillation period but also to oscillation amplitude growth. The most interesting fact is that we can choose such small β that the market exhibits a crash-like event (see Fig. 5(c)). The price and the number of buyers grow progressively until the market is saturated and the crash-like event occurs. After this moment, the trading process stops as all agents want to sell and nobody wants to buy.

Market behavior characterized by small randomness can be useful to study a mechanism of price formation. To reveal this mechanism we compare value-time plots of the following variables: stock price (Fig. 6(a)), the number of active agents (i.e. agents who put their buy or sell orders) (Fig. 6(b)), the mean of the expected value of returns in agent forecasts (Fig. 6(c)).

Considering the first two plots, we conclude that when the number of potential buyers is bigger than the number of potential sellers the price goes down. Hence, the stock price in our model appears to be a non-decreasing function of excess demand. Also note that a period of price growth is accompanied by the higher trading activity then a period of price decline. This may be explained by the imbalance between money and stock in the agent portfolio (the agent has too much money in comparison with the equilibrium price and always has an opportunity to buy the stock).

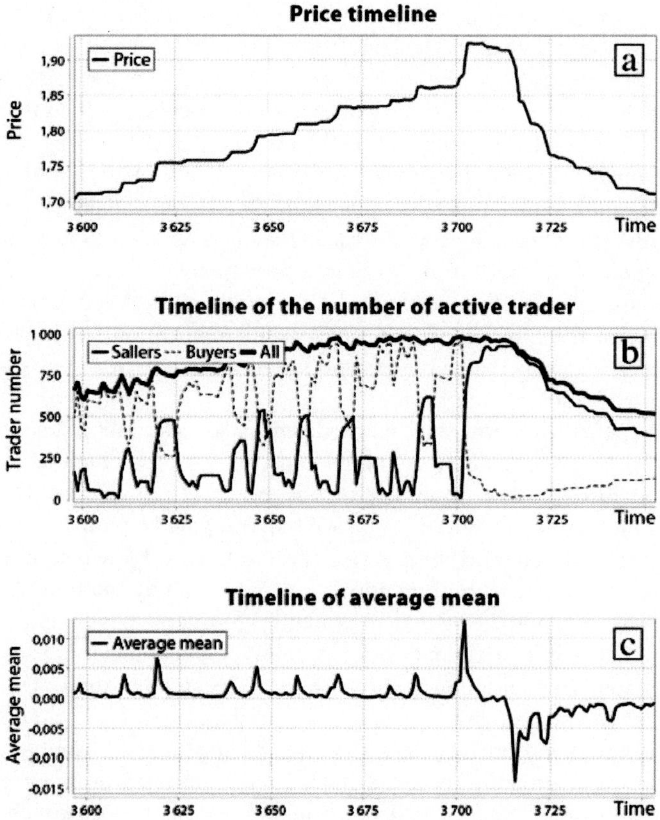

Fig. 6: A comparison of three value-time plots: (a) stock price, (b) the number of active agents (i.e. agents who put their buy or sell orders), (c) the mean of the expected value of returns in agent forecasts

According to the agent model, the sign of the forecasted mean of the return determines the agent's willingness to increase (positive mean) or reduce (negative mean) the fraction of wealth invested in shares. Looking at the first and the third plots, we conclude that sharp changes in average forecasted mean correspond to trend reversal.

Conclusion

In this paper, we suggest a microscopic model of the stock market in the framework of agent-based modeling. As a rather new modern approach, agent-based modeling seems to be the most adequate tool allowing investigation of complex systems consisting of many interacting autonomous elements. In the case of financial markets, behavior of such individual elements is clearer for the researcher than some general laws of market dynamics, since in reality such elements are people. Thus, an agent-based approach gives a simple and clear way to represent such complex systems as stock markets as it reproduces the behavior of the system as whole when features and properties of only individual elements are given. Another important thing is that this approach can give the possibility of exploring processes at the microscopic level (e.g. analysis of high-frequency market data).

Similar to some of the previous woks, we use a mathematical model based on the maximization of a utility function to describe the decision-making process. In comparison with the other microscopic models, the main feature of our simulator is a detailed comprehensive realization of the interaction between traders on the stock market. This realization includes an order filing system and implementation of an order book. One of the most important steps of this realization is the process of mutual price concessions between buyers and sellers, which seems to be consistent with that observed in the real markets.

Computer experiments show that the modeled market exhibits a steady trading process and realistic price dynamics. The wide diversity of the obtained dynamics includes the situation when the number of buyers grows progressively until the market is saturated and a crash-like event occurs. We want to point out that some statistical properties of generated time series agree with well-known stylized facts.

The developed computer program allows the user to study the trading activity of agents on the market and the statistical properties of time series generated by the system. Researcher may experiment with the obtained dynamics by varying parameters of the model. In addition, this software provides an opportunity for the user to enter the modeled market and take part in the trading process. Thus, the user is able to make an exogenous influence on the system and study its reaction.

We developed our program by means of an object-oriented programming language in order to be able to easily update the model (e.g. we can easily change the agent model or introduce a new step of interaction between agents). Because of the implemented user-trading mode, our program may be used as a simple trading trainer.

References

Arthur W.B., Holland J.H., LeBaron B., Palmer R., and Tayler P. (1997) Asset Pricing under Endogenous Expectations in an Articial Stock Market. The Economy as an Evolving Complex System, II, edited by W. Brian Arthur, Steven Durlauf, and David Lane, Vol. XXVII, SFI Studies in the Sciences of Complexity, Addison-Wesley, 1997.

Bottazzi G., Dosi G., and Rebesco I. (2005) Institutional Architectures and Behavioral Ecologies in the Dynamics of Financial Markets. Journal of Mathematical Economies, 2005, 41:197-228.

Brock W., and Hommes C. (1998) Heterogeneous beliefs and routes to chaos in a simple asset pricing model. Journal of Economic Dynamics and Control, 1998, 22:1235-1274.

Chiarella C. (1992) The Dynamics of Speculative Behaviour. Annals of Operational Research, 1992, 37:101-123.

Chiarella C., He X. (2001) Asset Price and Wealth Dynamics Under Heterogeneous Expectations. Quantitative Finance, 2001, 1:509-526.

Kim G. and Markowitz H. M. (1989) Investment rules, margin and market volatility. Journal of Portfolio Management, 1989, 16:45–52.

Levy M., Levy H., and Solomon S. (1994) A microscopic model of the stock market: Cycles, booms, and crashes. Economics Letters, 1994, 45:103-111.

Levy M., Levy H., and Solomon S. (1995) Microscopic simulation of the stock market: The effect of microscopic diversity. Journal de Physique I, 1995, 5:1087-1107.

Levy M., Levy H., and Solomon S. (2000) Microscopic Simulation of Financial Markets. Academic Press, New York, 2000.

Lux T. (1998) The socio-economic dynamics of speculative markets: Interacting agents, chaos, and the fat tails of return distributions. Journal of Economic Behavior and Organization, 1998, 33:143-165.

How can Information on CDS Contracts be Used to Estimate Liquidity Premium in the Bond Market

Polina Tarasova

National Research University Higher School of Economics, Moscow, Russia.
email: tarasovapolina@gmail.com

Abstract Liquidity is an important characteristic for any bond, but now in the literature there are no models for estimating the liquidity premium. Moreover, there is not even an exact definition of this notion. There are many facts proving the existence of the liquidity premium in the bond market. One of such fact, for example, is the difference between values of the bond spread and the credit default swap (CDS) premium. Following the Longstaff (2005) study, often, in practice, CDS data are used for the estimation of the pure credit risk of the underlying bond and hence for the separation of the bond risk premium from the liquidity premium and credit risk premium. However, the fact that CDS premium can be used for the pure credit risk measurement is a disputable proposition. The purpose of this paper is to make recommendations on the applicability of such approach for assessing liquidity premium. In this paper the risks associated with CDS transactions will be considered. Also, different approaches for assessing the liquidity bond premium and liquidity CDS premium will be reviewed as well as the correlation of these quantities. We will see that the CDS premium does not measure the pure credit risk component of the bond spread.

Keywords: Liquidity, Credit Default Swaps, negative CDS basis, Reduced Form Models

JEL classification: G12, G14

Introduction

One of the most challenging problems in the liquidity risk literature is the estimation of the liquidity risk premium in the bond market. The bond spread for a non-Treasury bond is usually defined as the difference between the bond's yield and the yield to maturity of a benchmark Treasury coupon security. It is measuring the compensation for additional option risk, credit risk, and liquidity risk that an investor is exposed to by investing in a non-Treasury security. Currently, there are a lot of procedures for estimation of credit spreads. However, almost all existing approaches for evaluating credit spread ignore the liquidity premium, which can be quite significant for low-liquidity markets (as the recent financial crisis has shown us). Therefore, the separation of the bond risk premium from the liquidity premium

D. Sornette et al. (Eds.), *Market Risk and Financial Markets Modeling*,
DOI 10.1007/978-3-642-27931-7_22, © Springer-Verlag Berlin Heidelberg 2012

and credit risk premium is a very relevant problem nowadays. In this paper we will discuss a new approach to resolving this problem. This approach involves simultaneous use of the data of CDS and bond markets. The CDS market has strongly increased in size since 2007 and has attracted a fairly large attention of dealers and investors. Since the CDS premium reflect an additional investor's view on default risk of the underlying bond, the simultaneous use of data from two different markets (CDS and bond markets) can give an appropriate estimation of credit risk premium.

The paper proceeds as follows. In section 2 we will discuss the mechanism of a CDS contract and the basic risks associated with this transaction. Global changes in the CDS market will be also considered. In section 3 we will describe a rather rough method of assessing the liquidity premium, the so-called "negative CDS basis approach". Then in section 4 we will discuss intensity models for CDS and liquidity, that have been proposed by Buhler and Trapp (2006, 2008) study. Section 5 concludes.

Credit Default Swaps

In order to understand the CDS pricing models, which will be considered in subsequent sections, we first need to discuss the mechanism of the CDS contract. Also we will consider global changes that have occurred in the CDS market since 2009, and risks associated with the CDS transaction.

A credit default swap is a swap contract that provides default protection against credit loss on a specified reference instrument (such an instrument can be a defined bond, a loan or another type of the liability). This contract allows an investor (protection buyer) to transfer a defined credit risk exposure to the protection seller. The basic cashflow of a CDS transaction is depicted below. The protection buyer (the risk seller) makes periodic payments (in most cases quarterly payments) to the protection seller (the risk buyer) until a credit event or CDS matures. In return, the protection seller receives default protection in case of a credit event.

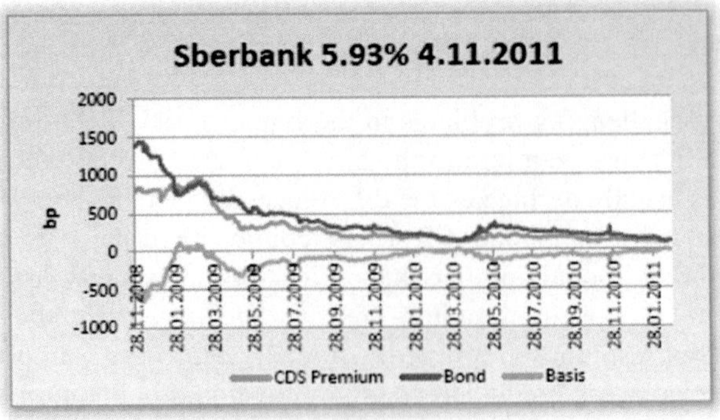

Fig. 1: Calculation of the "negative basis" for Sberbank of Russia

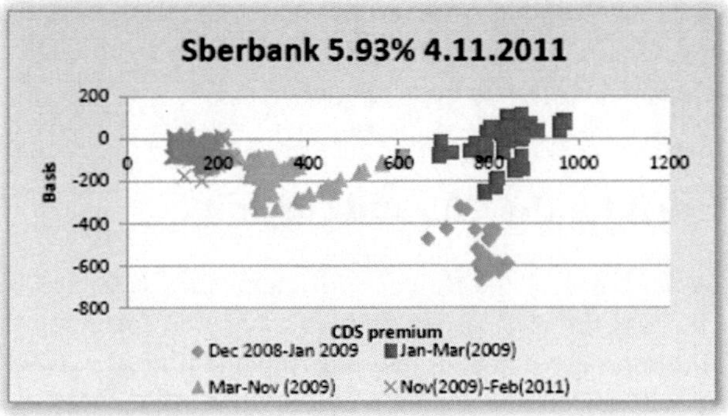

Fig. 2: Variations of the "negative basis" value for Sberbank of Russia[1]

As you can see in Figure 2, the difference between the Sberbank of Russia Eurobond nominal spread and the CDS premium is not zero. Moreover, this difference is time-varying. During December 2008 and January 2009 the mean value of this difference is *-514* basis points, during November 2009 – February 2011 the mean value is *-60* basis points (Figure 3). Thus there is a non-default component (liquidity risk), which influences the corporate bond spread. In the negative basis approach this difference is declared as the liquidity premium.

In the literature, the difference between the CDS premium and the corporate bond spread is called the negative basis (so the name of this approach for an estimation of the liquidity premium is the Negative CDS basis approach). Advantages of such an estimation are the following: it is easy to compute and interpret. All we need is simply to collect bond prices and CDS premiums with the equivalent maturities. Also, risk free rates are needed for estimation of the corporate bond spread (for example, some analysts use the Z-spread instead of the nominal spread or OAS spread). However, CDS trades are not available for all corporate bonds. Therefore, we should resolve an additional problem. It is necessary to build a model which will show the dependence of the liquidity premium on such liquidity indicators as the Bid-Ask spread, free-float, trade volume and so on. After finding a stable relationship between the bond liquidity premium and liquidity indicators, we can use this model for an estimation of the liquidity premium for bonds (with the same characteristics such as credit quality, maturity and so on) for which there are no CDS contracts.

The negative CDS basis approach doesn't take into account the CDS illiquidity. There also remains a little counterparty risk (the move to the central clearing reduces this risk, but a little part of counterparty risk is still present). However, the main disadvantage of this model lies in the fact that it is not quite correct simply to subtract the CDS premium from the corporate bond spread (the dimension of the corporate bond spread is the interest per annum but the dimension of the CDS

[1] In figure 2 and figure 3 "Bond" means Sberbank of Russia Eurobond nominal spread. "Basis" means the difference between the CDS premium and Russia Euro-bond nominal spread.

spread is percent of the nominal). Therefore you should first bring data to a single dimension (for example you can get the default intensity from CDS data and then construct the theoretical corporate bond spread).

Intensity Models for the CDS and Liquidity

In this section we will discuss the Buhler and Trapp study (2006, 2008). But firstly we will briefly discuss the intensity model (or a reduced form approach). A good explanation of this approach can be found in Brigo and Mercurio (2006) or in Brigo et al. (2010). We will use similar notation and definitions to those used in Brigo et al. (2010).

A reduced form approach assumes that the default is activated by an exogenous component that is independent of all default free market information. It also assumes that the default time is the first jump of a Cox process with intensity h_t. The survival probability in intensity models can be mathematically expressed as

$$Q(\tau \geq t) = E\ e^{-\int_0^t h(u)du}$$

We assume next τ is independent of interest rates. For simplicity, we also assume that in the case of a credit event the protection seller will not pay an accrual interest on the premium. We also remove the counterparty risk.

Then, the value for the premium leg of the CDS at time t equals

$$CDS^{premium\_leg} = \sum_{i=1}^{n} P(t,t_i) * D(t,t_i) * s ,$$

$$\text{where } P_t(t_1,t_2) = E_t\ e^{-\int_{t_1}^{t_2} h(u)du},\ D_t(t_1,t_2) = E_t\ e^{-\int_{t_1}^{t_2} r(u)du},$$

s is the value of the CDS premium.

Assume that the value of a notional of the CDS equals 1. Then the value for the default leg equals

$$CDS^{default\_leg} = (1-R) * \sum_{i=1}^{n} D(t,t_i) * P(t,t_{i-1}) * (1 - P_t(t_{i-1},t_i)),$$

where R is a recovery rate.

By imposing equality between the two legs, we obtain the fair value for the CDS premium

$$S = \frac{(1-R)*\sum_{i=1}^{n} D(t,t_i)*P(t,t_{i-1})*(1-P_t(t_{i-1},t_i))}{\sum_{i=1}^{n} P(t,t_i)*D(t,t_i)},$$

Now me move to Buhler and Trapp (2006). In this paper the authors study how liquidity influences the CDS and bond prices. They considered an intensity credit risk model, adding to it a new discount term l_t^b for the bonds of one entity and l_t^c for the CDS on these bonds. They assume that default free rates, default intensity and liquidity intensities are independent. Thus, the premium leg in their model at time t equals

$$CDS^{premium\_leg} = \sum_{i=1}^{n} P(t,t_{i-1})*D(t,t_i)*s*l^c(t,t_i),$$

$$\text{where } l_t^c(t_1,t_2) = E_t\, e^{-\int_{t_1}^{t_2}\gamma^c(u)du}.$$

The value of the defaulting leg in their model equals

$$CDS^{default\_leg} = \sum_{i=1}^{n} D(t,t_i)*P(t,t_{i-1})*(1-P_t(t_{i-1},t_i))-$$

$$R*\sum_{i=1}^{n} D(t,t_i)*P(t,t_{i-1})*(1-P_t(t_{i-1},t_i))*l^b(t,t_i),$$

$$\text{where } l_t^b(t_1,t_2) = E_t\, e^{-\int_{t_1}^{t_2}\gamma^b(u)du}.$$

By imposing equality between two legs, they obtain the fair value for the CDS premium

$$S = \frac{\sum_{i=1}^{n} D(t,t_i)*P(t,t_{i-1})*(1-P_t(t_{i-1},t_i))-R*\sum_{i=1}^{n} D(t,t_i)*P(t,t_{i-1})*(1-P_t(t_{i-1},t_i))*l^b(t,t_i)}{\sum_{i=1}^{n} P(t,t_{i-1})*D(t,t_i)*s*l^c(t,t_i)},$$

They use the following equation for the price of a default-risky bond at time t with face value 1

$$Bond\ \Pr ice = \sum_{i=1}^{n} P(t,t_i) * D(t,t_i) * (1 - P_t(t_{i-1},t_i)) * l^b(t,t_i) + P(t,t_n) * D(t,t_n) * l^b(t,t_n) +$$

$$R * \sum_{i=1}^{n} P(t,t_{i-1}) * (1 - P_t(t_{i-1},t_i)) * D(t,t_n) * l^b(t,t_i),$$

where c is the coupon of the bond.

The results of their study are the following. First, they show that the credit risk components in the corporate bonds spread and in the CDS premium are identical. The liquidity premium of corporate bonds is always positive and is correlated with the default risk premium (they show that the liquidity of bonds becomes worse as the default risk increases). They also find that the CDS liquidity premium in most cases has a very small value compared with the liquidity premium of the bond. Lastly, their approach explains the positive and negative values of the negative basis.

In 2008, Buhler and Trapp released another paper, in which they elaborate upon the previous model. They added the correlation between CDS and bond liquidity, the correlation between default and bond liquidity and the correlation between default and CDS liquidity. They also assumed different intensities for ask and bid CDS premiums. Finally, they managed to estimate the pure CDS liquidity premium (it averages 4% of the CDS premium) and the pure bond liquidity premium (it averages 35% of the corporate bond spread).

The order of magnitude of the results of their study, in principle, true, but the accuracy of the results is highly questionable, since too unrealistic assumptions were made (for example independence of the risk free interest rates of the default and liquidity intensities). Also their assumption that the liquidity intensities follow arithmetic Brownian motion is debatable, because the projected liquidity should oscillate at the same level, not to grow extremely at infinity.

Conclusion

In this paper we have considered several approaches for estimating the liquidity premium for corporate bonds using the CDS data. The CDS is a good tool for separating the credit risk from another market risk. The studies of Buhler and Trapp (2006, 2008) make it obvious that the liquidity risk is present in both CDS and bond markets. But they also concluded that the average value of the liquidity premium of the CDS premium is 4%, and the liquidity premium for the bonds averages 35% of the corporate bond spread. Therefore the negative basis approach, which we have considered in section 3 also can be acceptable under certain conditions. Of course, if we need a high accuracy, we should not forget about the fact that the CDS premium does not measure the pure credit risk. But for rough estimates, the negative basis approach is quite applicable.

References

Beumee, J., & Brigo, D., & Schiemert, D., & Stoyle, G. (2009). Charting a course through the CDS Big Bang. Global Special Report FitcSolutions. Available at SSRN: http://ssrn.com/abstract=1374407.

Bongaerts, D., & Frank, de J., & Driessen, J. (2009). Liquidity and liquidity risk premia in the CDS market. Preliminary version. University of Amsterdam, Tilburg University.

Bongaerts, D., & Frank, de J., & Driessen, J. (November 11, 2009). Derivative Pricing with Liquidity Risk: Theory and Evidence from the Credit Default Swap Market. Journal of Finance, Forthcoming; EFA 2007 Ljubljana Meetings Paper. Available at SSRN: http://ssrn.com/abstract=966167.

Buhler, W., & Trapp, M. (2006). Credit and liquidity risk in bond and CDS market. Working paper. University of Mannheim.

Buhler, W., & Trapp, M. (2008). Time-Varying Credit Risk and Liquidity Premia in Bond and CDS Markets. Working paper. University of Mannheim.

Brigo, D., & Predescu, M., & Capponi, A. (2010). Credit Default Swaps Liquidity modeling: A survey. Available at SSRN: http://ssrn.com/abstract=1564327.

Brigo, D., & Mercurio, F. (2006). Rate Models: Theory and Practice – with Smile, Inflation and Credit. Second Edition Springer Verlag.

Duffee., G. R. (1999). Estimating the price of default risk. The Review of Financial Studies,12:187-226.

Galai, D., & Landskroner, Y., & Raviv, A., & Wiener, Z. (2011). A Balance sheet Approach for Sovereign Debt. Available at SSRN: http://ssrn.com/abstract=1740253.

Giovanni, C., & Chen, J., & Williams, J. (2010). Liquidity interactions in credit Markets: A Preliminary Analysis of the Eurozone Sovereign Dept Crisis. Preprint. University of Southampton-school of management, University of Aberdeen Business School

Jonson, G., & Gallo, A., & Kakodkar, A., & Galiani, S. (2006). A Guide to the Exotics Credit Derivatives Market. Credit Derivatives Handbook Vol.2.

Hull, J. (2006) Option, futures and other derivatives. 6th edition.

Keating, C., & Marshall, B. (2010). Banking on Liquidity, Liquidity, Collateral and Derivatives. EDHEC Business School.

Lin, H., & Liu, S., & Wu, C. (2009). Liquidity Premia in the credit Default Swap and corporate Bond Markets. Washington State University and university of Missouri-Columbia.

Longstaff, F. A., & Mithal, S., & Neis, E. (2005). Corporate Yield Spreads: Default Risk or Liquidity? New Evidence from the Credit Default Swap Market. The Journal of Finance, Vol. 60, No. 5, pp. 2213-2253.

Merton, R. C. (1974). On the pricing of corporate debt: The risk structure of interest rates. Journal of Finance 29, 449-470.

Navneet, A., & Jeffrey, R., & Fanlin, Z. (2005). Reduced form vs. Structural models of credit Risk: A Case study of three models. Moody's KMV.

Nelson, C. R., & Siegel, A. F. (1987). Parsimonious Modeling of Yield Curves. The Journal of Business, Vol. 60, No. 4. pp. 473-489.

Rozenberg, S. (2009). A 'Big Bang' in the Credit Derivatives Universe. Derivatives Week.

Tang, D., & Yan, H. (2008). Liquidity and credit Default Swap Spreads. University of Hong Kong, University of South Carolina.

Smirnov, S. & Zakharov, A. (2006). A Liquidity-Based Robust Spline Fitting of Spot Yield Curve Providing Positive Forward Rates. www.effas-ebc.org/EBC Presentation/2006 Feb Luxembourg/zero yield curve fitting-version 270106.pdf.

Svensson, L. O. E. (1994). Estimating and Interpreting Forward Interest Rates: Sweden 1992-1994. NBER Working Paper Series, Sep 1994.
Vasicek, O. A. & Fong, H. G. (1982). Term Structure Modeling Using Exponential Splines. The Journal of Finance.

Adelic Theory of the Stock Market

Victor Zharkov

Natural science institute of Perm state university, Perm, Russia. email: vita@psu.ru

Abstract The p-adic theory of the stock market is presented. It is shown that the price dynamics is very naturally described by the adelic function. The procedure of derivation of the functional integral formulation of an adelic type is derived from microscopic models using generalized supercoherent states.

Introduction

We live in a high technology world. In finance we use artificial neural nets, genetic and evolutionary algorithms to investigate financial markets. Econophysics is the bright example of a new high technology theory in finance (Zharkov, 2001). Today, new scientific concepts penetrate to modern economic theory. For example, nonlinear dynamics, deterministic chaos, fractals, fuzzy sets, and others – promising us new discoveries, but at the same time, their appearance prompts the revision of earlier theories. It is shown in this article that there exists a relationship between the Elliott theory and the p-adic description of the dynamics of prices in the stock market. It is reasonable to talk about the existence of a new type of waves in the form of steps that are absent in the Elliott theory. A new theory of the stock market, describing the ensemble of traders and containing an adelic description of price dynamics has been developed.

Elliott Theory

In nanotechnology, magnetism, high-temperature superconductivity and in many physical phenomena we have fractal behavior in the experimental data. The peculiarity of this phenomenon is that the behavior of physical quantities that depend on time or the magnetic field is non-analytic. A one-dimensional fractal as a function of time, the magnetic field or temperature, is described by curve, nowhere nondifferentiable, then there is a function value or its derivative will be discontinuous at any point. In the late 1920s, R. Elliott developed the theory of waves, assuming some kind of regularity in the stock market, contrary to popular assumptions about the random nature of price movement. He found that price movements have repetitive cycles, which are associated with the emotions of investors as a result of external influences of news or mass psychology prevailing at the time. Elliott said that the ascending and descending oscillations of mass psychology always manifest themselves in the same repetitive patterns, which he called "waves".

D. Sornette et al. (Eds.), *Market Risk and Financial Markets Modeling*,
DOI 10.1007/978-3-642-27931-7_23, © Springer-Verlag Berlin Heidelberg 2012

The wave principle posits that collective investor psychology or crowd psychology moves from optimism to pessimism and back again in a natural sequence. These swings create patterns, as evidenced in the price movements of a market at every degree of trend. Elliott's model says that market prices alternate between five waves and three waves at all degrees of trend, as the illustration shows. Within the dominant trend, waves 1, 3, and 5 are "motive" waves, and each motive wave itself subdivides into five waves. Waves 2 and 4 are "corrective" waves, and subdivide into three waves. In a bear market the dominant trend is downward, so the pattern is reversed—five waves down and three up. Motive waves always move with the trend, while corrective waves move against it.

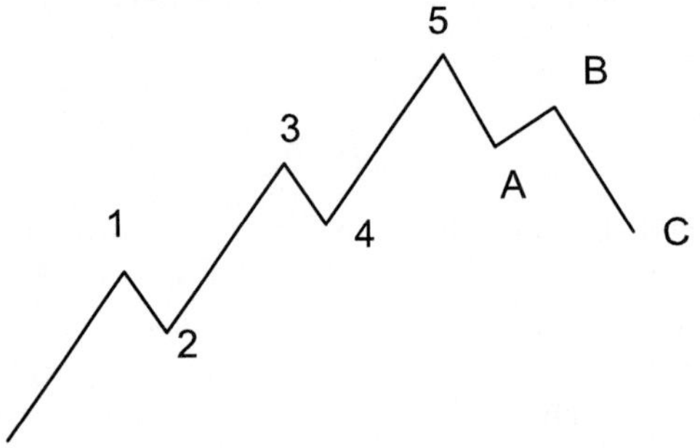

Fig. 1: Fractal of the first level – the curve that is not differentiable at a finite number of points 1, 2, 3, 4, 5, A, B, C

In a paper he co-authored in 1996, the physicist Didier Sornette said, "It is intriguing that the log-periodic structures documented here bear some similarity with the "Elliott waves" of technical analysis. A lot of effort has been developed in finance both by academic and trading institutions and more recently by physicists (using some of their statistical tools developed to deal with complex times series) to analyze past data to get information on the future. The 'Elliott wave' technique is probably the most famous in this field. We speculate that the "Elliott waves", so strongly rooted in the financial analysts' folklore, could be a signature of an underlying critical structure of the stock market" (Sornette et al., 1996).

How P-Adic Mathematics Appears in the Finance

It is a fact that we never have a case of irrational real numbers in everyday life or in scientific experiments. The results of any action can be expressed only in rational numbers. Of course, there is a common belief that if we measure with greater precision, we can get any number of decimals and interpret the result as a real number. However, this is an idealization, and we must be careful with such statements. Therefore, we take as our starting point the field of rational numbers Q. P-adic analysis and p-adic mathematical physics today attract great interest. P-adic models have been introduced to string theory, quantum theory and quantum gravity. Even a p-adic theory of consciousness has been developed. We would like to discuss the applicability of p-adic numbers and adeles to the stock market. Let us give the arguments for the appearance of p-adic numbers in the general class of systems. For the appearance of such a p-adic formalism, it is necessary to apply the functional integral for formulation of systems dynamics, which gives the possibility of a nontrivial change of variables in the functional integral from the real valued fields to the p-adic valued fields. This transformation of the fields gives us the new formulation of representation of the systems dynamics. As a result, we have obtained an effective theory with another set of fields and a different symmetry. In the first step, we have used the most evident procedure of introduction the p-adic numbers. We began with systems which had some set of dynamic fields or variables. These variables have some experimental meaning and that is why they have values in the field of rational numbers. Usually, securities have values such as the following – 10/12, 45/12. Securities mean shares and it is natural that their values fall in the field of rational numbers. In reality it is impossible to obtain an irrational number of an investor's share of the capital. As a result, we have come to the following statement: all the variables which describe securities are the elements of the rational field (Vladimirov et al., 1994).

In January 2000, the Commission on the Securities and Exchange Commission gave guidance to all major U.S. stock exchanges to transfer all stock quotation systems and systems of registration of transactions with shares and options to the format of the decimal point.

The second step of the construction of any theory is the choice of some method for evaluating of the final quantities. Here we need here a certain procedure for the evaluating of absolute values, as well as a procedure for the comparison of two numbers. According to the Ostrovskyi theorem, we have two possible modules for the completion of rational numbers: a real module (the real numbers field) or p-adic module (the p-adic number field). We have an infinite number of p-adic norms, which are characterized by a prime number p. At present, the real numbers are used by the vast majority of theories describing the reality, and the usual consensus is that the real numbers are the main elements for presenting the reality. We intend to show here that p-adic numbers are more suitable for the purposes of describing financial market price dynamics. Let us define some basic notation. An arbitrary rational number x can be written in the form (Vladimirov et al., 1994):

$$x = p^{\upsilon} \frac{m}{n}$$

with n and m not divisible by p, where p denotes a prime number. The p-adic norm of the rational number is equal to:

$$|x|_p = \frac{1}{p^{\upsilon}}$$

The field of p-adic numbers, Q_p is the completion of the field of rational numbers Q with the p-adic norm. The most interesting property of p-adic numbers is their ultrametricity. This means that they obey the strong triangle inequality:

$$|x+y|_p \leq \max(|x|_p, |y|_p)$$

Let us remind ourselves that a real number may be expressed by the following expansion:

$$10^{\upsilon} \sum_{n=0}^{\infty} b_n \left(\frac{1}{10}\right)^n,$$

where b_n=(0,1,....,p-1). A p-adic number has the following expansion:

$$x = p^{\upsilon} \sum_{n=0}^{\infty} a_n p^n,$$

where a_n=(0,1,....,p-1). Furthermore, we can define addition, subtraction, multiplication and division operations. Today there exists algebra and analysis for the field of p-adic numbers.

Let consider the free p-adic theory, which gives the following formal solution of x=Ct+B, with C, B p-adic constants. This is the geodesics of the free theory. To obtain the final result we need to construct some type of mapping from p-adic numbers to real numbers. This will give us the opportunity to compare our results with the price dynamics. Let us take the following form of the mapping:

$$a_n \longrightarrow (a_n)^D$$

A parameter D is called the dimension of the fractal space. Readers can learn about the current knowledge in this sphere in (Zharkov, 2001). In the figures below, two different kinds of waves are compared real data – sawlike and steplike waves are shown.

It is seen that the p-adic function can be very effective for the interpolation of these types of signals.

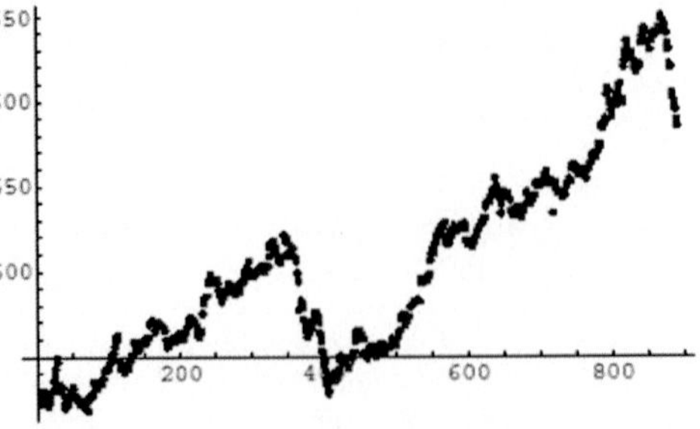

Fig. 2: Russian stock index

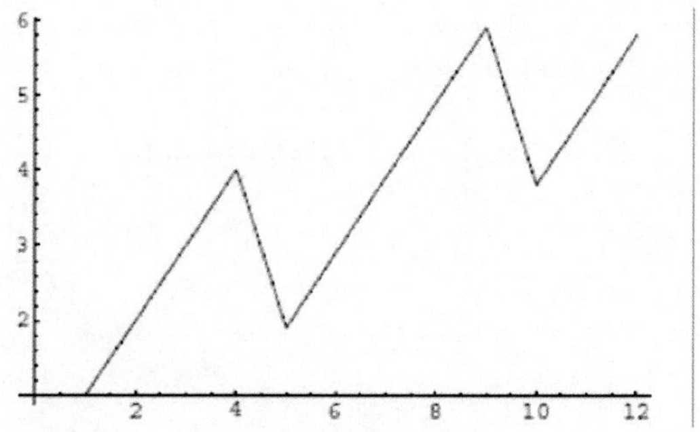

Fig. 3: Subcritical wave (First Level of Fractal) for D>1, p=3

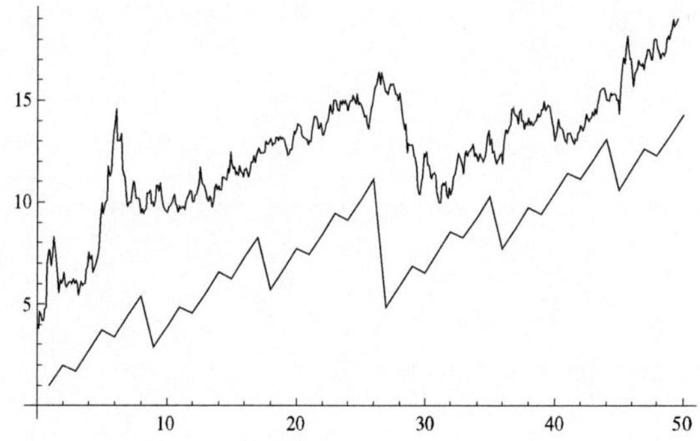

Fig. 4: Subcritical wave (Third Level of Fractal) for D>1, p=3. The second curve shows the real data

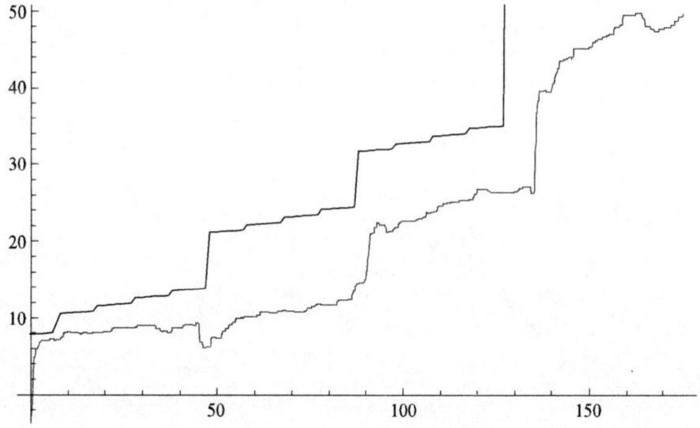

Fig. 5: Supercritcal wave (third Level of Fractal) for D<1, p=3. This type of wave is not presented in the Elliott theory.

One can see that these are the basic elements of Eliott wave analysis, which is well known among financial analysts. We have here two types of waves: (1) is the supercritical wave and (2) is the subcritical one. So we see that the p-adic and the adelic theories give us the foundation of Eliott type theory.

The figure below shows that graphs of stock market crashes are very similar to the simple p-adic configuration (Sornette).

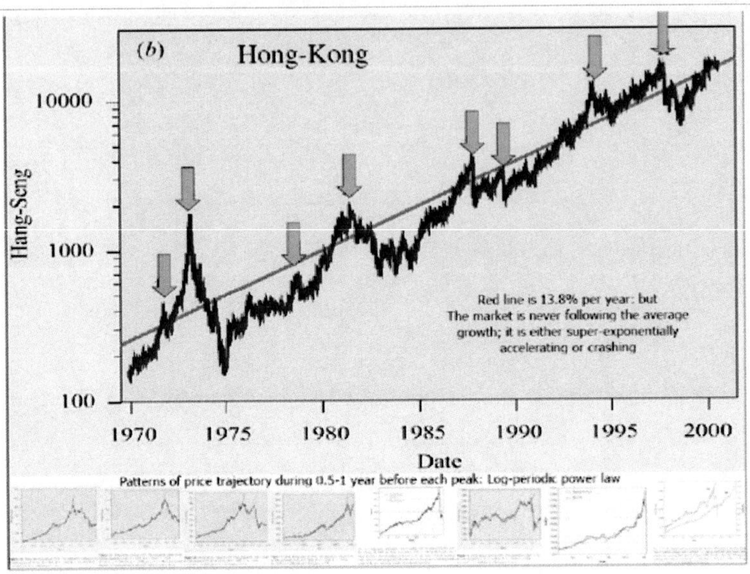

Fig. 6: Hong-Kong stock index dynamics

Figures of Gazprom and IBM shares and the RTS Index are shown below. The first curve shows the a p-adic interpolation of the real data. The second curve shows the real data. Different time scales are used.

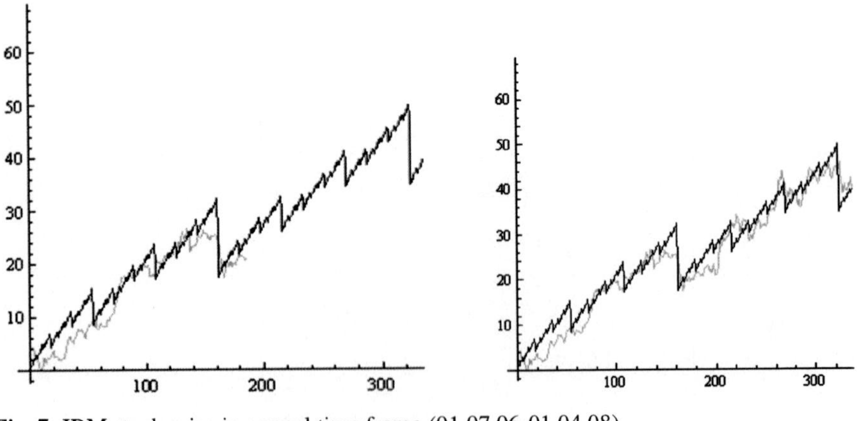

Fig. 7: IBM stock price in annual time frame (01.07.06-01.04.08)

In the first figure, an interpolation of the real data is shown. A forecast of future value was made. In the second figure this forecast was compared with real data.

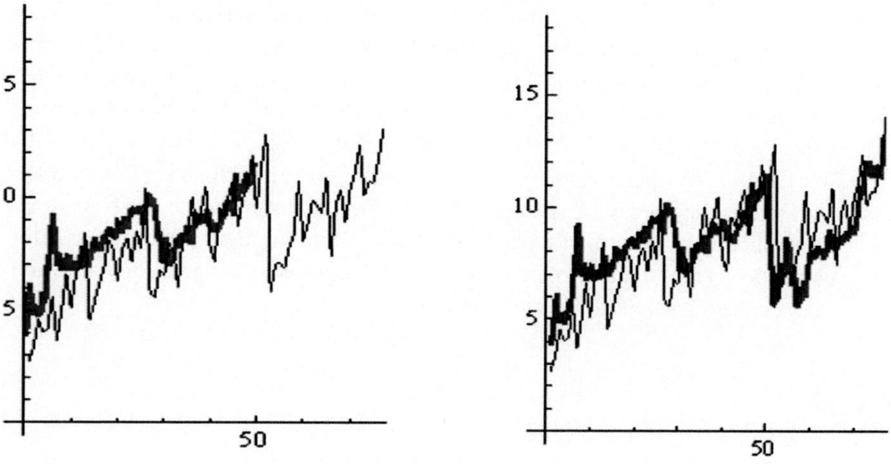

Fig. 8: Gazprom stock price in daily time frame (01.06.09-02.06.09)

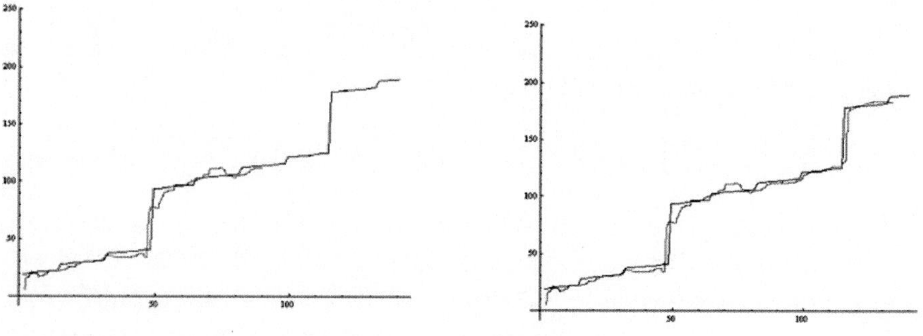

Fig. 9: RTS Index in weekly time frame (27.05.09-01.06.09)

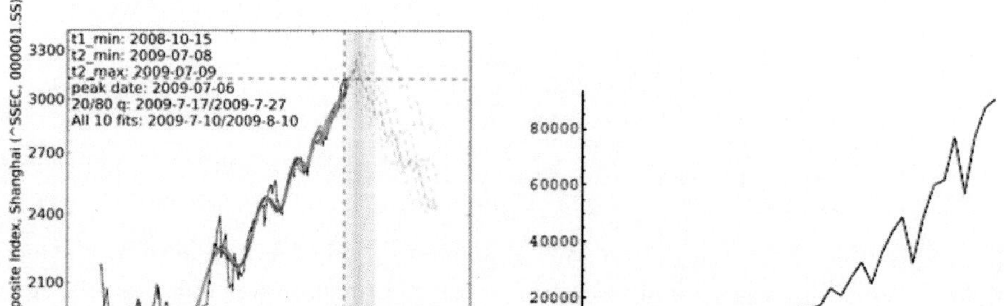

Fig. 10: LPPL compared to p-adic power law function x^3 with D=0.45

In Fig.10 a comparison was made between a typical bubble and a p-adic x^3 function with fractal dimension 0.45. Thus, our hypothesis that the financial market can be described by p-adic numbers and maps, was confirmed. P-adic mathematics provides a good mathematical framework to describe the Elliott Wave. With the use of even a simple database (p = 2, 3) for a fractal approximation, it is possible to qualitatively describe the Elliott wave patterns and other so-called "ladders", which are not described in the theory of waves, but are rather common in the Russian stock market. Application of the p-adic approach to the small number of parameters simplifies and accelerates the approximation of wave patterns in financial markets, and also allows extrapolation of the price trend.

Adele

Adele a is the set of the following type (Vladimirov at al., 1994):

$$a = \left(a_\infty, a_2, \ldots., a_j, \ldots\right),$$

For us, it will be very important that an adele group has an additive character (the analog of exponential function of plane wave):

$$\chi(xy) = \chi_\infty(x_\infty y_\infty)\prod{}_p \chi_p(x_p y_p) = \exp(-2\pi i x_\infty y_\infty)\prod{}_p \exp(2\pi i\{x_\infty y_\infty\}_p),$$

is the fractional part of $x_p y_p$. It is evident that an adele plane wave contains infinite numbers of the different p-adic projections of it. The multiplicative character of an adele group has the following expression:

$$\pi(b) = \pi_\infty(b_\infty)\pi_2(b_2)\ldots\pi_p(b_p). = |b_\infty|_\infty^s \prod{}_p |b|_p^s = |b|^s,$$

The price is described by a superposition of elementary Bruhat-Swarts functions:

$$\varphi(x) = \varphi_\infty(x_\infty)\prod{}_p \varphi_p(x_p)$$

$$x \in A^+; \varphi_\infty(x_\infty) \in S(R); \varphi_p(x_p) \in S(Q^p).$$

It will be shown later that each p-adic component of this function describes some fractal regime. That is why all components of this function together describe the multifractal behavior of the price. We restrict the set of adele function components to be from the following set of function:

$$(\varphi_\infty, \varphi_2, \varphi_3).$$

The remaining components of the adele function will be equal to a function:

$$\varphi_p(x_p) = \Omega(|x|_p).$$

In the microscopic theory, there exist three distinct regimes for describing the activity of traders. On the traders' level we have the theory with a set of fields which depend on the decision making variables of each individual trader. It is a high energy regime (analog of the UV regime in the field theory). At the medium range of energy there appears some p-adic formulation as a result of the spontaneous breaking of some symmetry. It gives us a description of trends and minitrends of prices, and it is an analog of the fractal description of price behavior. In the low energy limit (IR regime in the field theory) there appears the adelic (multifractal) description of the market.

Adele Functional Integral

All of the regimes mentioned above are described by three different types of quantum mechanics. According to Vladimirov et al. (1994), we have the following possibilities: the usual quantum mechanical formalism describes the microscopic mechanisms which exist between traders; the p-adic quantum mechanical formalism describes the typical pattern behavior of prices and the last one, an adelic quantum mechanical formalism, corresponds to the total dynamics of the securities price. These types of quantum description are represented by the following triplet of objects:

usual quantum mechanics: $(L_2(R), W(z_\infty), U(t_\infty))$,

p-adic quantum mechanics: $(L_2(Q_p), W_p(z), U_p(t))$,

adelic quantum mechanics: $(L_2(A), W_p(z), U_p(t))$,

where Q_p is the p-adic number field; $z=q,x$ are p-adic coordinates and momentums, $L_2(Q_p)$ is the space of square integrable functions in the Hilbert space of the system;

$W_p(z)$ is a unitary representation of the Heisenberg-Weil group; $U_p(t)$ is an evolutionary operator; W is an operator which gives the Weil representation for the commutation relations and acts according to the integral operator:

$$W_p(z)\psi_p(x) = \int_{Q_p} W(z; x, y)\psi_p(y)dy,$$

where $\psi_p \in L_2(Q_p)$ with the following integral kernel:

$$W_p(z;x,y) = \chi_p(2kx + qz) * \delta(x - y + q).,$$

An evolutionary operator is given by the following integral kernel. In adelic quantum mechanics the state of a system is given by the function:

$$\Psi_c(x,t) = \Psi_\infty(x_\infty, t_\infty)\prod_p \Psi_p(x_p, t_p)\prod_{p \in c} \Omega(|x|_p).$$

An adelic evolution operator has infinite numbers of p-adic components:

$$U(x,t) = \prod_p U_p(x_p, t_p)$$

The action of a concrete component is defined by the integer operator:

$$U_p(x_p, t_p)\psi_p(x) = \quad {}_{Q_p} K_p^t(x,y)\psi_p(y)dy$$

the kernel $K_p(x_p'', t_p''; x_p', t_p')$ is defined through the functional integral:

$$K_p(x_p'', t_p''; x_p', t_p') = \quad \chi_p(-S[x])Dx =$$

$$\chi_p(- {}_{t'}^{t''} L[x_m, t_m, x_m']dt_m)\prod_{t_m} dx(t_m).$$

Minority Game

Recently, some versions of the microscopic stock market description have been presented in many papers. The most famous of them is the so called minority game model, introduced by Zhang and Challet (1997). It is the agent based model of a stock market. In this model, the traders execute operations (buy and sell), which can be described by spin variables s_i. The minority game involves N traders, labeled with Roman indices i,j,k, etc. In each round of the game, all the traders act on the basis of exactly the same external information *I(k)*. Each trader i has at his disposal *S* number of strategies. The volatility of the market is described by the expression:

$$\sigma^2 = \quad {}_{\mu} (A^\mu)^2 - (\quad {}_{\mu} A^\mu)^2 ,$$

where $A^{\mu} = N^{-\frac{1}{2}} \sum_{i} [\varpi_i^{\mu} + s_i \xi_i^{\mu}]$ is the action of all traders. This gives:

$$\sum_{\mu} A^{\mu} = \frac{1}{N\sqrt{N}} \sum_{\mu} s_i \Big(\sum_{\mu} \xi_i^{\mu} \Big),$$

$$\sum_{\mu} \left(A^{\mu}\right)^2 = \frac{1}{2} + \frac{1}{N} \Big[\sum_{i} h_i s_i + \frac{1}{2} \sum_{ij} J_{ij} s_i s_j \Big],$$

Where $J_{ij} = \xi_i^{\mu} \xi_j^{\mu}$ are some coefficients describing the traders strategies and μ =(1,2,3,...K) is a variable describing the history (Challet, Zhang, 1997). The second expression formally coincides with the Hamiltonian of a spin glass.

Hubbard-type Microscopic Model

At the present time it is very desirable to generalize this model, to make it more adequate to traders' activities and to take into account three or four states of traders (buy, sell, hold and ground state). It is well known in condensed matter theory that the spin glass model or Heisenberg model is a "square root" of the Hubbard model. It is natural here to use a Hubbard-type model:

$$H = -t \sum_{<r,r'>,s} \alpha_{r,s}^{+} \alpha_{r',s} + U \sum_{r} n_{r,\uparrow} n_{r,\downarrow} =$$

$$\sum_{r} U X_r^{22} + \sum_{A,C,r,r'} t_{-AC}(r-r') X_r^{-A} X_{r'}^{C}$$

where $< r, r' >$ denote the sum over the nearest neighbors and *r* parameterize trader *i*.

Traders are described by $(\alpha_{r,s}^{+}, \alpha_{r',s})$, which are creation and destruction operators and *s*, which is the spin (gives the decision making variable) of traders. We give two different forms of this model; the first form is a standard one, the second form contains the Hubbard operators X^A (in fact they are projectors $X_r^A = |pr >< qr|$). These operators act in space of following states: $|0>$ is the ground state of a trader, $|\uparrow>= \alpha_{\uparrow}^{+} |0>$ is the buy state of a trader, $|\downarrow>= \alpha_{\downarrow}^{+} |0>$ is the sell state of a trader, $|2>= \alpha_{\uparrow}^{+} | \alpha_{\downarrow}^{+} 0>$ is the hold state of a trader. Such types of states of the traders appear in the paper of Thomas Lux in his theory of stock market (Lux, 1998). Here the first term describes the trading activity: buying by an i(r) trader and selling by a j(r) trader. The second term describes the distribution of the capital among the traders. These models give us the description of the microscopic picture of trading. This formulation contains some variables which are determined by the strategies of the traders. After integration over these variables in the functional integral we obtain an effective theory. But the theory which describes price dynamics as the result of collective behavior of an ensemble of traders can be derived from the previous theory by the application of the generalized supercoherent state. In this way, we obtain an effective functional formulation:

$$L_{eff} = \frac{< G(\theta, r, t') \,|\, (\partial / \partial t' - H) \,|\, G(\theta, r, t') >}{< G(\theta, r, t') \,|\, G(\theta, r, t') >},$$

where $| G >$ is a supercoherent state, which is expressed through generators of the dynamic superalgebra; $\{r, t', \theta\}$ are supercoordinates of superspace.

$| G >$ can be constructed in the following way (Zharkov, 1984):

$$| G > = e^{-\sum_{k=1}^{6} X^k b^k (r,t,\theta) - \sum_{j=1}^{2} X^{-j} \chi^j (r,t,\theta)} \, | 0 >$$

where $| 0 > = \otimes_r \, | 0 >_r, \{b^C\} = \{\{E_i\}, \{h_i\}\}, i = 1,2,3$.

$| G >$ has four components, two of them are fermionic (odd-valued Grassmanian nonlinear composite fields), and two are bosonic also composite and nonlinear in χ, E, h (Zharkov, 1991). This theory, as shown in recent papers, gives the p-adic functional integral and the description and can be regarded as a microscopic model of the market. Let us describe the possible scenario of this functional integral investigation. We have the very nonlinear representation which contain a quantum group. This quantum group formulation can be transformed through so called q-analysis. When q=1/p we have a p-adic representation for our functional integral. This p-adic regime was described at the beginning of this article.

Conclusion

The main conclusion of this work is that the stock market price is an adelic function. We formulate in this article a deep program of investigation of the microscopic theory of the stock market.

References

Sornette D., Johansen A., Bouchaud J. (1996). Stock market crashes, precursors and replicas. Journal de Physique I France 6, No.1, pp. 167–175.

Vladimirov V.S., Volovich I.V., Zelenov E.I. (1994). p-Adic Analysis and Mathematical Physics, World Scientific, Singapore.

Challet D., Zhang Y.C. (1997). Emergence of cooperation and organization in an evolutionary game. Physica A, 407.

Lux T. (1998). The Socio-Economic Dynamics of Speculative Markets: Interacting Agents, Chaos, and the Fat Tails of Return Distributions , Journal of Economic Behavior and Organization 33, 143-165.

Zharkov V. (1984) Teor. Mat. Fiz., 60, 404, (1988), 77,107.

Zharkov V. (1991) Teor. Mat. Fiz., 86, 262, (1992), 90,75.

Zharkov V. (2001) Modelling of complex system with information exchange by physical methods. Bulletin of Perm University, Information systems and Technologies, 5.115-125.